ABOUT THIS PUBLICATION

FOR SERVICE ASSISTANCE

Customer Service
1.704.898.0770

North Carolina General Statues is published by The Muliti-Media Group of Greater Charlotte in Charlotte, North Carolina. Copyright 2015 by the Multi-Media Group of Greater Charlotte. This book or parts thereof may not be reproduced in any form, stored in a retrieval system, or transmitted in any form by any means—electronic, mechanical, photocopy, recording or otherwise—without prior written permission of the publisher, except as provided by United States of America copyright law.

The records required by U.S. Code 2257(a) through (c) and the pertinent regulations 28 C.F.R. Cli. 1, Part 75 with respect to this publication and all materials associated with such records are maintained by The Multi-Media Group of Greater Charlotte, Publisher and available for review by Attorney General.

www.visionbooks.org

Copyright © 2015 by MMGGC
All rights reserved!

TID: 5061773
ISBN (10) digit: 1502915693
ISBN (13) digit: 978-1502915696

123-4-56789-01239-Paperback
123-4-56789-01239-Hardback

First Edition

090520140547

Printed in the United States of America

2015 EDITION

North Carolina Criminal Law And Procedure-Pamphlet # 53

Printed In conjunction with the Administration of the Courts

North Carolina Criminal Law and Procedure
Pamphlet Reference Guide

Chapters	Pamphlet
Chapter 1 Civil Procedure	1
Chapter 1 Civil Procedure (Continue)	2
Chapter 1A Rules of Civil Procedure	2
Chapter 1B Contribution.	2
Chapter 1C Enforcement of Judgments.	2
Chapter 1D Punitive Damages.	2
Chapter 1E Eastern Band of Cherokee Indians.	2
Chapter 1F North Carolina Uniform Interstate Depositions and Discovery Act.	2
Chapter 2 - Clerk of Superior Court [Repealed and Transferred.]	3
Chapter 3 - Commissioners of Affidavits and Deeds [Repealed.]	3
Chapter 4 - Common Law	3
Chapter 5 - Contempt [Repealed.]	3
Chapter 5A - Contempt	3
Chapter 6 - Liability for Court Costs	3
Chapter 7 - Courts [Repealed and Transferred.]	3
Chapter 7A – Judicial Department	3
Chapter 7A – Continuation (Judicial Department)	4
Chapter 7A – Continuation (Judicial Department)	5
Chapter 7B - Juvenile Code	5
Chapter 8 - Evidence	6
Chapter 8A - Interpreters for Deaf Persons [Recodified.]	6
Chapter 8B - Interpreters for Deaf Persons	6
Chapter 8C - Evidence Code	6
Chapter 9 - Jurors	6
Chapter 10 - Notaries [Repealed.]	6
Chapter 10A - Notaries [Recodified.]	6
Chapter 10B - Notaries	6
Chapter 11 - Oaths	6
Chapter 12 - Statutory Construction	6
Chapter 13 - Citizenship Restored	6
Chapter 14 - Criminal Law	7
Chapter 14 –Criminal Law (Continuation)	8
Chapter 15 - Criminal Procedure	9
Chapter 15A - Criminal Procedure Act (Continuation)	10
Chapter 15A - Criminal Procedure Act (Continuation)	11
Chapter 15B - Victims Compensation	11
Chapter 15C - Address Confidentiality Program	11
Chapter 16 - Gaming Contracts and Futures	11
Chapter 17 - Habeas Corpus	11

Chapter 17A - Law-Enforcement Officers [Recodified.]	11
Chapter 17B - North Carolina Criminal Justice Education and Training System [Recodified.] Chapter 17C - North Carolina Criminal Justice Education and Training Standards Commission	11
	11
Chapter 17D - North Carolina Justice Academy	11
Chapter 17E - North Carolina Sheriffs' Education and Training Standards Commission	11
Chapter 18 - Regulation of Intoxicating Liquors [Repealed.]	12
Chapter 18A - Regulation of Intoxicating Liquors [Repealed.]	12
Chapter 18B - Regulation of Alcoholic Beverages	12
Chapter 18C - North Carolina State Lottery	12
Chapter 19 - Offenses against Public Morals	12
Chapter 19A - Protection of Animals	12
Chapter 20 - Motor Vehicles	13
Chapter 20 - Motor Vehicles (Continuation)	14
Chapter 20 - Motor Vehicles (Continuation)	15
Chapter 20 - Motor Vehicles (Continuation)	16
Chapter 21 - Bills of Lading	17
Chapter 22 - Contracts Requiring Writing	17
Chapter 22A - Signatures	17
Chapter 22B - Contracts Against Public Policy	17
Chapter 22C - Payments to Subcontractors	17
Chapter 23 - Debtor and Creditor	17
Chapter 24 – Interest	17
Chapter 25 – Uniform Commercial Code	18
Chapter 25 – Uniform Commercial Code (Continuation)	19
Chapter 25A – Retail Installment Sales Act	20
Chapter 25B - Credit	20
Chapter 25C - Sales of Artwork	20
Chapter 26 - Suretyship	20
Chapter 27 - Warehouse Receipts [Repealed.]	20
Chapter 28 - Administration [Repealed.]	20
Chapter 28A - Administration of Decedents' Estates	20
Chapter 28B - Estates of Absentees in Military Service	20
Chapter 28C - Estates of Missing Persons	20
Chapter 29 - Intestate Succession	21
Chapter 30 - Surviving Spouses	21
Chapter 31 - Wills	21
Chapter 31A - Acts Barring Property Rights	21
Chapter 31B - Renunciation of Property and Renunciation of Fiduciary Powers Act	21
Chapter 31C - Uniform Disposition of Community Property Rights at Death Act	21
Chapter 32 - Fiduciaries	21
Chapter 32A - Powers of Attorney	21
Chapter 33 - Guardian and Ward [Repealed and Recodified.]	21

Chapter 33A - North Carolina Uniform Transfers to Minors Act	21
Chapter 33B - North Carolina Uniform Custodial Trust Act	21
Chapter 34 - Veterans' Guardianship Act	22
Chapter 35 - Sterilization Procedures	22
Chapter 35A - Incompetency and Guardianship	22
Chapter 36 - Trusts and Trustees [Repealed.]	22
Chapter 36A - Trusts and Trustees	22
Chapter 36B - Uniform Management of Institutional Funds Act [Repealed.]	22
Chapter 36C - North Carolina Uniform Trust Code	22
Chapter 36D - North Carolina Community Third Party Trusts, Pooled Trusts	23
Chapter 36E - Uniform Prudent Management of Institutional Funds Act	23
Chapter 37 - Allocation of Principal and Income [Repealed.]	23
Chapter 37A - Uniform Principal and Income Act	23
Chapter 38 - Boundaries	23
Chapter 38A - Landowner Liability	23
Chapter 39 - Conveyances	23
Chapter 39A - Transfer Fee Covenants Prohibited	23
Chapter 40 - Eminent Domain [Repealed.]	23
Chapter 40A - Eminent Domain	23
Chapter 41 - Estates	23
Chapter 41A - State Fair Housing Act	23
Chapter 42 - Landlord and Tenant	23
Chapter 42A - Vacation Rental Act	23
Chapter 43 - Land Registration	23
Chapter 44 - Liens	24
Chapter 44A - Statutory Liens and Charges	24
Chapter 45 - Mortgages and Deeds of Trust	24
Chapter 45A - Good Funds Settlement Act	24
Chapter 46 - Partition	24
Chapter 47 - Probate and Registration	25
Chapter 47A - Unit Ownership	25
Chapter 47B - Real Property Marketable Title Act	25
Chapter 47C - North Carolina Condominium Act	25
Chapter 47D - Notice of Settlement Act [Expired.]	25
Chapter 47E - Residential Property Disclosure Act	25
Chapter 47F - North Carolina Planned Community Act	25
Chapter 47G - Option to Purchase Contracts	25
Chapter 47H - Contracts for Deed	25
Chapter 48 - Adoptions +	26
Chapter 48A - Minors	26
Chapter 49 - Bastardy	26
Chapter 49A - Rights of Children	26
Chapter 50 - Divorce and Alimony	26
Chapter 50A - Uniform Child-Custody Jurisdiction and	

Enforcement Act	26
Chapter 50B - Domestic Violence	26
Chapter 50C - Civil No-Contact Orders	26
Chapter 51 - Marriage	26
Chapter 52 - Powers and Liabilities of Married Persons	27
Chapter 52A - Uniform Reciprocal Enforcement of Support Act [Repealed.]	27
Chapter 52B - Uniform Premarital Agreement Act	27
Chapter 52C - Uniform Interstate Family Support Act	27
Chapter 53 - Banks	27
Chapter 53A - Business Development Corporations and North Carolina Capital Resource Corporations	28
Chapter 53B - Financial Privacy Act	28
Chapter 54 - Cooperative Organizations	28
Chapter 54A - Capital Stock Savings and Loan Associations [Repealed.]	28
Chapter 54B - Savings and Loan Associations	29
Chapter 54C - Savings Banks	29
Chapter 55 - North Carolina Business Corporation Act	30
Chapter 55A - North Carolina Nonprofit Corporation Act	31
Chapter 55B - Professional Corporation Act	31
Chapter 55C - Foreign Trade Zones	31
Chapter 55D - Filings, Names, and Registered Agents for Corporations, Nonprofit Corporations, and Partnerships	31
Chapter 56 - Electric, Telegraph and Power Companies [Repealed.]	31
Chapter 57 - Hospital, Medical and Dental Service Corporations [Recodified.]	31
Chapter 57A - Health Maintenance Organization Act [Recodified.]	31
Chapter 57B - Health Maintenance Organization Act [Recodified.]	31
Chapter 57C - North Carolina Limited Liability Company Act.	31
Chapter 58 - Insurance.	32
Chapter 58 - Insurance (Continuation)	33
Chapter 58 - Insurance (Continuation)	34
Chapter 58 - Insurance (Continuation)	35
Chapter 58 - Insurance (Continuation)	36
Chapter 58 - Insurance (Continuation)	37
Chapter 58 - Insurance (Continuation)	38
Chapter 58A - North Carolina Health Insurance Trust Commission [Recodified.]	38
Chapter 59 - Partnership.	39
Chapter 59B - Uniform Unincorporated Nonprofit Association Act.	39
Chapter 60 - Railroads and Other Carriers [Repealed and Transferred.]	39
Chapter 61 - Religious Societies	39
Chapter 62 - Public Utilities	39

Chapter 62 - Public Utilities (Continuation)	40
Chapter 62A - Public Safety Telephone Service And Wireless Telephone Service	40
Chapter 63 - Aeronautics	40
Chapter 63A - North Carolina Global TransPark Authority	40
Chapter 64 - Aliens	40
Chapter 65 – Cemeteries	40
Chapter 66 - Commerce and Business	41
Chapter 67 - Dogs	41
Chapter 68 - Fences and Stock Law	41
Chapter 69 - Fire Protection	41
Chapter 70 - Indian Antiquities, Archaeological Resources and Unmarked Human Skeletal Remains Protection	42
Chapter 71 - Indians [Repealed]	42
Chapter 71A - Indians	42
Chapter 72 - Inns, Hotels and Restaurants	42
Chapter 73 - Mills	42
Chapter 74 - Mines and Quarries	42
Chapter 74A - Company Police [Repealed]	42
Chapter 74B - Private Protective Services Act [Repealed]	42
Chapter 74C - Private Protective Services	42
Chapter 74D - Alarm Systems	42
Chapter 74E - Company Police Act	42
Chapter 74F - Locksmith Licensing Act	42
Chapter 74G - Campus Police Act	42
Chapter 75 - Monopolies, Trusts and Consumer Protection	42
Chapter 75A - Boating and Water Safety	43
Chapter 75B - Discrimination in Business	43
Chapter 75C - Motion Picture Fair Competition Act	43
Chapter 75D - Racketeer Influenced and Corrupt Organizations	43
Chapter 75E - Unlawful Activities in Connection With Certain Corporate Transactions	43
Chapter 76 - Navigation	43
Chapter 76A - Navigation and Pilotage Commissions	43
Chapter 77 - Rivers, Creeks, and Coastal Waters	43
Chapter 78 - Securities Law [Repealed]	43
Chapter 78A - North Carolina Securities Act	43
Chapter 78B - Tender Offer Disclosure Act [Repealed]	43
Chapter 78C - Investment Advisers	43
Chapter 78D - Commodities Act	43
Chapter 79 - Strays [Repealed]	43
Chapter 80 - Trademarks, Brands, etc.	44
Chapter 81 - Weights and Measures [Recodified]	44
Chapter 81A - Weights and Measures Act of 1975.	44
Chapter 82 - Wrecks [Repealed]	44
Chapter 83 - Architects [Recodified]	44

Chapter 83A - Architects	44
Chapter 84 - Attorneys-at-Law	44
Chapter 84A - Foreign Legal Consultants	44
Chapter 85 - Auctions and Auctioneers [Repealed.]	44
Chapter 85A - Bail Bondsmen and Runners [Recodified.]	44
Chapter 85B - Auctions and Auctioneers	44
Chapter 85C - Bail Bondsmen and Runners [Recodified.]	44
Chapter 86 - Barbers [Recodified.]	44
Chapter 86A - Barbers	44
Chapter 87 - Contractors	44
Chapter 88 - Cosmetic Art [Repealed.]	44
Chapter 88A - Electrolysis Practice Act	44
Chapter 88B - Cosmetic Art	45
Chapter 89 - Engineering and Land Surveying [Recodified.]	45
Chapter 89A - Landscape Architects	45
Chapter 89B - Foresters	45
Chapter 89C - Engineering and Land Surveying	45
Chapter 89D - Landscape Contractors	45
Chapter 89E - Geologists Licensing Act	45
Chapter 89F - North Carolina Soil Scientist Licensing Act	45
Chapter 89G - Irrigation Contractors	45
Chapter 90 - Medicine and Allied Occupations	45
Chapter 90 - Medicine and Allied Occupations (Continuation)	46
Chapter 90 - Medicine and Allied Occupations (Continuation)	47
Chapter 90 - Medicine and Allied Occupations (Continuation)	48
Chapter 90A - Sanitarians and Water and Wastewater Treatment Facility Operators	48
Chapter 90B - Social Worker Certification and Licensure Act	48
Chapter 90C - North Carolina Recreational Therapy Licensure Act	48
Chapter 90D - Interpreters and Transliterators	48
Chapter 91 - Pawnbrokers [Repealed.]	48
Chapter 91A - Pawnbrokers Modernization Act of 1989	48
Chapter 92 - Photographers [Deleted.]	48
Chapter 93 - Certified Public Accountants	48
Chapter 93A - Real Estate License Law	49
Chapter 93B - Occupational Licensing Boards	49
Chapter 93C - Watchmakers [Repealed.]	49
Chapter 93D - North Carolina State Hearing Aid Dealers and Fitters Board.	49
Chapter 93E - North Carolina Appraisers Act	49
Chapter 94 - Apprenticeship	49
Chapter 95 - Department of Labor and Labor Regulations	49
Chapter 95 - Department of Labor and Labor Regulations (Continuation)	50
Chapter 96 - Employment Security	50
Chapter 97 - Workers' Compensation Act	50
Chapter 97 - Workers' Compensation Act (Continuation)	51

Chapter 98 - Burnt and Lost Records	51
Chapter 99 - Libel and Slander	51
Chapter 99A - Civil Remedies for Criminal Actions	51
Chapter 99B - Products Liability	51
Chapter 99C - Actions Relating to Winter Sports Safety and Accidents	51
Chapter 99D - Civil Rights	51
Chapter 99E - Special Liability Provisions	51
Chapter 100 - Monuments, Memorials and Parks	51
Chapter 101 - Names of Persons	51
Chapter 102 - Official Survey Base	51
Chapter 103 - Sundays, Holidays and Special Days	51
Chapter 104 - United States Lands	51
Chapter 104A - Degrees of Kinship	51
Chapter 104B - Hurricanes or Other Acts of Nature	51
Chapter 104C - Atomic Energy, Radioactivity and Ionizing Radiation [Repealed and Recodified.]	51
Chapter 104D - Southern States Energy Compact	51
Chapter 104E - North Carolina Radiation Protection Act	51
Chapter 104F - Southeast Interstate Low-Level Radioactive Waste Management Compact [Repealed]	51
Chapter 104G - North Carolina Low-Level Radioactive Waste Management Authority Act of 1987 [Repealed]	51
Chapter 105 - Taxation	51
Chapter 105 - Taxation (Continuation)	52
Chapter 105 - Taxation (Continuation)	53
Chapter 105 - Taxation (Continuation)	54
Chapter 105A - Setoff Debt Collection Act	55
Chapter 105B - Defaulted Student Loan Recovery Act	55
Chapter 106 - Agriculture	55
Chapter 106 - Agriculture (Continue)	56
Chapter 106 - Agriculture (Continue)	57
Chapter 107 - Agricultural Development Districts [Repealed.]	57
Chapter 108 - Social Services [Repealed and Recodified.]	57
Chapter 108A - Social Services	57
Chapter 108B - Community Action Programs	58
Chapter 108C Medicaid and Health Choice Provider Requirements.	58
Chapter 108D Medicaid Managed Care for Behavioral Health Services.	58
Chapter 109 - Bonds [Recodified.]	58
Chapter 110 - Child Welfare	58
Chapter 111 - Aid to the Blind	58
Chapter 112 - Confederate Homes and Pensions [Repealed.]	58
Chapter 113 - Conservation and Development	58
Chapter 113 - Conservation and Development (Continuation)	59

Chapter 83A - Architects	44
Chapter 84 - Attorneys-at-Law	44
Chapter 84A - Foreign Legal Consultants	44
Chapter 85 - Auctions and Auctioneers [Repealed.]	44
Chapter 85A - Bail Bondsmen and Runners [Recodified.]	44
Chapter 85B - Auctions and Auctioneers	44
Chapter 85C - Bail Bondsmen and Runners [Recodified.]	44
Chapter 86 - Barbers [Recodified.]	44
Chapter 86A - Barbers	44
Chapter 87 - Contractors	44
Chapter 88 - Cosmetic Art [Repealed.]	44
Chapter 88A - Electrolysis Practice Act	44
Chapter 88B - Cosmetic Art	45
Chapter 89 - Engineering and Land Surveying [Recodified.]	45
Chapter 89A - Landscape Architects	45
Chapter 89B - Foresters	45
Chapter 89C - Engineering and Land Surveying	45
Chapter 89D - Landscape Contractors	45
Chapter 89E - Geologists Licensing Act	45
Chapter 89F - North Carolina Soil Scientist Licensing Act	45
Chapter 89G - Irrigation Contractors	45
Chapter 90 - Medicine and Allied Occupations	45
Chapter 90 - Medicine and Allied Occupations (Continuation)	46
Chapter 90 - Medicine and Allied Occupations (Continuation)	47
Chapter 90 - Medicine and Allied Occupations (Continuation)	48
Chapter 90A - Sanitarians and Water and Wastewater Treatment Facility Operators	48
Chapter 90B - Social Worker Certification and Licensure Act	48
Chapter 90C - North Carolina Recreational Therapy Licensure Act	48
Chapter 90D - Interpreters and Transliterators	48
Chapter 91 - Pawnbrokers [Repealed.]	48
Chapter 91A - Pawnbrokers Modernization Act of 1989	48
Chapter 92 - Photographers [Deleted.]	48
Chapter 93 - Certified Public Accountants	48
Chapter 93A - Real Estate License Law	49
Chapter 93B - Occupational Licensing Boards	49
Chapter 93C - Watchmakers [Repealed.]	49
Chapter 93D - North Carolina State Hearing Aid Dealers and Fitters Board.	49
Chapter 93E - North Carolina Appraisers Act	49
Chapter 94 - Apprenticeship	49
Chapter 95 - Department of Labor and Labor Regulations	49
Chapter 95 - Department of Labor and Labor Regulations (Continuation)	50
Chapter 96 - Employment Security	50
Chapter 97 - Workers' Compensation Act	50
Chapter 97 - Workers' Compensation Act (Continuation)	51

Chapter 98 - Burnt and Lost Records	51
Chapter 99 - Libel and Slander	51
Chapter 99A - Civil Remedies for Criminal Actions	51
Chapter 99B - Products Liability	51
Chapter 99C - Actions Relating to Winter Sports Safety and Accidents	51
Chapter 99D - Civil Rights	51
Chapter 99E - Special Liability Provisions	51
Chapter 100 - Monuments, Memorials and Parks	51
Chapter 101 - Names of Persons	51
Chapter 102 - Official Survey Base	51
Chapter 103 - Sundays, Holidays and Special Days	51
Chapter 104 - United States Lands	51
Chapter 104A - Degrees of Kinship	51
Chapter 104B - Hurricanes or Other Acts of Nature	51
Chapter 104C - Atomic Energy, Radioactivity and Ionizing Radiation [Repealed and Recodified.]	51
Chapter 104D - Southern States Energy Compact	51
Chapter 104E - North Carolina Radiation Protection Act	51
Chapter 104F - Southeast Interstate Low-Level Radioactive Waste Management Compact [Repealed]	51
Chapter 104G - North Carolina Low-Level Radioactive Waste Management Authority Act of 1987 [Repealed]	51
Chapter 105 - Taxation	51
Chapter 105 - Taxation (Continuation)	52
Chapter 105 - Taxation (Continuation)	53
Chapter 105 - Taxation (Continuation)	54
Chapter 105A - Setoff Debt Collection Act	55
Chapter 105B - Defaulted Student Loan Recovery Act	55
Chapter 106 - Agriculture	55
Chapter 106 - Agriculture (Continue)	56
Chapter 106 - Agriculture (Continue)	57
Chapter 107 - Agricultural Development Districts [Repealed.]	57
Chapter 108 - Social Services [Repealed and Recodified.]	57
Chapter 108A - Social Services	57
Chapter 108B - Community Action Programs	58
Chapter 108C Medicaid and Health Choice Provider Requirements.	58
Chapter 108D Medicaid Managed Care for Behavioral Health Services.	58
Chapter 109 - Bonds [Recodified.]	58
Chapter 110 - Child Welfare	58
Chapter 111 - Aid to the Blind	58
Chapter 112 - Confederate Homes and Pensions [Repealed.]	58
Chapter 113 - Conservation and Development	58
Chapter 113 - Conservation and Development (Continuation)	59

Chapter 113A - Pollution Control and Environment	59
Chapter 113A - Pollution Control and Environment (Continuation)	60
Chapter 113B - North Carolina Energy Policy Act of 1975	60
Chapter 114 - Department of Justice	60
Chapter 115 - Elementary and Secondary Education [Repealed.]	60
Chapter 115A - Community Colleges, Technical Institutes, and Industrial Education Centers [Repealed.]	60
Chapter 115B - Tuition and Fee Waivers	60
Chapter 115C - Elementary and Secondary Education	60
Chapter 115C - Elementary and Secondary Education (Continuation)	61
Chapter 115C - Elementary and Secondary Education (Continuation)	62
Chapter 115C - Elementary and Secondary Education (Continuation)	63
Chapter 115D - Community Colleges	63
Chapter 115E - Private Educational Facilities Finance Act [Recodified]	63
Chapter 116 - Higher Education	63
Chapter 116 - Higher Education (Continuation)	63
Chapter 116A - Escheats and Abandoned Property [Repealed.]	64
Chapter 116B - Escheats and Abandoned Property	64
Chapter 116C - Continuum of Education Programs	64
Chapter 116D - Higher Education Bonds	64
Chapter 117 - Electrification	64
Chapter 118 - Firemen's and Rescue Squad Workers' Relief and Pension Funds [Recodified.]	64
Chapter 118A - Firemen's Death Benefit Act [Repealed.]	64
Chapter 118B - Members of a Rescue Squad Death Benefit Act [Repealed.]	64
Chapter 119 - Gasoline and Oil Inspection and Regulation	64
Chapter 120 - General Assembly	65
Chapter 120 - General Assembly (Continuation)	66
Chapter 120 - General Assembly (Continuation)	67
Chapter 120C - Lobbying	67
Chapter 121 - Archives and History	67
Chapter 122 - Hospitals for the Mentally Disordered [Repealed.]	67
Chapter 122A - North Carolina Housing Finance Agency	67
Chapter 122B - North Carolina Agricultural Facilities Finance Act [Repealed.]	67
Chapter 122C - Mental Health, Developmental Disabilities, and Substance Abuse Act of 1985	67
Chapter 122C - Mental Health, Developmental Disabilities, and Substance Abuse Act of 1985 (Continuation)	68
Chapter 122D - North Carolina Agricultural Finance Act	68

Chapter 122E - North Carolina Housing Trust and Oil Overcharge Act	68
Chapter 123 - Impeachment	69
Chapter 123A - Industrial Development [Repealed.]	69
Chapter 124 - Internal Improvements	69
Chapter 125 - Libraries	69
Chapter 126 - State Personnel System	69
Chapter 127 - Militia [Repealed.]	69
Chapter 127A - Militia	69
Chapter 127B - Military Affairs	69
Chapter 127C - Advisory Commission on Military Affairs	69
Chapter 128 - Offices and Public Officers	69
Chapter 128 - Offices and Public Officers (Continuation)	70
Chapter 129 - Public Buildings and Grounds	70
Chapter 130 - Public Health [Repealed.]	70
Chapter 130A - Public Health	70
Chapter 130A - Public Health (Continuation)	71
Chapter 130A - Public Health (Continuation)	72
Chapter 130B - Hazardous Waste Management Commission [Repealed.]	72
Chapter 131 - Public Hospitals [Repealed.]	72
Chapter 131A - Health Care Facilities Finance Act	72
Chapter 131B - Licensing of Ambulatory Surgical Facilities [Repealed.]	72
Chapter 131C - Charitable Solicitation Licensure Act [Repealed.]	72
Chapter 131D - Inspection and Licensing of Facilities	72
Chapter 131E - Health Care Facilities and Services	72
Chapter 131E - Health Care Facilities and Services (Continuation)	73
Chapter 131F - Solicitation of Contributions	73
Chapter 132 - Public Records	73
Chapter 133 - Public Works	74
Chapter 134 - Youth Development [Recodified.]	74
Chapter 134A - Youth Services [Repealed.]	74
Chapter 135 - Retirement System for Teachers and State Employees; Social Security; Health Insurance Program for Children	74
Chapter 135 - Retirement System for Teachers and State Employees; Social Security; Health Insurance Program for Children	75
Chapter 136 - Transportation	75
Chapter 136 - Transportation (Continuation)	76
Chapter 137 - Rural Rehabilitation [Repealed.]	76
Chapter 138 - Salaries, Fees and Allowances	76
Chapter 138A - State Government Ethics Act	76
Chapter 139 - Soil and Water Conservation Districts	76

Chapter 140 - State Art Museum; Symphony and Art Societies	76
Chapter 140A - State Awards System	76
Chapter 141 - State Boundaries	76
Chapter 142 - State Debt	76
Chapter 143 - State Departments, Institutions, and Commissions	77
Chapter 143 - State Departments, Institutions, and Commissions (Continuation)	78
Chapter 143 - State Departments, Institutions, and Commissions (Continuation)	79
Chapter 143 - State Departments, Institutions, and Commissions (Continuation)	80
Chapter 143A - State Government Reorganization	80
Chapter 143B - Executive Organization Act of 1973	80
Chapter 143B - Executive Organization Act of 1973 (Continuation)	81
Chapter 143B - Executive Organization Act of 1973 (Continuation)	82
Chapter 143C - State Budget Act	83
Chapter 143D - The State Governmental Accountability and Internal Control Act	83
Chapter 144 - State Flag, Official Governmental Flags, Motto, and Colors	83
Chapter 145 - State Symbols and Other Official Adoptions.	83
Chapter 146 - State Lands	83
Chapter 147 - State Officers	83
Chapter 148 - State Prison System	84
Chapter 149 - State Song and Toast	84
Chapter 150 - Uniform Revocation of Licenses [Repealed.]	84
Chapter 150A - Administrative Procedure Act [Recodified.]	84
Chapter 150B - Administrative Procedure Act	84
Chapter 151 - Constables [Repealed.]	84
Chapter 152 - Coroners	84
Chapter 152A - County Medical Examiner [Repealed.]	84
Chapter 152A - County Medical Examiner [Repealed.] (Continuation)	85
Chapter 153 - Counties and County Commissioners [Repealed.]	85
Chapter 153A - Counties	85
Chapter 153B - Mountain Resources Planning Act	85
Chapter 153C - Uwharrie Regional Resources Act	85
Chapter 154 - County Surveyor [Repealed.]	85
Chapter 155 - County Treasurer [Repealed.]	85
Chapter 156 - Drainage	85
Chapter 156 – Drainage (Continuation)	86

Chapter 157 - Housing Authorities and Projects	86
Chapter 157A - Historic Properties Commissions [Transferred.]	86
Chapter 158 - Local Development	86
Chapter 159 - Local Government Finance	86
Chapter 159 - Local Government Finance (Continuation)	87
Chapter 159A - Pollution Abatement and Industrial Facilities Financing Act [Unconstitutional.]	87
Chapter 159B - Joint Municipal Electric Power and Energy Act	87
Chapter 159C - Industrial and Pollution Control Facilities Financing Act	87
Chapter 159D - The North Carolina Capital Facilities Financing Act	87
Chapter 159E - Registered Public Obligations Act	87
Chapter 159F - North Carolina Energy Development Authority [Repealed.]	87
Chapter 159G - Water Infrastructure	87
Chapter 159H - [Reserved.]	87
Chapter 159I - Solid Waste Management Loan Program and Local Government Special Obligation Bonds	87
Chapter 160 - Municipal Corporations [Repealed And Transferred.]	87
Chapter 160A - Cities and Towns	88
Chapter 160A - Cities and Towns (Continuation)	89
Chapter 160B - Consolidated City-County Act	89
Chapter 160C - Baseball Park Districts [Repealed.]	90
Chapter 161 - Register of Deeds	90
Chapter 162 - Sheriff	90
Chapter 162A - Water and Sewer Systems	90
Chapter 162B Continuity of Local Government in Emergency.	90
Chapter 163 Elections and Election Laws.	90
Chapter 163 Elections and Election Laws. (Continuation)	91
Chapter 164 Concerning the General Statutes of North Carolina.	92
Chapter 165 Veterans.	92
Chapter 166 Civil Preparedness Agencies [Repealed.]	92
Chapter 166A North Carolina Emergency Management Act.	92
Chapter 167 State Civil Air Patrol [Repealed.]	92
Chapter 168 Persons with Disabilities.	92
Chapter 168A Persons With Disabilities Protection Act.	92

§ 105-164.7. Retailer to collect sales tax from purchaser as trustee for State.

The sales tax imposed by this Article is intended to be passed on to the purchaser of a taxable item and borne by the purchaser instead of by the retailer. A retailer must collect the tax due on an item when the item is sold at retail. The tax is a debt from the purchaser to the retailer until paid and is recoverable at law by the retailer in the same manner as other debts. A retailer is considered to act as a trustee on behalf of the State when it collects tax from the purchaser of a taxable item. The tax must be stated and charged separately on the invoices or other documents of the retailer given to the purchaser at the time of the sale except for either of the following:

(1)   Vending machine sales.

(2)   Where a retailer displays a statement indicating the sales price includes the tax. (1957, c. 1340, s. 5; 1973, c. 476, s. 193; 2000-19, s. 1.3; 2006-162, s. 7; 2009-451, s. 27A.3(j); 2012-79, s. 2.9.)

§ 105-164.8. Retailer's obligation to collect tax; remote sales subject to tax.

(a)   Obligation. - A retailer is required to collect the tax imposed by this Article notwithstanding any of the following:

(1)   That the purchaser's order or the contract of sale is delivered, mailed, or otherwise transmitted by the purchaser to the retailer at a point outside this State as a result of solicitation by the retailer through the medium of a catalogue or other written advertisement.

(2)   That the purchaser's order or the contract of sale is made or closed by acceptance or approval outside this State, or before any tangible personal property or digital property that is part of the order or contract enters this State.

(3)   That the purchaser's order or the contract of sale provides that the property shall be or is in fact procured or manufactured at a point outside this State and shipped directly to the purchaser from the point of origin.

(4)   That the property is mailed to the purchaser in this State or a point outside this State or delivered to a carrier outside this State f.o.b. or otherwise

and directed to the purchaser in this State regardless of whether the cost of transportation is paid by the retailer or by the purchaser.

(5)   That the property is delivered directly to the purchaser at a point outside this State.

(6)   Any combination in whole or in part of any two or more of the foregoing statements of fact, if it is intended that the property purchased be brought to this State for storage, use, or consumption in this State.

(b)   Remote Sales. - A retailer who makes a remote sale is engaged in business in this State and is subject to the tax levied under this Article if at least one of the following conditions is met:

(1)   The retailer is a corporation engaged in business under the laws of this State or a person domiciled in, a resident of, or a citizen of, this State.

(2)   The retailer maintains retail establishments or offices in this State, whether the remote sales thus subject to taxation by this State result from or are related in any other way to the activities of the establishments or offices.

(3)   The retailer solicits or transacts business in this State by employees, independent contractors, agents, or other representatives, whether the remote sales thus subject to taxation by this State result from or are related in any other way to the solicitation or transaction of business. A retailer is presumed to be soliciting or transacting business by an independent contractor, agent, or other representative if the retailer enters into an agreement with a resident of this State under which the resident, for a commission or other consideration, directly or indirectly refers potential customers, whether by a link on an Internet Web site or otherwise, to the retailer. This presumption applies only if the cumulative gross receipts from sales by the retailer to purchasers in this State who are referred to the retailer by all residents with this type of agreement with the retailer is in excess of ten thousand dollars ($10,000) during the preceding four quarterly periods. This presumption may be rebutted by proof that the resident with whom the retailer has an agreement did not engage in any solicitation in the State on behalf of the seller that would satisfy the nexus requirement of the United States Constitution during the four quarterly periods in question.

(4)   Repealed by Session Laws 1991, c. 45, s. 16.

(5) The retailer, by purposefully or systematically exploiting the market provided by this State by any media-assisted, media-facilitated, or media-solicited means, including direct mail advertising, distribution of catalogs, computer-assisted shopping, television, radio or other electronic media, telephone solicitation, magazine or newspaper advertisements, or other media, creates nexus with this State. A nonresident retailer who purchases advertising to be delivered by television, by radio, in print, on the Internet, or by any other medium is not considered to be engaged in business in this State based solely on the purchase of the advertising.

(6) Through compact or reciprocity with another jurisdiction of the United States, that jurisdiction uses its taxing power and its jurisdiction over the retailer in support of this State's taxing power.

(7) The retailer consents, expressly or by implication, to the imposition of the tax imposed by this Article. For purposes of this subdivision, evidence that a retailer engaged in the activity described in subdivision (5) is prima facie evidence that the retailer consents to the imposition of the tax imposed by this Article.

(8) The retailer is a holder of a wine shipper permit issued by the ABC Commission pursuant to G.S. 18B-1001.1.

(c) Local Tax. - A retailer who is required to collect the tax imposed by this Article must collect a local use tax on a transaction if a local sales tax does not apply to the transaction. The sourcing principles in G.S. 105-164.4B determine whether a local sales tax or a local use tax applies to a transaction. A "local sales tax" is a tax imposed under Chapter 1096 of the 1967 Session Laws or by Subchapter VIII of this Chapter, and a local use tax is a use tax imposed under that act or Subchapter. (1957, c. 1340, s. 5; 1987 (Reg. Sess., 1988), c. 1096, s. 4; 1991, c. 45, s. 16; 2001-347, s. 2.10; 2003-402, s. 13; 2003-416, s. 24(b), (c); 2009-451, s. 27A.3(a).)

§ 105-164.9. Advertisement to absorb tax unlawful.

Any retailer who shall by any character or public advertisement offer to absorb the tax levied in this Article or in any manner directly or indirectly advertise that the tax herein imposed is not considered an element in the price to the purchaser shall be guilty of a Class 1 misdemeanor. Any violations of the provisions of this section reported to the Secretary shall be reported by him to the Attorney General of the State to the end that such violations may be brought to the attention of the solicitor of the court of the county or district whose duty it is to prosecute misdemeanors in the jurisdiction. It shall be the duty of such solicitor to investigate such alleged violations and if he finds that this section has been violated prosecute such violators in accordance with the law. (1957, c. 1340, s. 5; 1973, c. 476, s. 193; 1993, c. 539, s. 704; 1994, Ex. Sess., c. 24, s. 14(c).)

§ 105-164.10. Retail tax calculation.

For the convenience of the retailer in collecting the tax due under this Article, the Secretary must prescribe tables that compute the tax due on sales by rounding off the amount of tax due to the nearest whole cent. The Secretary must issue a separate table for each rate of tax that may apply to a sale. (1957, c. 1340, s. 5; 1961, c. 826, s. 2; 1973, c. 476, s. 193; 1991, c. 689, s. 313; 2013-316, s. 5(e).)

§ 105-164.11. Excessive and erroneous collections.

(a) Remittance of Overcollections to Secretary. - When tax is collected for any period on a taxable sale in excess of the total amount that should have been collected or is collected on an exempt or nontaxable sale, the total amount collected must be remitted to the Secretary. If the Secretary determines that the seller overcollected the sales tax on a transaction, the Secretary shall take only one of the actions listed in this subsection. This subsection shall be construed with other provisions of this Article and given effect so as to result in the payment to the Secretary of the total amount collected as tax if it is in excess of the amount that should have been collected.

(1) If the Secretary determines that the seller overcollected tax on a transaction, the Secretary may allow a refund of the tax. The Secretary may allow the refund only if the seller gives the purchaser credit for or a refund of the overcollected tax. The Secretary shall not refund the overcollected tax to the seller if the seller has elected to offset a use tax liability on a related transaction with the overcollected sales tax under subdivision (2) of this subsection.

(2) If the Secretary determines that a seller who overcollected sales tax on a transaction is instead liable for a use tax on a related transaction, the Secretary may allow the seller to offset the use tax liability with the overcollected sales tax. The Secretary shall not allow an offset if the seller has elected to receive a refund of the overcollected tax under subdivision (1) of this subsection. The decision by a seller to receive an offset of tax liability rather than a refund of the overcollected tax does not affect the liability of the seller to the purchaser for the overcollected tax.

(3) If neither subdivision (1) nor (2) of this subsection applies, the Secretary shall retain the total amount collected on the transaction.

(b) Refund Procedures First Remedy. - The first course of remedy available to purchasers seeking a refund of over-collected sales or use taxes from the seller are the customer refund procedures provided in this Chapter or otherwise provided by administrative rule, bulletin, or directive on the law issued by the Secretary.

(c) Cause of Action Against Seller. - A cause of action against the seller for over-collected sales or uses taxes does not accrue until a purchaser has provided written notice to a seller and the seller has had 60 days to respond. The notice to the seller must contain the information necessary to determine the validity of the request.

(d) Presumption of Reasonable Business Practice. - In connection with a purchaser's request from the seller of over-collected sales or use taxes, a seller shall be presumed to have a reasonable business practice if, in the collection of sales and use taxes, the seller uses either a provider or a system, including a proprietary system, that is certified by the State and the seller has remitted to the State all taxes collected less any deductions, credits, or collection allowances.

(e) Reliance on Written Advice. - A seller who requests specific written advice from the Secretary and who collects and remits sales or use tax in accordance with the written advice the Secretary gives the seller is not liable to a purchaser for any overcollected sales or use tax that was collected in accordance with the written advice. Subsection (a) of this section governs when a seller may obtain a refund for overcollected tax. (1957, c. 1340, s. 5; 1959, c. 1259, s. 5; 1961, c. 826, s. 2; 1973, c. 476, s. 193; 1991 (Reg. Sess., 1992), c. 1007, s. 4; 2004-22, s. 1; 2009-413, s. 1; 2011-293, s. 1.)

§ 105-164.12: Repealed by Session Laws 2001-347, s. 2.11.

§ 105-164.12A. Electric golf cart and battery charger considered a single article.

The sale of an electric golf cart and a battery charger that is not physically attached to the golf cart is considered the sale of a single article of tangible personal property in imposing tax under this Article if the battery charger is designed to recharge the golf cart and is sold to the purchaser of the golf cart when the golf cart is sold. (1985 (Reg. Sess., 1986), c. 901.)

§ 105-164.12B. Tangible personal property sold below cost with conditional service contract.

(a)   Conditional Service Contract Defined. - A conditional service contract is a contract in which all of the following conditions are met:

(1)   A seller transfers an item of tangible personal property to a consumer on the condition that the consumer enter into an agreement to purchase services on an ongoing basis for a minimum period of at least six months.

(2)   The agreement requires the consumer to pay a cancellation fee to the seller if the consumer cancels the contract for services within the minimum period.

(3)   For the item transferred, the seller charges the consumer a price that, after any price reduction the seller gives the consumer, is below the purchase price the seller paid for the item. The seller's purchase price is presumed to be no greater than the price the seller paid, as shown on the seller's purchase invoice, for the same item within 12 months before the seller entered into the conditional service contract.

(b)   Tax. - If a seller transfers an item of tangible personal property as part of a conditional service contract, a sale has occurred. The sales price of the item is presumed to be the retail price at which the item would sell in the absence of the conditional service contract. Sales tax is due at the time of the transfer on the following:

(1) Any part of the presumed sales price the consumer pays at that time, if the service in the contract is taxable at the combined general rate.

(2) The presumed sales price, if the service in the contract is not taxable at the combined general rate.

(c)-(f). Repealed by Session Laws 2007-244, s. 3, effective October 1, 2007. (1996, 2nd Ex. Sess., c. 13, s. 5.1; 2001-414, ss. 16, 17; 2006-151, s. 6; 2007-244, s. 3.)

§ 105-164.12C. Items given away by merchants.

If a retailer engaged in the business of selling prepared food and drink for immediate or on-premises consumption also gives prepared food or drink to its patrons or employees free of charge, for the purpose of this Article, the property given away is considered sold along with the property sold. If a retailer gives an item of inventory to a customer free of charge on the condition that the customer purchase similar or related property, the item given away is considered sold along with the Item sold. In all other cases, property given away or used by any retailer or wholesale merchant is not considered sold, whether or not the retailer or wholesale merchant recovers its cost of the property from sales of other property. (2012-79, s. 2.10(a).)

§ 105-164.13. Retail sales and use tax.

The sale at retail and the use, storage, or consumption in this State of the following tangible personal property, digital property, and services are specifically exempted from the tax imposed by this Article:

Agricultural Group.

(1) (See notes for delayed repeal of subdivision) Any of the following items sold to a farmer for use by the farmer in the planting, cultivating, harvesting, or curing of farm crops or in the production of dairy products, eggs, or animals. A "farmer" includes a dairy operator, a poultry farmer, an egg producer, a livestock farmer, a farmer of crops, and a farmer of an aquatic species, as defined in G.S. 106-758.

a. Commercial fertilizer, lime, land plaster, plastic mulch, plant bed covers, potting soil, baler twine, and seeds.

b. Farm machinery, attachment and repair parts for farm machinery, and lubricants applied to farm machinery. The term "machinery" includes implements that have moving parts or are operated or drawn by an animal. The term does not include implements operated wholly by hand or motor vehicles required to be registered under Chapter 20 of the General Statutes.

c. A horse or mule.

d. Fuel.

(1a) (See notes for delayed repeal of subdivision) Sales of the following to a farmer, as defined in subdivision (1) of this section:

a. A container used for a purpose set out in subdivision (1) of this section or in packaging and transporting the farmer's product for sale.

b. A grain, feed, or soybean storage facility, and parts and accessories attached to the facility.

(1b) (See notes for delayed repeal of subdivision) Electricity sold to a farmer to be used for any farming purpose other than preparing food, heating dwellings, and other household purposes.

(2) Repealed by Session Laws 2001, c. 514, s. 1, effective February 1, 2002.

(2a) (See notes for delayed repeal of subdivision) Any of the following substances when purchased for use on animals or plants, as appropriate, held or produced for commercial purposes. This exemption does not apply to any equipment or devices used to administer, release, apply, or otherwise dispense these substances:

a. Remedies, vaccines, medications, litter materials, and feeds for animals.

b. Rodenticides, insecticides, herbicides, fungicides, and pesticides.

c. Defoliants for use on cotton or other crops.

d. Plant growth inhibitors, regulators, or stimulators, including systemic and contact or other sucker control agents for tobacco and other crops.

e. Semen.

(3) Products of forests and mines in their original or unmanufactured state when such sales are made by the producer in the capacity of producer.

(4) Cotton, tobacco, peanuts or other farm products sold to manufacturers for further manufacturing or processing.

(4a) (See notes for delayed repeal of subdivision) Baby chicks and poults sold for commercial poultry or egg production.

(4b) Products of a farm sold in their original state by the producer of the products if the producer is not primarily a retail merchant and ice used to preserve agriculture, aquaculture and commercial fishery products until the products are sold at retail.

(4c) (See notes for delayed repeal of subdivision) Any of the following items concerning the housing, raising, or feeding of animals:

a. Commercially manufactured facilities to be used for commercial purposes for housing, raising, or feeding animals or for housing equipment necessary for these commercial activities.

b. Building materials, supplies, fixtures, and equipment that become a part of and are used in the construction, repair, or improvement of an enclosure or a structure specifically designed, constructed, and used for housing, raising, or feeding animals or for housing equipment necessary for one of these commercial activities.

c. Commercially manufactured equipment, and parts and accessories for the equipment, used in a facility that is exempt from tax under this subdivision or in an enclosure or a structure whose building materials are exempt from tax under this subdivision.

(4d) (See notes for delayed repeal of subdivision) Any of the following tobacco items:

a. The lease or rental of tobacco sheets used in handling tobacco in the warehouse and transporting tobacco to and from the warehouse.

b. A metal flue sold for use in curing tobacco, whether the flue is attached to a handfired furnace or used in connection with a mechanical burner.

c. A bulk tobacco barn or rack, parts and accessories attached to the tobacco barn or rack, and any similar apparatus, part, or accessory used to cure or dry tobacco or another crop.

(4e) Repealed by Session Laws 2006-162, s. 8(b), effective July 24, 2006.

(4f) Sales of the following to a person who is engaged in the commercial logging business:

a. Logging machinery. - Logging machinery is machinery used to harvest raw forest products for transport to first market.

b. Attachments and repair parts for logging machinery.

c. Lubricants applied to logging machinery.

d. Fuel used to operate logging machinery.

Industrial Group.

(4g) A wood chipper that meets all of the following requirements:

a. It is designed to be towed by a motor vehicle.

b. It is assigned a 17-digit vehicle identification number by the National Highway Transportation Safety Association.

c. It is sold to a person who purchases a motor vehicle in this State that is to be registered in another state and who uses the purchased motor vehicle to tow the wood chipper to the state in which the purchased motor vehicle is to be registered.

(5) Manufactured products produced and sold by manufacturers or producers to other manufacturers, producers, or registered retailers or wholesale merchants, for the purpose of resale except as modified by G.S. 105-

164.3(51). This exemption does not extend to or include retail sales to users or consumers not for resale.

(5a)   Products that are subject to tax under Article 5F of this Chapter.

(5b)   Sales to a telephone company regularly engaged in providing telecommunications service to subscribers on a commercial basis of central office equipment, switchboard equipment, private branch exchange equipment, terminal equipment other than public pay telephone terminal equipment, and parts and accessories attached to the equipment.

(5c)   Sales of towers, broadcasting equipment, and parts and accessories attached to the equipment to a radio or television company licensed by the Federal Communications Commission.

(5d)   Sales of broadcasting equipment and parts and accessories attached to the equipment to a cable service provider. For the purposes of this subdivision, "broadcasting equipment" does not include cable.

(6)   Repealed by Session Laws 1989 (Regular Session, 1990), c. 1068, s. 1.

(7)   Sales of products of waters in their original or unmanufactured state when such sales are made by the producer in the capacity of producer. Fish and seafoods are likewise exempt when sold by the fisherman in that capacity.

(8)   Sales to a manufacturer of tangible personal property that enters into or becomes an ingredient or component part of tangible personal property that is manufactured. This exemption does not apply to sales of electricity.

(8a)   Sales to a small power production facility, as defined in 16 U.S.C. § 796(17)(A), of fuel used by the facility to generate electricity.

(9)   Boats, fuel oil, lubricating oils, machinery, equipment, nets, rigging, paints, parts, accessories, and supplies sold to any of the following:

a.   The holder of a standard commercial fishing license issued under G.S. 113-168.2 for principal use in commercial fishing operations.

b.   The holder of a shellfish license issued under G.S. 113-169.2 for principal use in commercial shellfishing operations.

c. The operator of a for-hire boat, as defined in G.S. 113-174, for principal use in the commercial use of the boat.

(10) Sales of the following to commercial laundries or to pressing and dry cleaning establishments:

a. Articles or materials used for the identification of garments being laundered or dry cleaned, wrapping paper, bags, hangers, starch, soaps, detergents, cleaning fluids and other compounds or chemicals applied directly to the garments in the direct performance of the laundering or the pressing and cleaning service.

b. Laundry and dry-cleaning machinery, parts and accessories attached to the machinery, and lubricants applied to the machinery.

c. Fuel, other than electricity, used in the direct performance of the laundering or the pressing and cleaning service.

Motor Fuels Group.

(10a) Sales of the following to a major recycling facility:

a. Lubricants and other additives for motor vehicles or machinery and equipment used at the facility.

b. Materials, supplies, parts, and accessories, other than machinery and equipment, that are not capitalized by the taxpayer and are used or consumed in the manufacturing and material handling processes at the facility.

c. Electricity used at the facility.

(10b) Recodified as G.S. 105-164.13(10a)c. by Session Laws 2005-276, s. 33.9, effective January 1, 2006.

(11) Any of the following fuel:

a. Motor fuel, as taxed in Article 36C of this Chapter, except motor fuel for which a refund of the per gallon excise tax is allowed under G.S. 105-449.105A or G.S. 105-449.107.

b. Alternative fuel taxed under Article 36D of this Chapter, unless a refund of that tax is allowed under G.S. 105-449.107.

(11a) Sales of diesel fuel to railroad companies for use in rolling stock other than motor vehicles. The definitions in G.S. 105-333 apply in this subdivision.

Medical Group.

(12) Sales of any of the following items:

a. Prosthetic devices for human use.

b. Mobility enhancing equipment sold on a prescription.

c. Durable medical equipment sold on prescription.

d. Durable medical supplies sold on prescription.

(13) All of the following drugs, including their packaging materials and any instructions or information about the drugs included in the package with them:

a. Drugs required by federal law to be dispensed only on prescription.

b. Over-the-counter drugs sold on prescription.

c. Insulin.

(13a) Repealed by Session Laws 1996, Second Extra Session, c. 14, s. 16.

(13b) Repealed by Session Laws 1999, c. 438, s. 7, effective October 1, 1999.

(13c) Repealed by Session Laws 2013-316, s. 3.2(a), effective January 1, 2014, and applicable to sales made on or after that date.

Printed Materials Group.

(14) Public school books on the adopted list, the selling price of which is fixed by State contract.

(14a) Recodified as subdivision (33a) by Session Laws 2000-120, s. 5, effective July 14, 2000.

Transactions Group.

(15) Accounts of purchasers, representing taxable sales, on which the tax imposed by this Article has been paid, that are found to be worthless and actually charged off for income tax purposes may, at corresponding periods, be deducted from gross sales. In the case of a municipality that sells electricity, the account may be deducted if it meets all the conditions for charge-off that would apply if the municipality were subject to income tax. Any accounts deducted pursuant to this subdivision must be added to gross sales if afterwards collected.

(16) Sales of an article repossessed by the vendor if tax was paid on the sales price of the article.

Exempt Status Group.

(17) Sales which a state would be without power to tax under the limitations of the Constitution or laws of the United States or under the Constitution of this State.

Unclassified Group.

(18) Repealed by Session Laws 2005-276, s. 33.9, effective January 1, 2006.

(19) Repealed by Session Laws 1991, c. 618, s. 1.

(20) Sales by blind merchants operating under supervision of the Department of Health and Human Services.

(21) The lease or rental of motion picture films used for exhibition purposes where the lease or rental of such property is an established business or part of an established business or the same is incidental or germane to said business of the lessee.

(22) The lease or rental of films, motion picture films, transcriptions and recordings to radio stations and television stations operating under a certificate from the Federal Communications Commission.

(22a) Sales of audiovisual masters made or used by a production company in making visual and audio images for first generation reproduction. For the purpose of this subdivision, an "audiovisual master" is an audio or video film, tape, or disk or another audio or video storage device from which all other copies are made.

(23)   Sales of the following packaging items:

a.   Wrapping paper, labels, wrapping twine, paper, cloth, plastic bags, cartons, packages and containers, cores, cones or spools, wooden boxes, baskets, coops and barrels, including paper cups, napkins and drinking straws and like articles sold to manufacturers, producers and retailers, when such materials are used for packaging, shipment or delivery of tangible personal property which is sold either at wholesale or retail and when such articles constitute a part of the sale of such tangible personal property and are delivered with it to the customer.

b.   A container that is used as packaging by the owner of the container or another person to enclose tangible personal property for delivery to a purchaser of the property and is required to be returned to its owner for reuse.

(24)   Sales of fuel and other items of tangible personal property for use or consumption by or on ocean-going vessels which ply the high seas in interstate or foreign commerce in the transport of freight and/or passengers for hire exclusively, when delivered to an officer or agent of such vessel for the use of such vessel; provided, however, that sales of fuel and other items of tangible personal property made to officers, agents, members of the crew or passengers of such vessels for their personal use shall not be exempted from payment of the sales tax.

(25)   Sales by merchants on the Cherokee Indian Reservation when such merchants are authorized to do business on the Reservation and are paying the tribal gross receipts levy to the Tribal Council.

(26)   Food and prepared food sold not for profit by a nonpublic or public school, including a charter school and a regional school, within the school building during the regular school day.

(26a)   Food and prepared food sold not for profit by a public school cafeteria to a child care center that participates in the Child and Adult Care Food Program of the Department of Health and Human Services.

(27) Repealed by Session Laws 2013-316, s. 3.2(a), effective January 1, 2014, and applicable to sales made on or after that date.

(27a) (See notes for delayed repeal of subdivision) Bread, rolls, and buns sold at a bakery thrift store. A "bakery thrift store" is a retail outlet of a bakery that sells at wholesale over ninety percent (90%) of the items it makes and sells at the retail outlet day-old bread, rolls, and buns returned to it by retailers that acquired these items from the bakery.

(28) Repealed by Session Laws 2013-316, s. 3.2(a), effective January 1, 2014, and applicable to sales made on or after that date.

(29) Repealed by Session Laws 2005-435, s. 30, effective September 27, 2005.

(29a) Repealed by Session Laws 1995 (Regular Session, 1996), c. 646, s. 5.

(30) Sales from vending machines when sold by the owner or lessee of said machines at a price of one cent (1¢) per sale.

(31) Sales of meals not for profit to elderly and incapacitated persons by charitable or religious organizations not operated for profit which are entitled to the refunds provided by G.S. 105-164.14(b), when such meals are delivered to the purchasers at their places of abode.

(31a) Food and prepared food sold by a church or religious organization not operated for profit when the proceeds of the sales are actually used for religious activities.

(31b) Repealed by Session Laws 1996, Second Extra Session, c. 14, s. 16.

(32) Sales of motor vehicles, the sale of a motor vehicle body to be mounted on a motor vehicle chassis when a certificate of title has not been issued for the chassis, and the sale of a motor vehicle body mounted on a motor vehicle chassis that temporarily enters the State so the manufacturer of the body can mount the body on the chassis.

(33) Tangible personal property purchased solely for the purpose of export to a foreign country for exclusive use or consumption in that or some other foreign country, either in the direct performance or rendition of professional or commercial services, or in the direct conduct or operation of a trade or business,

all of which purposes are actually consummated, or purchased by the government of a foreign country for export which purpose is actually consummated. "Export" shall include the acts of possessing and marshalling such property, by either the seller or the purchaser, for transportation to a foreign country, but shall not include devoting such property to any other use in North Carolina or the United States. "Foreign country" shall not include any territory or possession of the United States.

In order to qualify for this exemption, an affidavit of export indicating compliance with the terms and conditions of this exemption, as prescribed by the Secretary of Revenue, must be submitted by the purchaser to the seller, and retained by the seller to evidence qualification for the exemption.

If the purposes qualifying the property for exemption are not consummated, the purchaser shall be liable for the tax which was avoided by the execution of the aforesaid affidavit as well as for applicable penalties and interest and the affidavit shall contain express provision that the purchaser has recognized and assumed such liability.

The principal purpose of this exemption is to encourage the flow of commerce through North Carolina ports that is now moving through out-of-state ports. However, it is not intended that property acquired for personal use or consumption by the purchaser, including gifts, shall be exempt hereunder.

(33a)   Tangible personal property sold by a retailer to a purchaser inside or outside this State, when the property is delivered by the retailer in this State to a common carrier or to the United States Postal Service for delivery to the purchaser or the purchaser's designees outside this State and the purchaser does not subsequently use the property in this State. This exemption includes printed material sold by a retailer to a purchaser inside or outside this State when the printed material is delivered directly to a mailing house, to a common carrier, or to the United States Postal Service for delivery to a mailing house in this State that will preaddress and presort the material and deliver it to a common carrier or to the United States Postal Service for delivery to recipients outside this State designated by the purchaser.

(34)   Sales of items by a nonprofit civic, charitable, educational, scientific or literary organization when the net proceeds of the sales will be given or contributed to the State of North Carolina or to one or more of its agencies or instrumentalities, or to one or more nonprofit charitable organizations, one of

whose purposes is to serve as a conduit through which such net proceeds will flow to the State or to one or more of its agencies or instrumentalities.

(35) Sales by a nonprofit civic, charitable, educational, scientific, literary, or fraternal organization when all of the following conditions are met:

a. The sales are conducted only upon an annual basis for the purpose of raising funds for the organization's activities.

b. The proceeds of the sale are actually used for the organization's activities.

c. The products sold are delivered to the purchaser within 60 days after the first solicitation of any sale made during the organization's annual sales period.

(36) Advertising supplements and any other printed matter ultimately to be distributed with or as part of a newspaper.

(37) Repealed by Session Laws 2001-424, s. 34.23(a), effective December 1, 2001, and applicable to sales made on or after that date.

(38) Food and other items lawfully purchased under the Food Stamp Program, 7 U.S.C. § 2011, and supplemental foods lawfully purchased with a food instrument issued under the Special Supplemental Nutrition Program, 42 U.S.C. § 1786, and supplemental foods purchased for direct distribution by the Special Supplemental Nutrition Program.

(39) Sales of paper, ink, and other tangible personal property to commercial printers and commercial publishers for use as ingredients or component parts of free distribution periodicals and sales by printers of free distribution periodicals to the publishers of these periodicals. As used in this subdivision, the term "free distribution periodical" means a publication that is continuously published on a periodic basis monthly or more frequently, is provided without charge to the recipient, and is distributed in any manner other than by mail.

(40) Sales to the Department of Transportation.

(41) Sales of mobile classrooms to local boards of education or to local boards of trustees of community colleges.

(42) Tangible personal property that is purchased by a retailer for resale or is manufactured or purchased by a wholesale merchant for resale and then withdrawn from inventory and donated by the retailer or wholesale merchant to either a governmental entity or a nonprofit organization, contributions to which are deductible as charitable contributions for federal income tax purposes.

(43) Custom computer software. - Custom computer software and the portion of prewritten computer software that is modified or enhanced if the modification or enhancement is designed and developed to the specifications of a specific purchaser and the charges for the modification or enhancement are separately stated.

(43a) Computer software that meets any of the following descriptions:

a. It is purchased to run on an enterprise server operating system. The exemption includes a purchase or license of computer software for high-volume, simultaneous use on multiple computers that is housed or maintained on an enterprise server or end users' computers. The exemption includes software designed to run a computer system, an operating program, or application software.

b. It is sold to a person who operates a datacenter and is used within the datacenter.

c. It is sold to a person who provides cable service, telecommunications service, or video programming and is used to provide ancillary service, cable service, Internet access service, telecommunications service, or video programming.

(43b) Computer software or digital property that becomes a component part of other computer software or digital property that is offered for sale or of a service that is offered for sale.

(44) (See notes for delayed repeal of subdivision) Piped natural gas. - This item is exempt because it is taxed under Article 5E of this Chapter.

(45) Sales of aircraft lubricants, aircraft repair parts, and aircraft accessories to an interstate passenger air carrier for use at its hub.

(45a) Sales to an interstate air business of tangible personal property that becomes a component part of or is dispensed as a lubricant into commercial aircraft during its maintenance, repair, or overhaul. For the purpose of this subdivision, commercial aircraft includes only aircraft that has a certified maximum take-off weight of more than 12,500 pounds and is regularly used to carry for compensation passengers, commercial freight, or individually addressed letters and packages.

(45b) Sales of the following items to an interstate air courier for use at its hub:

a. Aircraft lubricants, aircraft repair parts, and aircraft accessories.

b. Materials handling equipment, racking systems, and related parts and accessories for the storage or handling and movement of tangible personal property at an airport or in a warehouse or distribution facility.

(45c) Sales of aircraft simulators to a company for flight crew training and maintenance training.

(46) Sales of electricity by a municipality whose only wholesale supplier of electric power is a federal agency and who is required by a contract with that federal agency to make payments in lieu of taxes.

(47) An amount charged as a deposit on a beverage container that is returnable to the vendor for reuse when the amount is refundable or creditable to the vendee, whether or not the deposit is separately charged.

(48) An amount charged as a deposit on an aeronautic, automotive, industrial, marine, or farm replacement part that is returnable to the vendor for rebuilding or remanufacturing when the amount is refundable or creditable to the vendee, whether or not the deposit is separately charged. This exemption does not include tires or batteries.

(49) Installation charges when the charges are separately stated on an invoice or similar billing document given to the purchaser at the time of sale.

(49a) Delivery charges for delivery of direct mail if the charges are separately stated on an invoice or similar billing document given to the purchaser at the time of sale.

(50) Fifty percent (50%) of the sales price of tangible personal property sold through a coin-operated vending machine, other than tobacco.

(51) Water delivered by or through main lines or pipes for either commercial or domestic use or consumption.

(52) Items subject to sales and use tax under G.S. 105-164.4, other than electricity, telecommunications service, and ancillary service as defined in G.S. 105-164.4, if all of the following conditions are met:

a. The items are purchased by a State agency for its own use and in accordance with G.S. 105-164.29A.

b. The items are purchased pursuant to a valid purchase order issued by the State agency that contains the exemption number of the agency and a description of the property purchased, or the items purchased are paid for with a State-issued check, electronic deposit, credit card, procurement card, or credit account of the State agency.

c. For all purchases other than by an agency-issued purchase order, the agency must provide to or have on file with the retailer the agency's exemption number.

(53) Sales to a professional land surveyor of tangible personal property on which custom aerial survey data is stored in digital form or is depicted in graphic form. Data is custom if it was created to the specifications of the professional land surveyor purchasing the property. A professional land surveyor is a person licensed as a surveyor under Chapter 89C of the General Statutes.

(54) The following telecommunications services and charges:

a. Telecommunications service that is a component part of or is integrated into a telecommunications service that is resold. This exemption does not apply to service purchased by a pay telephone provider who uses the service to provide pay telephone service. Examples of services that are resold include carrier charges for access to an intrastate or interstate interexchange network, interconnection charges paid by a provider of mobile telecommunications service, and charges for the sale of unbundled network elements. An unbundled network element is a network element, as defined in 47 U.S.C. § 153(29), to which access is provided on an unbundled basis pursuant to 47 U.S.C. § 251(c)(3).

b. Pay telephone service.

c. 911 charges imposed under G.S. 62A-43 and remitted to the 911 Fund under that section.

d. Charges for telecommunications service made by a hotel, motel, or another entity whose gross receipts are taxable under G.S. 105-164.4(a)(3) when the charges are incidental to the occupancy of the entity's accommodations.

e. Telecommunications service purchased or provided by a State agency or a unit of local government for the State Network or another data network owned or leased by the State or unit of local government.

(55) Sales of electricity for use at an eligible Internet datacenter and eligible business property to be located and used at an eligible Internet datacenter. As used in this subdivision, "eligible business property" is property that is capitalized for tax purposes under the Code and is used either:

a. For the provision of a service included in the business of the primary user of the datacenter, including equipment cooling systems for managing the performance of the property.

b. For the generation, transformation, transmission, distribution, or management of electricity, including exterior substations and other business personal property used for these purposes.

c. To provide related computer engineering or computer science research.

If the level of investment required by G.S. 105-164.3(8e)d. is not timely made, then the exemption provided under this subdivision is forfeited. If the level of investment required by G.S. 105-164.3(8e)d. is timely made but any specific eligible business property is not located and used at an eligible Internet datacenter, then the exemption provided for such eligible business property under this subdivision is forfeited. If the level of investment required by G.S. 105-164.3(8e)d. is timely made but any portion of the electricity is not used at an eligible Internet datacenter, then the exemption provided for such electricity under this subdivision is forfeited. A taxpayer that forfeits an exemption under this subdivision is liable for all past taxes avoided as a result of the forfeited exemption, computed from the date the taxes would have been due if the exemption had not been allowed, plus interest at the rate established under G.S. 105-241.21. If the forfeiture is triggered due to the lack of a timely investment required by G.S. 105-164.3(8e)d., then interest is computed from the date the taxes would have been due if the exemption had not been allowed. For all other forfeitures, interest is computed from the time as of which the eligible business property or electricity was put to a disqualifying use. The past taxes and interest are due 30 days after the date the exemption is forfeited. A taxpayer that fails to pay the past taxes and interest by the due date is subject to the provisions of G.S. 105-236.

(56) Sales to the owner or lessee of an eligible railroad intermodal facility of intermodal cranes, intermodal hostler trucks, and railroad locomotives that reside on the premises of the facility and are used at the facility.

(57) Fuel and electricity sold to a manufacturer for use in connection with the operation of a manufacturing facility. The exemption does not apply to electricity used at a facility at which the primary activity is not manufacturing.

(58) Tangible personal property purchased with a client assistance debit card issued for disaster assistance relief by a State agency or a federal agency or instrumentality.

(59) Interior design services provided in conjunction with the sale of tangible personal property.

(60) Admission charges to any of the following entertainment activities:

a. An event that is held at an elementary or secondary school and is sponsored by the school.

b. A commercial agricultural fair that meets the requirements of G.S. 106-520.1, as determined by the Commissioner of Agriculture.

c. A festival or other recreational or entertainment activity that lasts no more than seven consecutive days and is sponsored by a nonprofit entity that is exempt from tax under Article 4 of this Chapter and uses the entire proceeds of the activity exclusively for the entity's nonprofit purposes. This exemption applies to the first two activities sponsored by the entity during a calendar year.

d. A youth athletic contest sponsored by a nonprofit entity that is exempt from tax under Article 4 of this Chapter. For the purpose of this subdivision, a youth athletic contest is a contest in which each participating athlete is less than 20 years of age at the time of enrollment.

e. A State attraction. A State attraction is a physical place supported with State funds that offers cultural, educational, historical, or recreational opportunities. The term "State funds" has the same meaning as defined in G.S. 143C-1-1.

(61) A service contract for tangible personal property that is provided for any of the following:

a. An item exempt from tax under this Article, other than an item exempt from tax under G.S. 105-164.13(32).

b. A transmission, distribution, or other network asset contained on utility-owned land, right-of-way, or easement.

c. An item purchased by a professional motorsports racing team for which the team may receive a sales tax refund under G.S. 105-164.14A(5).

(62) An item used to maintain or repair tangible personal property pursuant to a service contract if the purchaser of the contract is not charged for the item. (1957, c. 1340, s. 5; 1959, c. 670; c. 1259, s. 5; 1961, c. 826, s. 2; cc. 1103, 1163; 1963, c. 1169, ss. 7-9; 1965, c. 1041; 1967, c. 756; 1969, c. 907; 1971, c. 990; 1973, c. 476, s. 143; c. 708, s. 1; cc. 1064, 1076; c. 1287, s. 8; 1975, 2nd Sess., c. 982; 1977, c. 771, s. 4; 1977, 2nd Sess., c. 1219, s. 43.6; 1979, c. 46, ss. 1, 2; c. 156, s. 1; c. 201; c. 625, ss. 1, 2; c. 801, ss. 74, 75; 1979, 2nd Sess., c. 1099, s. 1; 1981, cc. 14, 207, 982; 1983, c. 156; c. 570, s. 21; c. 713, ss. 91, 92; c. 873; c. 887; 1983 (Reg. Sess., 1984), c. 1071, s. 1; 1985, c. 114, s. 4; c. 555; c. 656, ss. 24, 25; 1985 (Reg. Sess., 1986), c. 953; c. 973; c. 982, s. 2; 1987, c. 800, s. 1; 1987 (Reg. Sess., 1988), c. 937; 1989, c. 692, ss. 3.5, 3.6; c. 748, s. 1; 1989 (Reg. Sess., 1990), c. 989; c. 1060; c. 1068, ss. 1, 2; 1991, c. 45, s. 17; c. 79, s. 2; c. 618, s. 1; c. 689, s. 314; 1991 (Reg. Sess., 1992), c. 931, ss. 1, 2; c. 935, s. 1; c. 940, s. 1; c. 949, s. 1; c. 1007, s. 44; 1993, c. 484, s. 3; c. 513, s. 11; 1993 (Reg. Sess., 1994), c. 739, s. 1; 1995, c. 390, s. 14; c. 451, s. 1; c. 477, ss. 2, 3; 1995 (Reg. Sess., 1996), c. 646, ss. 4, 5; c. 649, s. 1; 1996, 2nd Ex. Sess., c. 14, ss. 15, 16; 1997-369, s. 2; 1997-370, s. 2; 1997-397, s. 1; 1997-423, s. 3; 1997-443, s. 11A.118(a); 1997-456, s. 27; 1997-506, s. 36; 1997-521, s. 1; 1998-22, s. 6; 1998-55, ss. 9, 15; 1998-98, ss. 14, 14.1, 49, 107; 1998-146, s. 9; 1998-171, s. 10(a), (b); 1998-225, s. 4.3; 1999-337, s. 31; 1999-360, s. 7(a)-(c); 1999-438, ss. 5-12; 2000-120, s. 5; 2000-153, s. 5; 2001-347, s. 2.12; 2001-424, s. 34.23(a); 2001-476, s. 17(e); 2001-509, s. 1; 2001-514, s. 1; 2002-184, s. 9; 2003-284, ss. 45.5, 45.5A; 2003-349, s. 11; 2003-416, ss. 18(a), 21; 2003-431, s. 1; 2004-124, ss. 32B.2, 32B.4; 2005-276, s. 33.9; 2005-435,

ss. 30, 31; 2006-19, s. 1; 2006-33, s. 5; 2006-66, s. 24.17(b); 2006-162, ss. 8(a), 8(b); 2006-168, s. 4.2; 2006-252, s. 2.25(b); 2007-244, s. 4; 2007-323, s. 31.23(c); 2007-368, s. 1; 2007-383, s. 6; 2007-397, ss. 10(g), 10(h); 2007-491, s. 44(1)a; 2007-500, s. 1; 2007-527, ss. 10, 27; 2008-107, ss. 28.6(a), 28.20(a); 2009-451, s. 27A.3(f), (k); 2009-511, s. 1; 2010-91, s. 3; 2010-147, s. 6.1; 2011-330, s. 18; 2012-79, s. 1.4; 2013-316, ss. 3.2(a), (b), 3.3(b), 3.4(a), 4.1(d), 5(c), 6(c); 2013-360, s. 7.4(e); 2013-414, ss. 11(a), 58(e).)

§ 105-164.13A. Service charges on food, beverages, or prepared food.

When a service charge is imposed on food, beverages, or prepared food, so much of the service charge that does not exceed twenty percent (20%) of the sales price is considered a tip and is specifically exempted from the tax imposed by this Article if it meets both of the following conditions:

(1) Is separately stated in the price list, menu, or written proposal and also in the invoice or bill.

(2) Is turned over to the personnel directly involved in the service of the food, beverages, or prepared food, in accordance with G.S. 95-25.6. (1979, c. 801, s. 76; 1979, 2nd Sess., c. 1101; 1999-438, s. 13; 2013-414, s. 11(b).)

§ 105-164.13B. Food exempt from tax.

(a) State Exemption. - Food is exempt from the taxes imposed by this Article unless the food is included in one of the subdivisions in this subsection. The following food items are subject to tax:

(1) Repealed by Session Laws 2005-276, s. 33.10, effective October 1, 2005.

(2) Dietary supplements.

(3) Food sold through a vending machine.

(4) Prepared food, other than bakery items sold without eating utensils by an artisan bakery. The term "bakery item" includes bread, rolls, buns, biscuits,

bagels, croissants, pastries, donuts, danish, cakes, tortes, pies, tarts, muffins, bars, cookies, and tortillas. An artisan bakery is a bakery that meets all of the following requirements:

a. It derives over eighty percent (80%) of its gross receipts from bakery items.

b. Its annual gross receipts, combined with the gross receipts of all related persons as defined in G.S. 105-163.010, do not exceed one million eight hundred thousand dollars ($1,800,000).

(5) Soft drinks.

(6) Repealed by Session Laws 2003-284, s. 45.6B, effective January 1, 2004.

(7) Candy.

(b) Administration of Local Food Tax. - The Secretary must administer local sales and use taxes imposed on food as if they were imposed under this Article. This applies to local taxes on food imposed under Subchapter VIII of this Chapter and under Chapter 1096 of the 1967 Session Laws. (1998-212, s. 29A.1(b); 2001-347, s. 2.13; 2001-489, s. 3(b); 2003-284, ss. 45.6, 45.6A, 45.6B; 2003-416, s. 22; 2005-276, s. 33.10; 2008-107, s. 28.19(a); 2009-445, s. 42.)

§ 105-164.13C. (Repealed effective July 1, 2014) Sales and use tax holiday.

(a) The taxes imposed by this Article do not apply to the following items of tangible personal property if sold between 12:01 A.M. on the first Friday of August and 11:59 P.M. the following Sunday:

(1) Clothing with a sales price of one hundred dollars ($100.00) or less per item.

(2) School supplies with a sales price of one hundred dollars ($100.00) or less per item.

(2a)   School instructional materials with a sales price of three hundred dollars ($300.00) or less per item.

(3)   Computers with a sales price of three thousand five hundred dollars ($3,500) or less per item.

(3a)   Computer supplies with a sales price of two hundred fifty dollars ($250.00) or less per item.

(4)   Sport or recreational equipment with a sales price of fifty dollars ($50.00) or less per item.

(b)   The exemption allowed by this section does not apply to the following:

(1)   Sales of clothing accessories or equipment.

(2)   Sales of protective equipment.

(3)   Sales of furniture.

(4)   Repealed by Session Laws 2003-284, s. 45.7, effective October 1, 2003.

(5)   Sales of an item for use in a trade or business.

(6)   Rentals.

(c)   Repealed by Session Laws 2003-284, s. 45.7, effective October 1, 2003. (2001-424, s. 34.16(a); 2001-476, s. 18(b); 2003-284, s. 45.7; 2005-276, s. 33.11; 2007-323, s. 31.14(b); 2013-316, s. 3.4(a).)

§ 105-164.13D. (Repealed effective July 1, 2014) Sales and use tax holiday for Energy Star qualified products.

(a)   The taxes imposed by this Article do not apply to the Energy Star qualified products listed in this section if sold between 12:01 A.M. on the first Friday of November and 11:59 P.M. the following Sunday. The qualified products are:

(1) Clothes washers.

(2) Freezers and refrigerators.

(3) Central air conditioners and room air conditioners.

(4) Air-source heat pumps.

(5) Ceiling fans.

(6) Dehumidifiers.

(7) Programmable thermostats.

(b) The exemption allowed by this section does not apply to the following:

(1) The sale of a product for use in a trade or business.

(2) The rental of a product. (2008-107, s. 28.12(b); 2011-330, s. 19; 2013-316, s. 3.4(a).)

§ 105-164.13E. (Effective July 1, 2014) Exemption for farmers.

The following tangible personal property, digital property, and services are exempt from sales and use tax if purchased by a qualifying farmer and for use by the farmer in the planting, cultivating, harvesting, or curing of farm crops or in the production of dairy products, eggs, or animals. A qualifying farmer is a farmer who has an annual gross income of ten thousand dollars ($10,000) or more from farming operations for the preceding calendar year and includes a dairy operator, a poultry farmer, an egg producer, a livestock farmer, a farmer of crops, and a farmer of an aquatic species, as defined in G.S. 106-758:

(1) Fuel and electricity that is measured by a separate meter or another separate device and used for a purpose other than preparing food, heating dwellings, and other household purposes.

(2) Commercial fertilizer, lime, land plaster, plastic mulch, plant bed covers, potting soil, baler twine, and seeds.

(3)   Farm machinery, attachment and repair parts for farm machinery, and lubricants applied to farm machinery. The term "machinery" includes implements that have moving parts or are operated or drawn by an animal. The term does not include implements operated wholly by hand or motor vehicles required to be registered under Chapter 20 of the General Statutes.

(4)   A container used in the planting, cultivating, harvesting, or curing of farm crops or in the production of dairy products, eggs, or animals or used in packaging and transporting the farmer's product for sale.

(5)   A grain, feed, or soybean storage facility and parts and accessories attached to the facility.

(6)   Any of the following substances when purchased for use on animals or plants, as appropriate, held or produced for commercial purposes. This exemption does not apply to any equipment or devices used to administer, release, apply, or otherwise dispense these substances:

a.   Remedies, vaccines, medications, litter materials, and feeds for animals.

b.   Rodenticides, insecticides, herbicides, fungicides, and pesticides.

c.   Defoliants for use on cotton or other crops.

d.   Plant growth inhibitors, regulators, or stimulators, including systemic and contact or other sucker control agents for tobacco and other crops.

e.   Semen.

(7)   Baby chicks and poults sold for commercial poultry or egg production.

(8)   Any of the following items concerning the housing, raising, or feeding of animals:

a.   A commercially manufactured facility to be used for commercial purposes for housing, raising, or feeding animals or for housing equipment necessary for these commercial activities. The exemption also applies to commercially manufactured equipment, and parts and accessories for the equipment, used in the facility.

b. Building materials, supplies, fixtures, and equipment that become a part of and are used in the construction, repair, or improvement of an enclosure or a structure specifically designed, constructed, and used for housing, raising, or feeding animals or for housing equipment necessary for one of these commercial activities. The exemption also applies to commercially manufactured equipment, and parts and accessories for the equipment, used in the enclosure or a structure.

(9) A bulk tobacco barn or rack, parts and accessories attached to the tobacco barn or rack, and any similar apparatus, part, or accessory used to cure or dry tobacco or another crop. (2013-316, s. 3.3(a); 2013-363, s. 11.4.)

§ 105-164.14. Certain refunds authorized.

(a) Interstate Carriers. - An interstate carrier is allowed a refund, in accordance with this section, of part of the sales and use taxes paid by it on the purchase in this State of railway cars and locomotives, and fuel, lubricants, repair parts, and accessories for a motor vehicle, railroad car, locomotive, or airplane the carrier operates. An "interstate carrier" is a person who is engaged in transporting persons or property in interstate commerce for compensation. The Secretary shall prescribe the periods of time, whether monthly, quarterly, semiannually, or otherwise, with respect to which refunds may be claimed, and shall prescribe the time within which, following these periods, an application for refund may be made.

An applicant for refund shall furnish the following information and any proof of the information required by the Secretary:

(1) A list identifying the railway cars, locomotives, fuel, lubricants, repair parts, and accessories purchased by the applicant inside or outside this State during the refund period.

(2) The purchase price of the items listed in subdivision (1) of this subsection.

(3) The sales and use taxes paid in this State on the listed items.

(4) The number of miles the applicant's motor vehicles, railroad cars, locomotives, and airplanes were operated both inside and outside this State

during the refund period. Airplane miles are not in this State if the airplane does not depart or land in this State.

(5)   Any other information required by the Secretary.

For each applicant, the Secretary shall compute the amount to be refunded as follows. First, the Secretary shall determine the mileage ratio. The numerator of the mileage ratio is the number of miles the applicant operated all motor vehicles, railroad cars, locomotives, and airplanes in this State during the refund period. The denominator of the mileage ratio is the number of miles the applicant operated all motor vehicles, railroad cars, locomotives, and airplanes both inside and outside this State during the refund period. Second, the Secretary shall determine the applicant's proportional liability for the refund period by multiplying this mileage ratio by the purchase price of the items identified in subdivision (1) of this subsection and then multiplying the resulting product by the tax rate that would have applied to the items if they had all been purchased in this State. Third, the Secretary shall refund to each applicant the excess of the amount of sales and use taxes the applicant paid in this State during the refund period on these items over the applicant's proportional liability for the refund period.

(a1)   Repealed by Session Laws 2010-166, s. 1.17, effective July 1, 2010.

(a2)   Utility Companies. - A utility company is allowed a refund, in accordance with this section, of part of the sales and use taxes paid by it on the purchase in this State of railway cars and locomotives and accessories for a railway car or locomotive the utility company operates. The Secretary shall prescribe the periods of time, whether monthly, quarterly, semiannually, or otherwise, with respect to which refunds may be claimed and shall prescribe the time within which, following these periods, an application for refund may be made.

An applicant for refund shall furnish the following information and any proof of the information required by the Secretary:

(1)   A list identifying the railway cars, locomotives, and accessories purchased by the applicant inside or outside this State during the refund period.

(2)   The purchase price of the items listed in subdivision (1) of this subsection.

(3)   The sales and use taxes paid in this State on the listed items.

(4) The number of miles the applicant's railway cars and locomotives were operated both inside and outside this State during the refund period.

(5) Any other information required by the Secretary.

For each applicant, the Secretary shall compute the amount to be refunded as follows. First, the Secretary shall determine the ratio of the number of miles the applicant operated its railway cars and locomotives in this State during the refund period to the number of miles it operated them both inside and outside this State during the refund period. Second, the Secretary shall determine the applicant's proportional liability for the refund period by multiplying this mileage ratio by the purchase price of the items identified in subdivision (1) of this subsection and then multiplying the resulting product by the tax rate that would have applied to the items if they had all been purchased in this State. Third, the Secretary shall refund to each applicant the excess of the amount of sales and use taxes the applicant paid in this State during the refund period on these items over the applicant's proportional liability for the refund period.

(b) (Effective until July 1, 2014) Nonprofit Entities and Hospital Drugs. – A nonprofit entity is allowed a semiannual refund of sales and use taxes paid by it under this Article on direct purchases of tangible personal property and services, other than electricity, telecommunications service, and ancillary service, for use in carrying on the work of the nonprofit entity. Sales and use tax liability indirectly incurred by a nonprofit entity through reimbursement to an authorized person of the entity for the purchase of tangible personal property and services, other than electricity, telecommunications service, and ancillary service, for use in carrying on the work of the nonprofit entity is considered a direct purchase by the entity. Sales and use tax liability indirectly incurred by a nonprofit entity on building materials, supplies, fixtures, and equipment that become a part of or annexed to any building or structure that is owned or leased by the nonprofit entity and is being erected, altered, or repaired for use by the nonprofit entity for carrying on its nonprofit activities is considered a sales or use tax liability incurred on direct purchases by the nonprofit entity. A request for a refund must be in writing and must include any information and documentation required by the Secretary. A request for a refund for the first six months of a calendar year is due the following October 15; a request for a refund for the second six months of a calendar year is due the following April 15.

The refunds allowed under this subsection do not apply to an entity that is owned and controlled by the United States or to an entity that is owned or controlled by the State and is not listed in this subsection. A hospital that is not listed in this subsection is allowed a semiannual refund of sales and use taxes paid by it on over-the-counter drugs purchased for use in carrying out its work. The following nonprofit entities are allowed a refund under this subsection:

(1) Hospitals not operated for profit, including hospitals and medical accommodations operated by an authority or other public hospital described in Article 2 of Chapter 131E of the General Statutes.

(2) An organization that is exempt from income tax under section 501(c)(3) of the Code, other than an organization that is properly classified in any of the following major group areas of the National Taxonomy of Exempt Entities:

a. Community Improvement and Capacity Building.

b. Public and Societal Benefit.

c. Mutual and Membership Benefit.

(2a) Volunteer fire departments and volunteer emergency medical services squads that are one or more of the following:

a. Exempt from income tax under the Code.

b. Financially accountable to a city as defined in G.S. 160A-1, a county, or a group of cities and counties.

(2b) An organization that is a single member LLC that is disregarded for income tax purposes and satisfies all of the following conditions:

a. The owner of the LLC is an organization that is exempt from income tax under section 501(c)(3) of the Code.

b. The LLC is a nonprofit entity that would be eligible for an exemption under 501(c)(3) of the Code if it were not disregarded for income tax purposes.

c. The LLC is not an organization that would be properly classified in any of the major group areas of the National Taxonomy of Exempt Entities listed in subdivision (2) of this subsection.

(3) Repealed by Session Laws 2008-107, s. 28.22(a), effective July 1, 2008, and applicable to purchases made on or after that date.

(4) Qualified retirement facilities whose property is excluded from property tax under G.S. 105-278.6A.

(5) A university affiliated nonprofit organization that procures, designs, constructs, or provides facilities to, or for use by, a constituent institution of The University of North Carolina. For purposes of this subdivision, a nonprofit organization includes an entity exempt from taxation as a disregarded entity of the nonprofit organization.

(b) (Effective July 1, 2014) Nonprofit Entities and Hospital Drugs. - A nonprofit entity is allowed a semiannual refund of sales and use taxes paid by it under this Article on direct purchases of tangible personal property and services, other than electricity, telecommunications service, and ancillary service, for use in carrying on the work of the nonprofit entity. Sales and use tax liability indirectly incurred by a nonprofit entity through reimbursement to an authorized person of the entity for the purchase of tangible personal property and services, other than electricity, telecommunications service, and ancillary service, for use in carrying on the work of the nonprofit entity is considered a direct purchase by the entity. Sales and use tax liability indirectly incurred by a nonprofit entity on building materials, supplies, fixtures, and equipment that become a part of or annexed to any building or structure that is owned or leased by the nonprofit entity and is being erected, altered, or repaired for use by the nonprofit entity for carrying on its nonprofit activities is considered a sales or use tax liability incurred on direct purchases by the nonprofit entity. A request for a refund must be in writing and must include any information and documentation required by the Secretary. A request for a refund for the first six months of a calendar year is due the following October 15; a request for a refund for the second six months of a calendar year is due the following April 15. The aggregate annual refund amount allowed an entity under this subsection for a fiscal year may not exceed thirty-one million seven hundred thousand dollars ($31,700,000).

The refunds allowed under this subsection do not apply to an entity that is owned and controlled by the United States or to an entity that is owned or controlled by the State and is not listed in this subsection. A hospital that is not listed in this subsection is allowed a semiannual refund of sales and use taxes paid by it on over-the-counter drugs purchased for use in carrying out its work. The following nonprofit entities are allowed a refund under this subsection:

(1) Hospitals not operated for profit, including hospitals and medical accommodations operated by an authority or other public hospital described in Article 2 of Chapter 131E of the General Statutes.

(2) An organization that is exempt from income tax under section 501(c)(3) of the Code, other than an organization that is properly classified in any of the following major group areas of the National Taxonomy of Exempt Entities:

a. Community Improvement and Capacity Building.

b. Public and Societal Benefit.

c. Mutual and Membership Benefit.

(2a) Volunteer fire departments and volunteer emergency medical services squads that are one or more of the following:

a. Exempt from income tax under the Code.

b. Financially accountable to a city as defined in G.S. 160A-1, a county, or a group of cities and counties.

(2b) An organization that is a single member LLC that is disregarded for income tax purposes and satisfies all of the following conditions:

a. The owner of the LLC is an organization that is exempt from income tax under section 501(c)(3) of the Code.

b. The LLC is a nonprofit entity that would be eligible for an exemption under 501(c)(3) of the Code if it were not disregarded for income tax purposes.

c. The LLC is not an organization that would be properly classified in any of the major group areas of the National Taxonomy of Exempt Entities listed in subdivision (2) of this subsection.

(3) Repealed by Session Laws 2008-107, s. 28.22(a), effective July 1, 2008, and applicable to purchases made on or after that date.

(4) Qualified retirement facilities whose property is excluded from property tax under G.S. 105-278.6A.

(5) A university affiliated nonprofit organization that procures, designs, constructs, or provides facilities to, or for use by, a constituent institution of The University of North Carolina. For purposes of this subdivision, a nonprofit organization includes an entity exempt from taxation as a disregarded entity of the nonprofit organization.

(c) Certain Governmental Entities. - A governmental entity listed in this subsection is allowed an annual refund of sales and use taxes paid by it under this Article on direct purchases of tangible personal property and services, other than electricity, telecommunications service, and ancillary service. Sales and use tax liability indirectly incurred by a governmental entity on building materials, supplies, fixtures, and equipment that become a part of or annexed to any building or structure that is owned or leased by the governmental entity and is being erected, altered, or repaired for use by the governmental entity is considered a sales or use tax liability incurred on direct purchases by the governmental entity for the purpose of this subsection. A request for a refund must be in writing and must include any information and documentation required by the Secretary. A request for a refund is due within six months after the end of the governmental entity's fiscal year.

This subsection applies only to the following governmental entities:

(1) A county.

(2) A city as defined in G.S. 160A-1.

(2a) A consolidated city-county as defined in G.S. 160B-2.

(2b), (2c) Repealed by Session Laws 2005-276, s. 7.51(a), effective July 1, 2005, and applicable to sales made on or after that date.

(3) A metropolitan sewerage district or a metropolitan water district in this State.

(4) A water and sewer authority created under Chapter 162A of the General Statutes.

(5) A lake authority created by a board of county commissioners pursuant to an act of the General Assembly.

(6) A sanitary district.

(7)   A regional solid waste management authority created pursuant to G.S. 153A-421.

(8)   An area mental health, developmental disabilities, and substance abuse authority, other than a single-county area authority, established pursuant to Article 4 of Chapter 122C of the General Statutes.

(9)   A district health department, or a public health authority created pursuant to Part 1A of Article 2 of Chapter 130A of the General Statutes.

(10)   A regional council of governments created pursuant to G.S. 160A-470.

(11)   A regional planning and economic development commission or a regional economic development commission created pursuant to Chapter 158 of the General Statutes.

(12)   A regional planning commission created pursuant to G.S. 153A-391.

(13)   A regional sports authority created pursuant to G.S. 160A-479.

(14)   A public transportation authority created pursuant to Article 25 of Chapter 160A of the General Statutes.

(14a)   A facility authority created pursuant to Part 4 of Article 20 of Chapter 160A of the General Statutes.

(15)   A regional public transportation authority created pursuant to Article 26 of Chapter 160A of the General Statutes, or a regional transportation authority created pursuant to Article 27 of Chapter 160A of the General Statutes.

(16)   A local airport authority that was created pursuant to a local act of the General Assembly.

(17)   A joint agency created by interlocal agreement pursuant to G.S. 160A-462 to operate a public broadcasting television station.

(18)   Repealed by Session Laws 2001-474, s. 7, effective November 29, 2001.

(19)   Repealed by Session Laws 2001-474, s. 7, effective November 29, 2001.

(20) A constituent institution of The University of North Carolina, but only with respect to sales and use tax paid by it for tangible personal property or services that are eligible for refund under this subsection acquired by it through the expenditure of contract and grant funds.

(21) The University of North Carolina Health Care System.

(22) A regional natural gas district created pursuant to Article 28 of Chapter 160A of the General Statutes.

(23) A special district created under Article 43 of this Chapter.

(24) A public library created pursuant to an act of the General Assembly or established pursuant to G.S. 153A-270.

(d) Late Applications. - Refunds applied for more than three years after the due date are barred.

(d1) Alcoholic Beverages. - The refunds authorized by this section do not apply to purchases of alcoholic beverages, as defined in G.S. 18B-101.

(d2) A city subject to the provisions of G.S. 160A-340.5 is not allowed a refund of sales and use taxes paid by it under this Article for purchases related to the provision of communications service as defined in Article 16A of Chapter 160A of the General Statutes.

(e) State Agencies. - The State is allowed quarterly refunds of local sales and use taxes paid indirectly by the State agency on building materials, supplies, fixtures, and equipment that become a part of or annexed to a building or structure that is owned or leased by the State agency and is being erected, altered, or repaired for use by the State agency.

A person who pays local sales and use taxes on building materials or other tangible personal property for a State building project shall give the State agency for whose project the property was purchased a signed statement containing all of the following information:

(1) The date the property was purchased.

(2) The type of property purchased.

(3) The project for which the property was used.

(4) If the property was purchased in this State, the county in which it was purchased.

(5) If the property was not purchased in this State, the county in which the property was used.

(6) The amount of sales and use taxes paid.

If the property was purchased in this State, the person shall attach a copy of the sales receipt to the statement. A State agency to whom a statement is submitted shall verify the accuracy of the statement.

Within 15 days after the end of each calendar quarter, every State agency shall file with the Secretary a written application for a refund of taxes to which this subsection applies paid by the agency during the quarter. The application shall contain all information required by the Secretary. The Secretary shall credit the local sales and use tax refunds directly to the General Fund.

(f) through (h) Repealed by Session Laws 2010-166, s. 1.17, effective July 1, 2010.

(i) Repealed by Session Laws 1999-360, s. 5, for taxes paid on or after January 1, 2008.

(j) through (o) Repealed by Session Laws 2010-166, s. 1.17, effective July 1, 2010.

(p) Not an Overpayment. - Taxes for which a refund is allowed under this section are not an overpayment of tax and do not accrue interest as provided in G.S. 105-241.21. (1957, c. 1340, s. 5; 1961, c. 826, s. 2; 1963, cc. 169, 1134; 1965, c. 1006; 1967, c. 1110, s. 6; 1969, c. 1298, s. 1; 1971, cc. 89, 286; 1973, c. 476, s. 193; 1977, c. 895, s. 1; 1979, c. 47; c. 801, ss. 77, 79-82; 1983, c. 594, s. 1; c. 891, s. 13; 1983 (Reg. Sess., 1984), c. 1097, s. 7; 1985, cc. 431, 523; 1985 (Reg. Sess., 1986), c. 863, s. 5; 1987, c. 557, ss. 8, 9; c. 850, s. 16; 1987 (Reg. Sess., 1988), c. 1044, s. 5; 1989, c. 168, s. 5; c. 251; c. 780, s. 1.1; 1989 (Reg. Sess., 1990), c. 936, s. 4; 1991, c. 356, s. 1; c. 689, s. 190.1(b); 1991 (Reg. Sess., 1992), c. 814, s. 1; c. 917, s. 1; c. 1030, s. 25; 1995, c. 17, s. 8; c. 21, s. 1; c. 458, s. 7; c. 461, s. 13; c. 472, s. 1; 1995 (Reg. Sess., 1996), c. 646, s. 6; 1996, 2nd Ex. Sess., c. 18, s. 15.7(a); 1997-340, s. 1; 1997-393, s. 2;

1997-423, s. 1; 1997-426, s. 5; 1997-502, s. 3; 1998-55, ss. 16, 17; 1998-98, s. 15; 1998-212, ss. 29A.4(a), 29A.14(i), 29A.18(b); 1999-360, ss. 4, 5(a), (b), 9; 1999-438, s. 14; 2000-56, s. 9; 2000-140, s. 92.A(c); 2001-414, s. 1; 2001-474, s. 7; 2003-416, ss. 18(b)-(e), 23; 2003-431, ss. 2, 3; 2003-435, 2nd Ex. Sess., s. 4.1; 2004-110, s. 5.1; 2004-124, s. 32B.1; 2004-170, s. 21(a); 2004-204, 1st Ex. Sess., s. 3; 2005-276, ss. 7.27(a), 7.51(a), 33.12; 2005-429, s. 2.12; 2005-435, ss. 32(a), 33(a)-(c), 61, 61.1; 2006-33, s. 6; 2006-66, ss. 24.6(a), (b), (c), 24.10(b), 24.13(b), 24A.1(a); 2006-162, ss. 9, 27; 2006-168, s. 3.1; 2006-252, ss. 2.2, 2.3; 2007-323, ss. 31.10(a), 31.20(b), 31.23(d); 2007-345, s. 14.6(a); 2007-491, s. 44(1)a; 2008-107, ss. 28.22(a), 28.23(a), (b); 2008-118, s. 3.10(a); 2008-154, s. 1; 2009-233, s. 1; 2009-445, ss. 13, 14(a); 2009-527, s. 2(d); 2009-550, s. 4.1; 2010-31, s. 31.5(c), (d); 2010-91, s. 4; 2010-95, s. 4(a); 2010-166, s. 1.17; 2011-84, s. 1(b); 2011-330, s. 26(a); 2012-79, s. 2.11; 2013-316, s. 3.4(b); 2013-414, ss. 12, 42(a), 54(a).)

§ 105-164.14A. Economic incentive refunds.

(a) Refund. - The following taxpayers are allowed an annual refund of sales and use taxes paid under this Article:

(1) (Repealed for purchases made on or after January 1, 2016) Passenger air carrier. - An interstate passenger air carrier is allowed a refund of the sales and use tax paid by it on fuel in excess of two million five hundred thousand dollars ($2,500,000). The amount of sales and use tax paid does not include a refund allowed to the interstate passenger air carrier under G.S. 105-164.14(a). This subdivision is repealed for purchases made on or after January 1, 2016.

(2) Major recycling facility. - An owner of a major recycling facility is allowed a refund of the sales and use tax paid by it on building materials, building supplies, fixtures, and equipment that become a part of the real property of the recycling facility. Liability incurred indirectly by the owner for sales and use taxes on these items is considered tax paid by the owner.

(3) Business in low-tier area. - A taxpayer that is engaged primarily in one of the businesses listed in G.S. 105-129.83(a) in a development tier one area and that places machinery and equipment in service in that area is allowed a refund of the sales and use tax paid by it on the machinery and equipment. For purposes of this subdivision, "machinery and equipment" includes engines, machinery, equipment, tools, and implements used or designed to be used in

one of the businesses listed in G.S. 105-129.83, capitalized for tax purposes under the Code, and not leased to another party. Liability incurred indirectly by the taxpayer for sales and use taxes on these items is considered tax paid by the taxpayer. The sunset for Article 3J of Chapter 105 of the General Statutes for development tier one areas applies to this subdivision.

(4) (Repealed for purchases made on or after January 1, 2016) Motorsports team or sanctioning body. - A professional motorsports racing team, a motorsports sanctioning body, or a related member of such a team or body is allowed a refund of the sales and use tax paid by it in this State on aviation fuel that is used to travel to or from a motorsports event in this State, to travel to a motorsports event in another state from a location in this State, or to travel to this State from a motorsports event in another state. For purposes of this subdivision, a "motorsports event" includes a motorsports race, a motorsports sponsor event, and motorsports testing. This subdivision is repealed for purchases made on or after January 1, 2016.

(5) (Repealed for purchases made on or after January 1, 2016) Professional motorsports team. - A professional motorsports racing team or a related member of a team is allowed a refund of fifty percent (50%) of the sales and use tax paid by it in this State on tangible personal property, other than tires or accessories, that comprises any part of a professional motorsports vehicle. For purposes of this subdivision, "motorsports accessories" includes instrumentation, telemetry, consumables, and paint. This subdivision is repealed for purchases made on or after January 1, 2016.

(6) (Repealed for purchases made on or after January 1, 2014) Analytical services business. - A taxpayer engaged in analytical services in this State is allowed a refund of sales and use tax paid by it. This subdivision is repealed for purchases made on or after January 1, 2014. The amount of the refund is the greater of the following:

a. Fifty percent (50%) of the eligible amount of sales and use tax paid by it on tangible personal property that is consumed or transformed in analytical service activities. The eligible amount of sales and use tax paid by the taxpayer in this State is the amount by which sales and use tax paid by the taxpayer in this State in the fiscal year exceed the amount paid by the taxpayer in this State in the 2006-2007 State fiscal year.

b. Fifty percent (50%) of the amount of sales and use tax paid by it in the fiscal year on medical reagents.

(7) (Repealed for purchases made on or after January 1, 2038) Railroad intermodal facility. - The owner or lessee of an eligible railroad intermodal facility is allowed a refund of sales and use tax paid by it under this Article on building materials, building supplies, fixtures, and equipment that become a part of the real property of the facility. Liability incurred indirectly by the owner or lessee of the facility for sales and use taxes on these items is considered tax paid by the owner or lessee. This subdivision is repealed for purchases made on or after January 1, 2038.

(b) Administration. - A request for a refund must be in writing and must include any information and documentation required by the Secretary. A request for a refund is due within six months after the end of the State's fiscal year. Refunds applied for after the due date are barred.

(c) Report. - The Department must include in the economic incentives report required by G.S. 105-256 the following information itemized by refund and by taxpayer:

(1) The number of taxpayers claiming a refund allowed in this section.

(2) The total amount of purchases with respect to which refunds were claimed.

(3) The total cost to the General Fund of the refunds claimed.

(d) Not an Overpayment. - Taxes for which a refund is allowed under this section are not an overpayment of tax and do not accrue interest as provided in G.S. 105-241.21. (2010-166, s. 1.18; 2011-330, ss. 15(c), 20(a), 26(b); 2012-36, s. 11(a); 2013-316, s. 3.5(a).)

§ 105-164.14B. (Repealed for sales made on or after January 1, 2014) Certain industrial facilities refunds.

(a) Definitions. - The following definitions apply in this section:

(1) Air courier services. - The furnishing of air delivery of individually addressed letters and packages for compensation, except by the United States Postal Service.

(2) Aircraft manufacturing. - The manufacturing or assembling of complete aircraft or of aircraft engines, blisks, fuselage sections, flight decks, flight deck systems or components, wings, fuselage fairings, fins, moving leading and trailing wing edges, wing boxes, nose sections, tailplanes, passenger doors, nacelles, thrust reversers, landing gear, braking systems, or any combination of these.

(3) Bioprocessing. - Biomanufacturing or processing that includes the culture of cells to make commercial products, the purification of biomolecules from cells, or the use of these molecules in manufacturing.

(4) Reserved.

(5) Reserved.

(6) Facility. - A single building or structure or a group of buildings or structures that are located on a single parcel of land or on contiguous parcels of land under common ownership and any other related real property contained on the parcel or parcels.

(7) Financial services, securities operations, and related systems development. - One or both of the following functions:

a. Performing analysis, operations, trading, or sales functions for investment banking, securities dealing and brokering, securities trading and underwriting, investment portfolio or mutual fund management, retirement services, or employee benefit administration.

b. Developing information technology systems and applications, managing and enhancing operating applications and databases, or providing, operating, and maintaining telecommunications networks and distributed and mainframe computing resources for investment banking, securities dealing and brokering, securities trading and underwriting, investment portfolio or mutual fund management, retirement services, or employee benefit administration.

(8) Reserved.

(9) Reserved.

(10) Reserved.

(11) Motor vehicle manufacturing. - Any of the following:

a. Manufacturing complete automobiles and light-duty motor vehicles.

b. Manufacturing heavy-duty truck chassis and assembling complete heavy-duty trucks, buses, heavy-duty motor homes, and other special purpose heavy-duty motor vehicles for highway use.

c. Manufacturing complete military armored vehicles, nonarmored military universal carriers, combat tanks, and specialized components for combat tanks.

(12) Owner. - The term includes a lessee under a capital lease.

(13) Paper-from-pulp manufacturing. - An industry primarily engaged in manufacturing or converting paper, other than newsprint or uncoated groundwood paper, from pulp or pulp products, or in converting purchased sanitary paper stock or wadding into sanitary paper products.

(14) Pharmaceutical and medicine manufacturing and distribution of pharmaceuticals and medicines. - Any of the following:

a. Manufacturing biological and medicinal products. For purposes of this sub-subdivision, a biological product is a preparation that is synthesized from living organisms or their products and used medically as a diagnostic, preventive, or therapeutic agent. For the purpose of this sub-subdivision, bacteria, viruses, and their parts are considered living organisms.

b. Processing botanical drugs and herbs by grading, grinding, and milling.

c. Isolating active medicinal principals from botanical drugs and herbs.

d. Manufacturing pharmaceutical products intended for internal and external consumption in forms such as ampoules, tablets, capsules, vials, ointments, powders, solutions, and suspensions.

(15) Reserved.

(16) Reserved.

(17) Related entity. - An entity for which the taxpayer possesses directly or indirectly at least eighty percent (80%) of the control and value.

(18) Semiconductor manufacturing. - The development and production of semiconductor material, devices, or components.

(19) Solar electricity generating materials manufacturing. - The development and production of one or more of the following:

a. Photovoltaic materials or modules used in producing electricity.

b. Polymers or polymer films primarily intended for incorporation into photovoltaic materials or modules used in producing electricity.

(20) Repealed by Session Laws 2011-3, s. 1(a), effective July 1, 2010, and applicable to sales made on or after that date.

(21) Reserved.

(22) Turbine manufacturing. - An industry primarily engaged in manufacturing turbines or complete turbine generator set units, such as steam, hydraulic, gas, and wind. The term does not include the manufacturing of aircraft turbines.

(b) Refund. - An owner of an industrial facility that meets the business, minimum investment, and industry-specific requirements of this section is allowed an annual refund of sales and use tax paid by it under this Article on building materials, building supplies, fixtures, and equipment that are installed in the construction of the facility and that become a part of the real property of the facility. Liability incurred indirectly by the owner for sales and use taxes on those items is considered tax paid by the owner. The requirements are:

(1) Business requirement. - The facility is primarily engaged in one or more of the following:

a. Air courier services.

b. Aircraft manufacturing.

c. Bioprocessing.

d. Financial services, securities operations, and related systems development.

e. Motor vehicle manufacturing.

e1. Paper-from-pulp manufacturing.

f. Pharmaceutical and medicine manufacturing and distribution of pharmaceuticals and medicines.

g. Semiconductor manufacturing.

h. Solar electricity generating materials manufacturing.

i. Turbine manufacturing.

(2) Minimum investment requirement. - The Secretary of Commerce has certified that the owner of the facility will invest at least the required amount of private funds to construct the facility in this State. For the purpose of this subsection, costs of construction may include costs of acquiring and improving land for the facility and costs of equipment for the facility. If the facility is located in a development tier one area, the required amount is fifty million dollars ($50,000,000). For all other facilities, the required amount is one hundred million dollars ($100,000,000). The owner may invest these funds either directly or indirectly through a related entity.

(3) Industry-specific requirements:

a. If the facility is primarily engaged in financial services, securities operations, and related systems development, it satisfies all of the following conditions:

1. It is owned and operated by the business for which the services are provided or by a related entity of that business as defined in G.S. 105-130.7A.

2. No part of it is leased to a third-party tenant that is not a related entity of the business.

b. If the facility is primarily engaged in solar electricity generating materials manufacturing, the business satisfies a wage standard at the facility. The wage standard is equal to one hundred five percent (105%) of the lesser of the average weekly wage for all insured private employers in the State and the average weekly wage for all insured private employers in the county. A business satisfies the wage standard if it pays an average weekly wage that is at least equal to the amount required by this sub-subdivision. In making the wage calculation, the business must include any jobs that were filled for at least 1,600 hours during the calendar year.

(c) Forfeiture. - If the owner of an eligible facility does not make the required minimum investment within five years after the first refund under this section with respect to the facility, the facility loses its eligibility and the owner forfeits all refunds already received under this subsection. Upon forfeiture, the owner is liable for tax under this Article equal to the amount of all past taxes refunded under this section, plus interest at the rate established in G.S. 105-241.21, computed from the date each refund was issued. The tax and interest are due 30 days after the date of the forfeiture. A person that fails to pay the tax and interest is subject to the penalties provided in G.S. 105-236.

(d) Administration. - A request for a refund must be in writing and must include any information and documentation required by the Secretary. A request for a refund is due within six months after the end of the State's fiscal year. Refunds applied for after the due date are barred.

(e) Report. - The Department must include in the economic incentives report required by G.S. 105-256 the following information itemized by refund and taxpayer:

(1) The number of taxpayers claiming a refund allowed in this section.

(2) The total amount of purchases with respect to which refunds were claimed.

(3) The location of facilities with respect to which refunds were claimed.

(4) The total cost to the General Fund of the refunds claimed.

(f) Sunset. - This section is repealed for sales made on or after January 1, 2014.

(g) Not an Overpayment. - Taxes for which a refund is allowed under this section are not an overpayment of tax and do not accrue interest as provided in G.S. 105-241.21. (2010-166, s. 1.19; 2011-3, ss. 1(a), (b); 2011-330, s. 26(c); 2012-36, s. 11(b).)

Part 4. Reporting and Payment.

§ 105-164.15: Repealed by Session Laws 2010-95, s. 13, effective July 17, 2010.

§ 105-164.15A. Effective date of tax changes.

(a) General Rate Items. - The effective date of a tax change for tangible personal property, digital property, or services taxable under this Article is administered as follows:

(1) For a taxable item that is provided and billed on a monthly or other periodic basis:

a. A new tax or a tax rate increase applies to the first billing period that is at least 30 days after enactment and that starts on or after the effective date.

b. A tax repeal or a tax rate decrease applies to bills rendered on or after the effective date.

(2) For a taxable item that is not billed on a monthly or other periodic basis, a tax change applies to amounts received for items provided on or after the effective date, except amounts received for items provided under a lump-sum or unit-price contract entered into or awarded before the effective date or entered into or awarded pursuant to a bid made before the effective date.

(b) Combined Rate Items. - The effective date of a rate change for an item that is taxable under this Article at the combined general rate is the effective date of any of the following:

(1) The effective date of a change in the State general rate of tax set in G.S. 105-164.4.

(2) For an increase in the authorization for local sales and use taxes, the date on which local sales and use taxes authorized by Subchapter VIII of this Chapter for every county become effective in the first county or group of counties to levy the authorized taxes.

(3) For a repeal in the authorization for local sales and use taxes, the effective date of the repeal. (2005-276, s. 33.13; 2006-162, s. 10; 2007-323, s. 31.17(c); 2009-451, s. 27A.3(l); 2011-330, s. 27; 2013-316, s. 3.2(c).)

§ 105-164.16. Returns and payment of taxes.

(a) General. - Sales and use taxes are payable when a return is due. A return is due quarterly or monthly as specified in this section. A return must be filed with the Secretary on a form prescribed by the Secretary and in the manner required by the Secretary. A return must be signed by the taxpayer or the taxpayer's agent.

A sales tax return must state the taxpayer's gross sales for the reporting period, the amount and type of sales made in the period that are exempt from tax under G.S. 105-164.13 or are elsewhere excluded from tax, the amount of tax due, and any other information required by the Secretary. A use tax return must state the purchase price of tangible personal property, digital property, or services that were purchased or received during the reporting period and are subject to tax under G.S. 105-164.6, the amount of tax due, and any other information required by the Secretary. Returns that do not contain the required information will not be accepted. When an unacceptable return is submitted, the Secretary will require a corrected return to be filed.

(b) Quarterly. - A taxpayer who is consistently liable for less than one hundred dollars ($100.00) a month in State and local sales and use taxes must file a return and pay the taxes due on a quarterly basis. A quarterly return covers a calendar quarter and is due by the last day of the month following the end of the quarter.

(b1) Monthly. - A taxpayer who is consistently liable for at least one hundred dollars ($100.00) but less than twenty thousand dollars ($20,000) a month in State and local sales and use taxes must file a return and pay the taxes due on a monthly basis. A monthly return is due by the 20th day of the month following the calendar month covered by the return.

(b2) Prepayment. - A taxpayer who is consistently liable for at least twenty thousand dollars ($20,000) a month in State and local sales and use taxes must make a monthly prepayment of the next month's tax liability. The prepayment is due on the date a monthly return is due. The prepayment must equal at least sixty-five percent (65%) of any of the following:

(1)   The amount of tax due for the current month.

(2)   The amount of tax due for the same month in the preceding year.

(3)   The average monthly amount of tax due in the preceding calendar year.

(b3)   Category. - The Secretary must monitor the amount of State and local sales and use taxes paid by a taxpayer or estimate the amount of taxes to be paid by a new taxpayer and must direct each taxpayer to pay tax and file returns as required by this section. In determining the amount of taxes due from a taxpayer, the Secretary must consider the total amount due from all places of business owned or operated by the same person as the amount due from that person. A taxpayer must file a return and pay tax in accordance with the Secretary's direction.

(c)   Repealed by Session Laws 2001-427, s. 6(a), effective January 1, 2002, and applicable to taxes levied on or after that date.

(d)   Use Tax on Out-of-State Purchases. - Use tax payable by an individual who purchases the items listed in this subsection outside the State for a nonbusiness purpose is due on an annual basis. For an individual who is not required to file an individual income tax return under Part 2 of Article 4 of this Chapter, the annual reporting period ends on the last day of the calendar year and a use tax return is due by the following April 15. For an individual who is required to file an individual income tax return, the annual reporting period ends on the last day of the individual's income tax year, and the use tax must be paid on the income tax return as provided in G.S. 105-269.14. The items are:

(1)   Tangible personal property other than a boat or an aircraft.

(2)   Digital property.

(3)   A service.

(e)   Simultaneous State and Local Changes. - When State and local sales and use tax rates change on the same date because one increases and the other decreases but the combined rate does not change, sales and use taxes payable on the following periodic payments are reportable in accordance with the changed State and local rates:

(1) Lease or rental payments billed after the effective date of the changes.

(2) Installment sale payments received after the effective date of the changes by a taxpayer who reports the installment sale on a cash basis. (1957, c. 1340, s. 5; 1967, c. 1110, s. 6; 1973, c. 476, s. 193; 1979, c. 801, s. 83; 1983 (Reg. Sess., 1984), c. 1097, s. 14; 1985, c. 656, s. 26; 1985 (Reg. Sess., 1986), c. 1007; 1987, c. 557, s. 6; 1989 (Reg. Sess., 1990), c. 945, s. 1; 1991, c. 690, s. 4; 1993, c. 450, s. 7; 1997-77, s. 1; 1998-121, s. 1; 1999-341, s. 1; 2000-120, s. 11; 2001-347, s. 2.14; 2001-414, s. 18; 2001-427, s. 6(a); 2001-430, s. 7; 2002-184, ss. 10, 11; 2003-284, ss. 44.1, 45.8; 2003-416, s. 26; 2005-276, s. 33.24; 2006-162, s. 5(b); 2006-33, s. 9; 2007-527, ss. 11, 12; 2008-134, s. 11; 2009-451, s. 27A.3(b), (c), (m); 2010-31, s. 31.3(a)-(d); 2010-95, s. 42; 2011-330, s. 21.)

§§ 105-164.17 through 105-164.18: Repealed by Session Laws 1993, c. 450, ss. 8, 9.

§ 105-164.19. Extension of time for making returns and payment.

The Secretary for good cause may extend the time for filing any return under the provisions of this Article and may grant additional time within which to file the return as he may deem proper, but the time for filing any return shall not be extended for more than 30 days after the regular due date of the return. If the time for filing a return is extended, interest accrues at the rate established pursuant to G.S. 105-241.21 from the time the return was due to be filed to the date of payment. (1957, c. 1340, s. 5; 1973, c. 476, s. 193; 1977, c. 1114, s. 10; 1985, c. 656, s. 30; 2007-491, s. 44(1)a; 2013-414, s. 1(f).)

§ 105-164.20. Cash or accrual basis of reporting.

Any retailer, except a retailer who sells electricity or telecommunications service, may report sales on either the cash or accrual basis of accounting upon making application to the Secretary for permission to use the basis selected. Permission granted by the Secretary to report on a selected basis continues in effect until revoked by the Secretary or the taxpayer receives permission from the Secretary to change the basis selected. A retailer who sells electricity or telecommunications service must report its sales on an accrual basis. A sale of electricity or telecommunications service is considered to accrue when the retailer bills its customer for the sale. (1957, c. 1340, s. 5; 1973, c. 476, s. 193; 1983 (Reg. Sess., 1984), c. 1097, s. 15; 1998-22, s. 7; 2001-430, s. 8.)

§ 105-164.21. Repealed by Session Laws 1987, c. 622, s. 10.

§ 105-164.21A. (Repealed effective July 1, 2014) Deduction for municipalities that sell electric power.

A municipality that pays the retail sales tax imposed by this Article on electricity may deduct from the amount of tax payable by the municipality an amount equal to three percent (3%) of the difference between its gross receipts from sales of electricity for the preceding reporting period and the amount paid by the municipality for purchased power and related services during that reporting period. (1983 (Reg. Sess., 1984), c. 1097, s. 12; 1989 (Reg. Sess., 1990), c. 945, s. 2; 2013-316, s. 4.1(a).)

§ 105-164.21B: Repealed by Session Laws 2006-151, s. 9, effective January 1, 2007.

Part 5. Records Required to Be Kept.

§ 105-164.22. Record-keeping requirements, inspection authority, and effect of failure to keep records.

Retailers, wholesale merchants, and consumers must keep for a period of three years records that establish their tax liability under this Article. The Secretary or a person designated by the Secretary may inspect these records at any reasonable time during the day.

A retailer's records must include records of the retailer's gross income, gross sales, net taxable sales, and all items purchased for resale. Failure of a retailer to keep records that establish that a sale is exempt under this Article subjects the retailer to liability for tax on the sale.

A wholesale merchant's records must include a bill of sale for each customer that contains the name and address of the purchaser, the date of the purchase, the item purchased, and the price at which the wholesale merchant sold the item. Failure of a wholesale merchant to keep these records for the sale of an item subjects the wholesale merchant to liability for tax at the rate that applies to the retail sale of the item.

A consumer's records must include an invoice or other statement of the purchase price of an item the consumer purchased from outside the State. Failure of the consumer to keep these records subjects the consumer to liability for tax on the purchase price of the item, as determined by the Secretary. (1957, c. 1340, s. 5; 1973, c. 476, s. 193; 1998-98, s. 51; 2009-451, s. 27A.3(n).)

§ 105-164.23: Repealed by Session Laws 2009-451, s. 27A.3(o), effective August 7, 2009.

§ 105-164.24: Repealed by Session Laws 2009-451, s. 27A.3(o), effective August 7, 2009.

§ 105-164.25: Repealed by Session Laws 2009-451, s. 27A.3(o), effective August 7, 2009.

§ 105-164.26. Presumption that sales are taxable.

For the purpose of the proper administration of this Article and to prevent evasion of the retail sales tax, the following presumptions apply:

(1)   That all gross receipts of wholesale merchants and retailers are subject to the retail sales tax until the contrary is established by proper records as required in this Article.

(2)   That tangible personal property sold by a person for delivery in this State is sold for storage, use, or other consumption in this State.

(3) That tangible personal property delivered outside this State and brought to this State by the purchaser is for storage, use, or consumption in this State.

(4) That digital property sold for delivery or access in this State is sold for storage, use, or consumption in this State.

(5) That a service purchased for receipt in this State is purchased for storage, use, or consumption in this State. (1957, c. 1340, s. 5; 1998-98, s. 108; 2009-451, s. 27A.3(p).)

§ 105-164.27. Repealed by Session Laws 1961, c. 826, s. 2.

§ 105-164.27A. Direct pay permit.

(a) General. - A general direct pay permit authorizes its holder to purchase any tangible personal property, digital property, or service without paying tax to the seller and authorizes the seller to not collect any tax on a sale to the permit holder. A person who purchases an item under a direct pay permit issued under this subsection is liable for use tax due on the purchase. The tax is payable when the property is placed in use or the service is received. A direct pay permit issued under this subsection does not apply to taxes imposed under G.S. 105-164.4 on sales of electricity or the gross receipts derived from rentals of accommodations.

A person who purchases an item for storage, use, or consumption in this State whose tax status cannot be determined at the time of the purchase because of one of the reasons listed below may apply to the Secretary for a general direct pay permit:

(1) The place of business where the item will be stored, used, or consumed is not known at the time of the purchase and a different tax consequence applies depending on where the item is used.

(2) The manner in which the item will be stored, used, or consumed is not known at the time of the purchase and one or more of the potential uses is taxable but others are not taxable.

(a1) Direct Mail. - A person who purchases direct mail may apply to the Secretary for a direct pay permit for the purchase of direct mail. A direct pay permit issued for direct mail does not apply to any purchase other than the purchase of direct mail. A person who purchases direct mail under a direct pay permit must file a return and pay the tax due monthly or quarterly to the Secretary.

(b) Telecommunications Service. - A direct pay permit for telecommunications service authorizes its holder to purchase telecommunications service and ancillary service without paying tax to the seller and authorizes the seller to not collect any tax on a sale to the permit holder. A person who purchases these services under a direct pay permit must file a return and pay the tax due monthly or quarterly to the Secretary. A direct pay permit issued under this subsection does not apply to any tax other than the tax on telecommunications service and ancillary service.

A call center that purchases telecommunications service that originates outside this State and terminates in this State may apply to the Secretary for a direct pay permit for telecommunications service and ancillary service. A call center is a business that is primarily engaged in providing support services to customers by telephone to support products or services of the business. A business is primarily engaged in providing support services by telephone if at least sixty percent (60%) of its calls are incoming.

(c) Application. - An application for a direct pay permit must be made on a form provided by the Secretary and contain the information required by the Secretary. The Secretary may grant the application if the Secretary finds that the applicant complies with the sales and use tax laws and that the applicant's compliance burden will be greatly reduced by use of the permit.

(d) Revocation. - A direct pay permit is valid until the holder returns it to the Secretary or the Secretary revokes it. The Secretary may revoke a direct pay permit if the holder of the permit does not file a sales and use tax return on time, does not pay sales and use tax on time, or otherwise fails to comply with the sales and use tax laws. (2000-120, s. 1; 2001-414, s. 20; 2001-430, s. 9; 2002-72, s. 18; 2003-284, s. 45.9; 2003-416, s. 16(b); 2006-33, s. 7; 2009-451, s. 27A.3(q); 2012-79, s. 2.12; 2013-414, s. 13.)

§ 105-164.28. Certificate of exemption.

(a) Relief From Liability. - Except as provided in subsection (b) of this section, a seller is not liable for the tax otherwise applicable if the Secretary determines that a purchaser improperly claimed an exemption, or if the seller within 90 days of the sale meets the following requirements:

(1) For a sale made in person, the seller obtains a certificate of exemption or a blanket certificate of exemption from a purchaser with which the seller has a recurring business relationship. If the purchaser provides a paper certificate, the certificate must be signed by the purchaser and state the purchaser's name, address, certificate of registration number, reason for exemption, and type of business. For purposes of this subdivision, a certificate received by fax is a paper certificate. If the purchaser does not provide a paper certificate, the seller must obtain and maintain the same information required had a certificate been provided by the purchaser.

(2) Repealed by Session Laws 2013-414, s. 43(a), effective August 23, 2013.

(3) For a sale made over the Internet or by other remote means, the seller obtains the purchaser's name, address, certificate of registration number, reason for exemption, and type of business and maintains this information in a retrievable format in its records. If a certificate of exemption is provided electronically for a remote sale, the requirements of subdivision (1) of this subsection apply except the electronic certificate is not required to be signed by the purchaser.

(4) In the case of drop shipment sales, a third-party vendor obtains a certificate of exemption provided by its customer or any other acceptable information evidencing qualification for a resale exemption, regardless of whether the customer is registered to collect and remit sales and use tax in the State.

(b) Substantiation Request. - If the Secretary determines that a certificate of exemption or the required data elements obtained by the seller are incomplete, the Secretary may request substantiation from the seller. A seller is not required to verify that a certificate of registration number provided by a purchaser is correct. If a seller does one of the following within 120 days after a request for substantiation by the Secretary, the seller is not liable for the tax otherwise applicable:

(1) Obtains a fully completed certificate of exemption from the purchaser provided in good faith. The certificate is provided in good faith if it claims an exemption that meets all of the following conditions:

a. It was statutorily available in this State on the date of the transaction.

b. It could be applicable to the item being purchased.

c. It is reasonable for the purchaser's type of business.

(2) Obtains other information to establish the transaction was not subject to tax.

(c) Fraud. - The relief from liability under this section does not apply to a seller who does any of the following:

(1) Fraudulently fails to collect tax.

(2) Solicits purchasers to participate in the unlawful claim of an exemption.

(3) Accepts an exemption certificate when the purchaser claims an entity-based exemption when the subject of the transaction sought to be covered by the exemption certificate is received by the purchaser at a location operated by the seller, and the claimed exemption is not available in this State.

(4) Had knowledge or had reason to know at the time information was provided relating to the exemption claimed that the information was materially false.

(5) Knowingly participated in activity intended to purposefully evade tax properly due on the transaction.

(d) Purchaser's Liability. - A purchaser who does not resell an item purchased under a certificate of exemption is liable for any tax subsequently determined to be due on the sale.

(e) Renewal of Information. - The Secretary may not require a seller to renew a blanket certificate of exemption or to update exemption certificate information or data elements when there is a recurring business relationship between the buyer and seller. For purposes of this section, a recurring business relationship exists when a period of no more than 12 months elapse between sales transactions. (1957, c. 1340, s. 5; 1973, c. 476, s. 193; 1991 (Reg. Sess., 1992), c. 914, s. 1; 2000-120, s. 6; 2005-276, s. 33.15; 2009-451, s. 27A.3(r); 2011-330, s. 28; 2013-414, s. 43(a).)

§ 105-164.28A. Other exemption certificates.

(a) Authorization. - The Secretary may require a person who purchases an item that is exempt from tax or is subject to a preferential rate of tax depending on the status of the purchaser or the intended use of the item to obtain an exemption certificate from the Department to receive the exemption or preferential rate. An exemption certificate authorizes a retailer to sell an item to the holder of the certificate and either collect tax at a preferential rate or not collect tax on the sale, as appropriate. A person who purchases an item under an exemption certificate is liable for any tax due on the sale if the Department determines that the person is not eligible for the certificate. The liability is relieved when the seller obtains the purchaser's name, address, type of business, reason for exemption, and exemption number in lieu of obtaining an exemption certificate.

(b) Scope. - This section does not apply to a direct pay permit or a certificate of exemption. G.S. 105-164.27A addresses a direct pay permit, and G.S. 105-164.28 addresses a certificate of exemption.

(c) Administration. - This section shall be administered in accordance with G.S. 105-164.28. (2002-184, s. 12; 2009-451, s. 27A.3(s); 2013-414, s. 43(b).)

§ 105-164.29. Application for certificate of registration by wholesale merchants and retailers.

(a) Requirement and Application. - Before a person may engage in business as a retailer or a wholesale merchant, the person must obtain a certificate of registration. To obtain a certificate of registration, a person must register with the Department. A wholesale merchant or retailer who has more than one business is required to obtain only one certificate of registration to cover all operations of the business throughout the State. An application for registration must be signed as follows:

(1) By the owner, if the owner is an individual.

(2) By a manager, member, or partner, if the owner is an association, a partnership, or a limited liability company.

(3) By an executive officer or some other person specifically authorized by the corporation to sign the application, if the owner is a corporation. If the application is signed by a person authorized to do so by the corporation, written evidence of the person's authority must be attached to the application.

(b) Issuance. - A certificate of registration is not assignable and is valid only for the person in whose name it is issued. A copy of the certificate of registration must be displayed at each place of business.

(c) Term. - A certificate of registration is valid unless it is revoked for failure to comply with the provisions of this Article or becomes void. A certificate issued to a retailer who makes taxable sales becomes void if, for a period of 18 months, the retailer files no returns or files returns showing no sales.

(d) Revocation. - The failure of a wholesale merchant or retailer to comply with this Article or G.S. 14-401.18 is grounds for revocation of the wholesale merchant's or retailer's certificate of registration. Before the Secretary revokes a wholesale merchant's or retailer's certificate of registration, the Secretary must notify the wholesale merchant or retailer that the Secretary proposes to revoke the certificate of registration and that the proposed revocation will become final unless the wholesale merchant or retailer objects to the proposed revocation and files a request for a Departmental review within the time set in G.S. 105-241.11 for requesting a Departmental review of a proposed assessment. The notice must be sent in accordance with the methods authorized in G.S. 105-241.20. The procedures in Article 9 of this Chapter for review of a proposed assessment apply to the review of a proposed revocation. (1957, c. 1340, s. 5; 1973, c. 476, s. 193; 1979, 2nd Sess., c. 1084; 1991, c. 690, s. 5; 1993, c. 354, s. 17; c. 539, s. 705; 1994, Ex. Sess., c. 24, s. 14(c); 1999-333, s. 8; 2000-140, s. 67(b); 2007-491, s. 19; 2009-451, s. 27A.3(t).)

§ 105-164.29A. State government exemption process.

(a) Application. - To be eligible for the exemption provided in G.S. 105-164.13(52), a State agency must obtain from the Department a sales tax exemption number. The application for exemption must be in the form required by the Secretary, be signed by the State agency's head, and contain any information required by the Secretary. The Secretary must assign a sales tax exemption number to a State agency that submits a proper application.

(b) Liability. - A State agency that does not use the items purchased with its exemption number must pay the tax that should have been paid on the items purchased, plus interest calculated from the date the tax would otherwise have been paid. (2003-431, s. 4; 2004-170, s. 22.)

§ 105-164.29B. Information to counties and cities.

The Secretary must give information on refunds of tax made under this Article to a designated county or city official within 30 days after the official makes a written request to the Secretary for the information. For a request made by a county official, the Secretary must give the official a list of each claimant that received a refund in the past 12 months of at least one thousand dollars ($1,000) of tax paid to the county. For a request made by a city official, the Secretary must give the official a list of each claimant that received a refund in the past 12 months of at least one thousand dollars ($1,000) of tax paid to all the counties in which the city is located. The list must include the name and address of each of these claimants and the amount of the refund received from each county covered by the request.

A claimant that has received a refund under this Article of tax paid to a county must give information on the refund to a designated official of the county or a city located in the county. The claimant must give the information to the county or city official within 30 days after the official makes a written request to the claimant for the information. For a request by a county or city official, the claimant must give the official a copy of the request for the refund and any supporting documentation requested by the official to verify the request. If a claimant determines that a refund it has received under this Article is incorrect, the claimant must file an amended request for a refund.

For purposes of this section, a designated county official is the chair of the board of county commissioners or a county official designated in a resolution adopted by the Board, and a designated city official is the mayor of the city or a city official designated in a resolution adopted by the city's governing board. Information given to a county or city official under this section is not a public record and may not be disclosed except as provided in G.S. 153A-148.1 or G.S. 160A-208.1. (2010-166, s. 1.20.)

Part 6. Examination of Records.

§ 105-164.30. Secretary or agent may examine books, etc.

For the purpose of enforcing the collection of the tax levied by this Article, the Secretary or his duly authorized agent is authorized to examine at all reasonable hours during the day the books, papers, records, documents or other data of all retailers or wholesale merchants bearing upon the correctness of any return or for the purpose of filing a return where none has been made as required by this Article, and may require the attendance of any person and take his testimony with respect to any such matter, with power to administer oaths to such person or persons. If any person summoned as a witness fails to obey any summons to appear before the Secretary or his authorized agent, or refuses to testify or answer any material question or to produce any book, record, paper, or other data when required to do so, the Secretary or his authorized agent shall report the failure or refusal to the Attorney General or the district solicitor, who shall thereupon institute proceedings in the superior court of the county where the witness resides to compel obedience to any summons of the Secretary or his authorized agent. Officers who serve summonses or subpoenas, and witnesses attending, shall receive like compensation as officers and witnesses in the superior courts, to be paid from the proper appropriation for the administration of this Article.

In the event any retailer or wholesale merchant fails or refuses to permit the Secretary or his authorized agent to examine his books, papers, accounts, records, documents or other data, the Secretary may require the retailer or wholesale merchant to show cause before the superior court of the county in which said taxpayer resides or has its principal place of business as to why the books, records, papers, or documents should not be examined and the superior court shall have jurisdiction to enter an order requiring the production of all necessary books, records, papers, or documents and to punish for contempt any person who violates the order. (1957, c. 1340, s. 5; 1973, c. 476, s. 193; 1998-98, s. 52; 2013-414, s. 1(g).)

§ 105-164.31: Repealed by Session Laws 2009-451, s. 27A.3(o), effective August 7, 2009.

§ 105-164.32. Incorrect returns; estimate.

If a retailer, a wholesale merchant or a consumer fails to file a return and pay the tax due under this Article or files a grossly incorrect or false or fraudulent return, the Secretary must estimate the tax due and assess the retailer, wholesale merchant, or consumer based on the estimate. (1957, c. 1340, s. 5; 1973, c. 476, s. 193; 2001-414, s. 21; 2009-451, s. 27A.3(u).)

Part 7. Failure to Make Returns; Overpayments.

§§ 105-164.33 through 105-164.34: Repealed by Session Laws 1963, c. 1169, s. 3.

§ 105-164.35. (Repealed effective August 23, 2013) Excessive payments; recomputing tax.

As soon as practicable after a return is filed, the Secretary shall examine it. If it then appears that the correct amount of tax is greater or less than the amount shown in the return, the tax shall be recomputed.

(1)   Excessive Payments. - If the amount already paid exceeds that which should have been paid on the basis of the tax so recomputed, the excess shall be credited or refunded to the taxpayer in accordance with the provisions of this Article.

(2)   to (5) Repealed by Session Laws 1959, c. 1259, s. 9. (1957, c. 1340, s. 5; 1959, c. 1259, s. 9; 1973, c. 476, s. 193; 2013-414, s. 14.)

§ 105-164.36. Repealed by Session Laws 1959, c. 1259, s. 9.

§ 105-164.37. Bankruptcy, receivership, etc.

If any taxpayer subject to the provisions of this Article goes into bankruptcy, receivership or turns over his stock of merchandise by voluntary transfer to creditors, the tax liability under this Article shall constitute a prior lien upon such stock of merchandise and shall become subject to levy under execution and it shall be the duty of the transferee in any such case to retain the amount of the tax due from the first sales of such stock of merchandise and pay the same to the Secretary. (1957, c. 1340, s. 5; 1973, c. 476, s. 193.)

§ 105-164.38. Tax is a lien.

(a) The tax imposed by this Article is a lien upon all personal property of any person who is required by this Article to obtain a certificate of registration to engage in business and who stops engaging in the business by transferring the business, transferring the stock of goods of the business, or going out of business. A person who stops engaging in business must file the return required by this Article within 30 days after transferring the business, transferring the stock of goods of the business, or going out of business.

(b) Any person to whom the business or the stock of goods was transferred must withhold from the consideration paid for the business or stock of goods an amount sufficient to cover the taxes due until the person selling the business or stock of goods produces a statement from the Secretary showing that the taxes have been paid or that no taxes are due. If the person who buys a business or stock of goods fails to withhold an amount sufficient to cover the taxes and the taxes remain unpaid after the 30-day period allowed, the buyer is personally liable for the unpaid taxes to the extent of the greater of the following:

(1) The consideration paid by the buyer for the business or the stock of goods.

(2) The fair market value of the business or the stock of goods.

(c) Assessment. - The period of limitations for assessing liability against the buyer of a business or the stock of goods of a business and for enforcing the lien against the property expires one year after the end of the period of limitations for assessment against the person who sold the business or the stock of goods. Except as otherwise provided in this section, the assessment procedures in Article 9 of this Chapter apply to a person who buys a business or the stock of goods of a business to the same extent as if the person had incurred the original tax liability. (1957, c. 1340, s. 5; 1963, c. 1169, s. 3; 1973,

c. 476, s. 193; 1991, c. 690, s. 6; 1991 (Reg. Sess., 1992), c. 949, s. 2; 2000-140, s. 67(c); 2007-491, s. 20.)

§ 105-164.39. Attachment.

In the event any retailer or wholesale merchant is delinquent in the payment of the tax herein provided for, the Secretary may give notice of the amount of such delinquency by registered mail to all persons having in their possession or under their control any credits or other personal property belonging to such retailer or wholesale merchant or owing any debts to such taxpayer at the time of the receipt by them of such notice and thereafter any person so notified shall neither transfer nor make any other disposition of such credits, other personal property or debts until the Secretary shall have consented to a transfer or disposition or until 30 days shall have elapsed from and after the receipt of such notice. All persons so notified must within five days after receipt of such notice advise the Secretary of any and all such credits, other personal property or debts in their possession, under their control or owing by them as the case may be. The remedy provided by this section shall be cumulative and optional and in addition to all other remedies now provided by law for the collection of taxes due the State. (1957, c. 1340, s. 5; 1973, c. 476, s. 193.)

§ 105-164.40. Jeopardy assessment.

If the Secretary is of the opinion that the collection of any tax or any amount of tax required to be collected and paid to the State under this Article will be jeopardized by delay, he shall make an assessment of the tax or amount of tax required to be collected and shall mail or issue a notice of such assessment to the taxpayer together with a demand for immediate payment of the tax or of the deficiency in tax declared to be in jeopardy including interest and penalties. In the case of a tax for a current period, the Secretary may declare the taxable period of the taxpayer immediately terminated and shall cause notice of such finding and declaration to be mailed or issued to the taxpayer together with a demand for immediate payment of the tax based on the period declared terminated and such tax shall be immediately due and payable, whether or not the time otherwise allowed by law for filing a return and paying the tax has expired. Assessments provided for in this section shall be immediately due and payable and proceedings for the collection shall commence at once and if any such tax, penalty or interest is not paid upon demand of the Secretary, he shall forthwith cause a levy to be made on the property of the taxpayer or, in his discretion the Secretary may require the taxpayer to file such indemnity bond as in his judgment may be sufficient to protect the interest of the State. (1957, c. 1340, s. 5; 1973, c. 476, s. 193.)

§ 105-164.41: Repealed by Session Laws 2011-330, s. 38, effective June 27, 2011.

§ 105-164.42: Repealed by Session Laws 1959, c. 1259, s. 9.

Part 7A. Uniform Sales and Use Tax Administration Act.

§ 105-164.42A. Short title.

This Part is the "Uniform Sales and Use Tax Administration Act" and may be cited by that name. (2001-347, s. 1.3; 2005-276, s. 33.31.)

§ 105-164.42B. Definitions.

The following definitions apply in this Part:

(1)   Agreement. - Streamlined Agreement, as defined in G.S. 105-164.3.

(2)   Certified automated system. - Software certified jointly by the states that are signatories to the Agreement to calculate the tax imposed by each jurisdiction on a transaction, determine the amount of tax to remit to the appropriate state, and maintain a record of the transaction.

(3)   Certified service provider. - An agent certified jointly by the states that are signatories to the Agreement to perform all of the seller's sales tax functions.

(4)   Member state. - A state that has entered into the Agreement.

(5)   Person. - Defined in G.S. 105-228.90.

(6)   Sales tax. - The tax levied in G.S. 105-164.4.

(7)   Seller. - A person making sales, leases, or rentals of personal property or services.

(8) State. - The term "this State" means the State of North Carolina. Otherwise, the term "state" means any state of the United States and the District of Columbia.

(9) Use tax. - The tax levied in G.S. 105-164.6. (2001-347, s. 1.3; 2005-276, ss. 33.16, 33.31.)

§ 105-164.42C. Authority to enter Agreement.

The Secretary is authorized to enter into the Agreement with one or more states to simplify and modernize sales and use tax administration in order to substantially reduce the burden of tax compliance for all sellers and for all types of commerce. The Secretary may act jointly with other member states to establish standards for certification of a certified service provider and a certified automated system and to establish performance standards for multistate sellers.

The Secretary is authorized to represent this State before the other member states. The Secretary may take any other actions reasonably required to implement this Part, including the joint procurement with other member states of goods and services in furtherance of the Agreement. (2001-347, s. 1.3; 2005-276, s. 33.31.)

§ 105-164.42D. Relationship to North Carolina law.

No provision of the Agreement authorized by this Part invalidates or amends any provision of the law of this State. Adoption of the Agreement by this State does not amend or modify any law of this State. Implementation of a condition of the Agreement in this State must be made pursuant to an act of the General Assembly. (2001-347, s. 1.3; 2005-276, s. 33.31.)

§ 105-164.42E. Agreement requirements.

The Secretary may not enter into the Agreement unless the Agreement requires each state to abide by the following requirements:

(1) Uniform state rate. - The Agreement must set restrictions to achieve more uniform state rates through the following:

a. Limiting the number of state rates.

b. Limiting maximums on the amount of state tax that is due on a transaction.

c. Limiting thresholds on the application of a state tax.

(2) Uniform standards. - The Agreement must establish uniform standards for all of the following:

a. The sourcing of transactions to taxing jurisdictions.

b. The administration of exempt sales.

c. The allowances a seller can take for bad debts.

d. Sales and use tax returns and remittances.

(3) Uniform definitions. - The Agreement must require states to develop and adopt uniform definitions of sales and use tax terms. The definitions must enable a state to preserve its ability to make policy choices not inconsistent with the uniform definitions.

(4) Central registration. - The Agreement must provide a central, electronic registration system that allows a seller to register to collect and remit sales and use taxes for all signatory states.

(5) No nexus attribution. - The Agreement must provide that registration with the central registration system and the collection of sales and use taxes in the signatory states will not be used as a factor in determining whether the seller has nexus with a state for any tax.

(6) Local sales and use taxes. - The Agreement must provide for reduction of the burdens of complying with local sales and use taxes through one or more of the following:

a. Restricting variances between the state and local tax bases.

b. Requiring states to administer any sales and use taxes levied by local jurisdictions within the state so that sellers collecting and remitting these taxes will not have to register or file returns with, remit funds to, or be subject to independent audits from local taxing jurisdictions.

c. Restricting the frequency of changes in the local sales and use tax rates and setting effective dates for the application of local jurisdictional boundary changes to local sales and use taxes.

d. Providing notice of changes in local sales and use tax rates and of changes in the boundaries of local taxing jurisdictions.

(7) Monetary allowances. - The Agreement must outline any monetary allowances that are to be provided by the states to sellers or certified service providers.

(8) State compliance. - The Agreement must require each state to certify compliance with the terms of the Agreement before becoming a member and to maintain compliance, under the laws of the member state, with all provisions of the Agreement while a member.

(9) Consumer privacy. - The Agreement must require each state to adopt a uniform policy for certified service providers that protects the privacy of consumers and maintains the confidentiality of tax information. (2001-347, s. 1.3; 2005-276, s. 33.31.)

§ 105-164.42F. Cooperating sovereigns.

The Agreement authorized by this Part is an accord among individual cooperating sovereigns in furtherance of their governmental functions. The Agreement provides a mechanism among the member states to establish and maintain a cooperative, simplified system for the application and administration of sales and use taxes under the laws of each member state. (2001-347, s. 1.3; 2005-276, s. 33.31.)

§ 105-164.42G. Effect of Agreement.

Entry of this State into the Agreement does not create a cause of action or a defense to an action. No person may challenge any action or inaction by a department, agency, or other instrumentality of this State, or a political subdivision of this State, on the ground that the action or inaction is inconsistent with the Agreement. No law of this State, or its application, may be declared invalid on the ground that the provision or application is inconsistent with the Agreement. (2001-347, s. 1.3; 2005-276, s. 33.31.)

§ 105-164.42H. Certification of certified automated system and effect of certification.

(a)   Certification. - The Secretary may certify a software program as a certified automated system if the Secretary determines that the program correctly determines all of the following and that the software can generate reports and returns required by the Secretary:

(1)   The applicable combined State and local sales and use tax rate for a sale, based on the sourcing principles in G.S. 105-164.4B.

(2)   Whether or not an item is exempt from tax, based on a uniform product code or another method.

(3)   Repealed by Session Laws 2006-33, s. 12, effective June 1, 2006.

(4)   The amount of tax to be remitted for each taxpayer for a reporting period.

(5)   Any other issue necessary for the application or calculation of sales and use tax due.

(b)   Liability. - A seller may choose to use a certified automated system in performing its sales tax administration functions. A seller that uses a certified automated system is liable for sales and use taxes due on transactions it processes using the certified automated system except for underpayments of tax attributable to errors in the functioning of the system. A person that provides a certified automated system is responsible for the proper functioning of that system and is liable for underpayments of tax attributable to errors in the functioning of the system. (2000-120, s. 2; 2001-347, ss. 1.1, 1.3; 2005-276, s. 33.31; 2006-33, s. 12.)

§ 105-164.42I. Contract with certified service provider and effect of contract.

(a) Certification. - The Secretary may certify an entity as a certified service provider if the entity meets all of the following requirements:

(1) The entity uses a certified automated system.

(2) The entity has agreed to update its program upon notification by the Secretary.

(3) The entity integrates its certified automated system with the system of a seller for whom the entity collects tax so that the tax due on a sale is determined at the time of the sale.

(4) The entity remits the taxes it collects at the time and in the manner specified by the Secretary.

(5) The entity agrees to file sales and use tax returns on behalf of the sellers for whom it collects tax.

(6) The entity enters into a contract with the Secretary and agrees to comply with all the conditions of the contract.

(b) Contract. - The Secretary may contract or authorize in writing the Streamlined Sales Tax Governing Board to contract on behalf of the Secretary with a certified service provider for the collection and remittance of sales and use taxes. A certified service provider must file with the Secretary or the Streamlined Sales Tax Governing Board a bond or an irrevocable letter of credit in the amount set by the Secretary. A bond or irrevocable letter of credit must be conditioned upon compliance with the contract, be payable to the State or the Streamlined Sales Tax Governing Board, and be in the form required by the Secretary. The amount a certified service provider charges under the contract is a cost of collecting the tax and is payable from the amount collected.

(c) Liability. - A seller may contract with a certified service provider to collect and remit sales and use taxes payable to the State on sales made by the seller. A certified service provider with whom a seller contracts is the agent of the seller. As the seller's agent, the certified service provider, rather than the seller, is liable for sales and use taxes due this State on all sales transactions the certified service provider processes for the seller unless the seller misrepresents the type of products it sells or commits fraud. A seller that misrepresents the type of products it sells or commits fraud is liable for taxes not collected as a result of the misrepresentation or fraud.

(d) Audit and Review. - In the absence of misrepresentation or fraud, a seller that contracts with a certified service provider is not subject to audit on the transactions processed by the certified service provider. A seller is subject to audit for transactions not processed by the certified service provider. The State may perform a system check of a seller and review a seller's procedures to determine if the certified service provider's system is functioning properly and the extent to which the seller's transactions are being processed by the certified service provider. A certified service provider is subject to audit. (2000-120, s. 2; 2001-347, ss. 1.1, 1.3; 2005-276, s. 33.31; 2013-414, s. 44.)

§ 105-164.42J. Performance standard for multistate seller.

The Secretary may establish a performance standard for a seller that is engaged in business in this State and at least 10 other states and has developed a proprietary system to determine the amount of sales and use taxes due on transactions. A seller that enters into an agreement with the Secretary that establishes a performance standard for that system is liable for the failure of the system to meet the performance standard. (2001-347, s. 1.3; 2005-276, s. 33.31.)

§ 105-164.42K. Registration and effect of registration.

Registration under the Agreement satisfies the registration requirements under this Article. A seller who registers under the Agreement within 12 months after the State becomes a member of the Agreement and who meets the following conditions is not subject to assessment for sales tax for any period before the effective date of the seller's registration:

(1) The seller was not registered with the State during the 12-month period before the effective date of this State's participation in the Agreement.

(2) When the seller registered, the seller had not received a letter from the Department notifying the seller of an audit.

(3) The seller continues to be registered under the Agreement and to remit tax to the State for at least 36 months. (2005-276, s. 33.17.)

§ 105-164.42L. Liability relief for erroneous information or insufficient notice by Department.

(a) The Secretary may develop databases that provide information on the boundaries of taxing jurisdictions and the tax rates applicable to those taxing jurisdictions. A person who relies on the information provided in these databases is not liable for underpayments of tax attributable to erroneous information provided by the Secretary in those databases.

(b) The Secretary may develop a taxability matrix that provides information on the taxability of certain items. A person who relies on the information provided in the taxability matrix is not liable for underpayments of tax attributable to erroneous information provided by the Secretary in the taxability matrix.

(c) A retailer is not liable for an underpayment of tax attributable to a rate change when the State fails to provide for at least 30 days between the enactment of the rate change and the effective date of the rate change if the conditions of this subsection are satisfied. However, if the State establishes the retailer fraudulently failed to collect tax at the new rate or solicited customers based on the immediately preceding effective rate, this liability relief does not apply. Both of the following conditions must be satisfied for liability relief:

(1) The retailer collected tax at the immediately preceding rate.

(2) The retailer's failure to collect at the newly effective rate does not extend beyond 30 days after the date of enactment of the new rate or the effective date applicable under G.S. 105-164.15A. (2005-276, s. 33.18; 2007-244, s. 5; 2013-414, s. 15.)

Part 8. Administration and Enforcement.

§ 105-164.43: Repealed by Session Laws 2007-491, s. 2, effective January 1, 2008.

§ 105-164.43A. (Recodified effective August 8, 2001 - See note) Certification of tax collector software and tax collector.

(a)   Recodified as § 105-164.42H(a) by Session Laws 2001-347, s. 1.1, effective August 8, 2001. See note.

(b)   Recodified as § 105-164.42I(a) by Session Laws 2001-347, s. 1.1, effective August 8, 2001. See note. (2000-120, s. 2; 2001-347, s. 1.1.)

§ 105-164.43B. (Recodified effective August 8, 2001 - See note) Contract with Certified Sales Tax Collector.

Recodified as § 105-164.42I(b) by Session Laws 2001-347, s. 1.1, effective August 8, 2001. See note. (2000-120, s. 2; 2001-347, s. 1.1.)

§ 105-164.43C: Repealed by Session Laws 2001-347, s. 1.2, effective August 8, 2001. See note.

§ 105-164.44. Penalty and remedies of Article 9 applicable.

All provisions not inconsistent with this Article in Article 9, entitled "General Administration - Penalties and Remedies" of Subchapter I of Chapter 105 of the General Statutes, including but not limited to, administration, auditing, making returns, promulgation of rules and regulations by the Secretary, additional taxes, assessment procedure, imposition and collection of taxes and the lien thereof, assessments, refunds and penalties are hereby made a part of this Article and shall be applicable thereto. (1957, c. 1340, s. 5; 1973, c. 476, s. 193.)

§ 105-164.44A: Repealed by Session Laws 1991, c. 45, s. 18.

§ 105-164.44B: Repealed by Session Laws 2011-145, s. 13.27(a), effective July 1, 2011.

§ 105-164.44C: Repealed by Session Laws 2001-424, s. 34.15(a)(1), as amended by Session Laws 2002-126, s. 30A.1, effective July 1, 2002.

§ 105-164.44D. Reimbursement for sales tax exemption for purchases by the Department of Transportation.

The amount of sales and use tax revenue that is not realized by the General Fund as the result of the sales and use tax exemption in G.S. 105-164.13 for purchases by the Department of Transportation shall be transferred from the Highway Fund to the General Fund in accordance with this section. This direct transfer is made in lieu of eliminating the Department of Transportation's sales and use tax exemption to alleviate the administrative and accounting burden that would be placed on the Department of Transportation by eliminating the exemption.

For the 1991-92 fiscal year, the State Treasurer shall transfer the sum of eight million seven hundred thousand dollars ($8,700,000) from the Highway Fund to the General Fund. The transfer shall be made on a quarterly basis by transferring one-fourth of the annual amount each quarter.

For each fiscal year following the 1991-92 fiscal year, the State Treasurer shall transfer the sum transferred the previous fiscal year plus or minus the percentage of that amount by which the total collection of State sales and use taxes increased or decreased during the previous fiscal year. In each fiscal year, the transfer shall be made on a quarterly basis by transferring one-fourth of the annual amount each quarter. (1991, c. 689, s. 322.)

§ 105-164.44E. (Repealed effective July 1, 2020) Transfer to the Dry-Cleaning Solvent Cleanup Fund.

(a)   Transfer. - At the end of each quarter, the Secretary must transfer to the Dry-Cleaning Solvent Cleanup Fund established under G.S. 143-215.104C an amount equal to fifteen percent (15%) of the net State sales and use taxes collected under G.S. 105-164.4(a)(4) during the previous fiscal year, as determined by the Secretary based on available data.

(b)   Sunset. - This section is repealed effective July 1, 2020. (2000-19, s. 1.1; 2009-483, ss. 6, 8.)

§ 105-164.44F. Distribution of part of telecommunications taxes to cities.

(a) Amount. - The Secretary must distribute part of the taxes imposed by G.S. 105-164.4(a)(4c) on telecommunications service and ancillary service. The Secretary must make the distribution within 75 days after the end of each calendar quarter. The amount the Secretary must distribute is the following percentages of the net proceeds of the taxes collected during the quarter:

(1) Eighteen and seventy one hundredths percent (18.70%) minus two million six hundred twenty thousand nine hundred forty-eight dollars ($2,620,948), must be distributed to cities in accordance with this section. The deduction is one-fourth of the annual amount by which the distribution to cities of the gross receipts franchise tax on telephone companies, imposed by former G.S. 105-20, was required to be reduced beginning in fiscal year 1995-96 as a result of the "freeze deduction."

(2) Seven and seven tenths percent (7.7%) must be distributed to counties and cities as provided in G.S. 105-164.44I.

(b) Share of Cities Incorporated on or After January 1, 2001. - The share of a city incorporated on or after January 1, 2001, is its per capita share of the amount to be distributed to all cities incorporated on or after this date. This amount is the proportion of the total to be distributed under this section that is the same as the proportion of the population of cities incorporated on or after January 1, 2001, compared to the population of all cities. In making the distribution under this subsection, the Secretary must use the most recent annual population estimates certified to the Secretary by the State Budget Officer.

(c) Share of Cities Incorporated Before January 1, 2001. - The share of a city incorporated before January 1, 2001, is its proportionate share of the amount to be distributed to all cities incorporated before this date. A city's proportionate share for a quarter is based on the amount of telephone gross receipts franchise taxes attributed to the city under G.S. 105-116.1 for the same quarter that was the last quarter in which taxes were imposed on telephone companies under repealed G.S. 105-120. The amount to be distributed to all cities incorporated before January 1, 2001, is the amount determined under subsection (a) of this section, minus the amount distributed under subsection (b) of this section.

The following changes apply when a city incorporated before January 1, 2001, alters its corporate structure. When a change described in subdivision (2) or (3) occurs, the resulting cities are considered to be cities incorporated before January 1, 2001, and the distribution method set out in this subsection rather than the method set out in subsection (b) of this section applies:

(1) If a city dissolves and is no longer incorporated, the proportional shares of the remaining cities incorporated before January 1, 2001, must be recalculated to adjust for the dissolution of that city.

(2) If two or more cities merge or otherwise consolidate, their proportional shares are combined.

(3) If a city divides into two or more cities, the proportional share of the city that divides is allocated among the new cities on a per capita basis.

(d) Share of Cities Served by a Telephone Membership Corporation. - The share of a city served by a telephone membership corporation, as described in Chapter 117 of the General Statutes, is computed as if the city was incorporated on or after January 1, 2001, under subsection (b) of this section. If a city is served by a telephone membership corporation and another provider, then its per capita share under this subsection applies only to the population of the area served by the telephone membership corporation.

(e) Ineligible Cities. - An ineligible city is disregarded for all purposes under this section. A city incorporated on or after January 1, 2000, is not eligible for a distribution under this section unless it meets both of the following requirements:

(1) It is eligible to receive funds under G.S. 136-41.2.

(2) A majority of the mileage of its streets is open to the public.

(f) Nature. - The General Assembly finds that the revenue distributed under this section is local revenue, not a State expenditure, for the purpose of Section 5(3) of Article III of the North Carolina Constitution. Therefore, the Governor may not reduce or withhold the distribution. (2001-424, s. 34.25(b); 2001-430, s. 10; 2001-487, s. 67(d); 2002-120, s. 4; 2004-203, s. 5(g); 2005-276, s. 33.19; 2005-435, s. 34(c); 2006-33, s. 8; 2006-66, ss. 24.1(d), (e), (f), (g); 2006-151, s. 7; 2007-145, s. 9(a); 2007-323, ss. 31.2(a), (b); 2009-451, s. 27A.2(c).)

§ 105-164.44G. (Repealed for sales made on or after January 1, 2014) Distribution of part of tax on modular homes.

The Secretary must distribute to counties twenty percent (20%) of the taxes collected under G.S. 105-164.4(a)(8) on modular homes. The Secretary must make the distribution on a monthly basis in accordance with the distribution formula in G.S. 105-486. (2003-400, s. 16; 2009-445, s. 15(a); 2013-316, s. 3.1(b).)

§ 105-164.44H. Transfer to State Public School Fund.

Each fiscal year, the Secretary of Revenue shall transfer at the end of each quarter from the State sales and use tax net collections received by the Department of Revenue under Article 5 of Chapter 105 of the General Statutes to the State Treasurer for the State Public School Fund, one-fourth of the amount transferred the preceding fiscal year plus or minus the percentage of that amount by which the total collection of State sales and use taxes increased or decreased during the preceding fiscal year. (2005-276, s. 7.51(b).)

§ 105-164.44I. Distribution of part of sales tax on video programming service and telecommunications service to counties and cities.

(a) Distribution. - The Secretary must distribute to the counties and cities part of the taxes imposed by G.S. 105-164.4(a)(4c) on telecommunications service and G.S. 105-164.4(a)(6) on video programming service. The Secretary must make the distribution within 75 days after the end of each calendar quarter. The amount the Secretary must distribute is the sum of the revenue listed in this subsection. From this amount, the Secretary must first make the distribution required by subsection (b) of this section and then distribute the remainder in accordance with subsections (c) and (d) of this section. The revenue to be distributed under this section consists of the following:

(1) The amount specified in G.S. 105-164.44F(a)(2).

(2) Twenty three and six tenths percent (23.6%) of the net proceeds of the taxes collected during the quarter on video programming, other than on direct-to-home satellite service.

(3) Thirty-seven and one tenths percent (37.1%) of the net proceeds of the taxes collected during the quarter on direct-to-home satellite service.

(b) Supplemental PEG Channel Support. - G.S. 105-164.44J sets out the requirements for receipt by a county or city of supplemental PEG channel support funds distributed under this subsection. The Secretary must include the applicable amount of supplemental PEG channel support in each quarterly distribution to a county or city. The amount to include is one-fourth of the share of each qualifying PEG channel certified by the city or county under G.S. 105-164.44J. The share of each certified PEG channel is the sum of four million dollars ($4,000,000) and the amount of any funds returned to the Secretary in the prior fiscal year under G.S. 105-164.44J(d) divided by the number of PEG channels certified under G.S. 105-164.44J. A county or city may not receive PEG channel support under this subsection for more than three qualifying PEG channels.

For purposes of this subsection, the term "qualifying PEG channel" has the same meaning as in G.S. 105-164.44J.

(c) 2006-2007 Fiscal Year Distribution. - The share of a county or city is its proportionate share of the amount to be distributed to all counties and cities under this subsection. The proportionate share of a county or city is the base amount for the county or city compared to the base amount for all other counties and cities. The base amount of a county or city that did not impose a cable franchise tax under G.S. 153A-154 or G.S. 160A-214 before July 1, 2006, is two dollars ($2.00) times the most recent annual population estimate for that county or city. The base amount of a county or city that imposed a cable franchise tax under either G.S. 153A-154 or G.S. 160A-214 before July 1, 2006, is the amount of cable franchise tax and subscriber fee revenue the county or city certifies to the Secretary that it imposed during the first six months of the 2006-2007 fiscal year. A county or city must make this certification by March 15, 2007. The certification must specify the amount of revenue that is derived from the cable franchise tax and the amount that is derived from the subscriber fee.

(c1) Revised Certification. - If a county or city determines that the amount of cable franchise tax it imposed during the first six months of the 2006-2007 fiscal year differs from the amount certified to the Secretary under subsection (c) of this section, the county or city may submit a new certification to the Secretary revising the amount. For distributions for quarters beginning on or after October 1, 2007, the Secretary must determine the proportionate share of a county or city based upon certifications submitted on or before October 1, 2007. For distributions for quarters beginning on or after April 1, 2008, the Secretary must determine the proportionate share of a county or city based upon certifications submitted on or before April 1, 2008. Certifications submitted after April 1, 2008, may not be used to adjust a county's or city's base amount under subsection (c) of this section.

(d) Subsequent Distributions. - For subsequent fiscal years, the Secretary must multiply the amount of a county's or city's share under this section for the preceding fiscal year by the percentage change in its population for that fiscal year and add the result to the county's or city's share for the preceding fiscal year to obtain the county's or city's adjusted amount. Each county's or city's proportionate share for that year is its adjusted amount compared to the sum of the adjusted amounts for all counties and cities.

(e) Use of Proceeds. - A county or city that imposed subscriber fees during the first six months of the 2006-2007 fiscal year must use a portion of the funds distributed to it each fiscal year under subsections (c) and (d) of this section for the operation and support of PEG channels. The amount of funds that must be used for PEG channel operation and support in fiscal year 2006-2007 is two times the amount of subscriber fee revenue the county or city certified to the Secretary that it imposed during the first six months of the 2006-2007 fiscal year. The amount of funds that must be used for PEG channel operation and support in subsequent fiscal years is the same proportionate amount of the funds that were distributed under subsections (c) and (d) of this section and used for this purpose in fiscal year 2006-2007.

A county or city that used part of its franchise tax revenue in fiscal year 2005-2006 for the operation and support of PEG channels or a publicly owned and operated television station must use the funds distributed to it under subsections (c) and (d) of this section to continue the same level of support for the PEG channels and public stations. The remainder of the distribution may be used for any public purpose.

(f) Late Information. - A county or city that does not submit information that the Secretary needs to make a distribution by the date the information is due is excluded from the distribution. If the county or city later submits the required information, the Secretary must include the county or city in the distribution for the quarter that begins after the date the information is received.

(g)   Population Determination. - In making population determinations under this section, the Secretary must use the most recent annual population estimates certified to the Secretary by the State Budget Officer. For purposes of the distributions made under this section, the population of a county is the population of its unincorporated areas plus the population of an ineligible city in the county, as determined under this section.

(h)   City Changes. - The following changes apply when a city alters its corporate structure or incorporates:

(1)   If a city dissolves and is no longer incorporated, the proportional shares of the remaining counties and cities must be recalculated to adjust for the dissolution of that city.

(2)   If two or more cities merge or otherwise consolidate, their proportional shares are combined.

(3)   If a city divides into two or more cities, the proportional share of the city that divides is allocated among the new cities on a per capita basis.

(4)   If a city incorporates after January 1, 2007, and the incorporation is not addressed by subdivisions (2) or (3) of this subsection, the share of the county in which the new city is located is allocated between the county and the new city on a per capita basis.

(i)   Ineligible Cities. - An ineligible city is disregarded for all purposes under this section. A city incorporated on or after January 1, 2000, is not eligible for a distribution under this section unless it meets both of the following requirements:

(1)   It is eligible to receive funds under G.S. 136-41.2.

(2)   A majority of the mileage of its streets is open to the public.

(j)   Nature. - The General Assembly finds that the revenue distributed under this section is local revenue, not a State expenditure, for the purpose of Section 5(3) of Article III of the North Carolina Constitution. Therefore, the Governor may not reduce or withhold the distribution. (2006-151, s. 8; 2006-66, ss.

24.1(h), (i); 2007-145, s. 9(a); 2007-323, ss. 31.2(a), (b); 2007-527, s. 28; 2008-148, ss. 1, 2; 2009-451, s. 27A.2(d); 2010-158, s. 11(b); 2013-414, s. 45.)

§ 105-164.44J. Supplemental PEG channel support.

(a) Definitions. - The following definitions apply in this section:

(1) Existing agreement. - Defined in G.S. 66-350.

(2) PEG channel. - Defined in G.S. 66-350.

(3) PEG channel operator. - An entity that does one or more of the following:

a. Produces programming for delivery on a PEG channel.

b. Provides facilities for the production of programming or playback of programming for delivery on a PEG channel.

(4) Qualifying PEG channel. - A PEG channel that operates for at least 90 days during a fiscal year and that meets all of the following programming requirements:

a. It delivers at least eight hours of scheduled programming a day.

b. It delivers at least six hours and 45 minutes of scheduled, non-character-generated programming a day.

c. Its programming content does not repeat more than fifteen percent (15%) of the programming content on any other PEG channel provided to the same county or city.

(5) Supplemental PEG channel support funds. - The amount distributed to a county or city under G.S. 105-164.44I(b).

(b) Certification. - A county or city must certify to the Secretary by July 15 of each year all of the qualifying PEG channels provided for its use during the preceding fiscal year by a cable service provider under either G.S. 66-357 or an existing agreement. A county or city may not certify more than three qualifying PEG channels. The certification must include all of the following:

(1) An identification of each channel as a public, an education, or a government channel.

(2) The name and signature of the PEG channel operator for each channel. If a qualifying PEG channel has more than one PEG channel operator, the county or city must include the name of each operator of the PEG channel. A PEG channel operator may be included on the certification of only one county or city for each type of PEG channel that it operates.

(3) Any other information required by the Secretary.

(c) Use of Funds. - A county or city must use the supplemental PEG channel support funds distributed to it for the operation and support of each of the qualifying PEG channels it certifies by allocating the amount it receives equally among each of the qualifying PEG channels. A county or city must distribute the supplemental PEG channel support funds to the PEG channel operator of the qualifying PEG channel within 30 days of its receipt of the supplemental PEG channel support funds from the Department, or as specified in an interlocal agreement. If a qualifying PEG channel has more than one PEG channel operator, the county or city must distribute the amount allocated for that PEG channel equally to each PEG channel operator, or as specified in an interlocal agreement.

(d) Errors in Certification. - If a county or city determines that it certified a PEG channel in error, the county or city must submit a revised certification to the Secretary, and the county or city must return all supplemental PEG channel support funds distributed to it as a result of the error. The Secretary must add the funds returned to the total amount of supplemental PEG channel support funds to be allocated in the following fiscal year. (2008-148, s. 3; 2010-158, s. 11(c).)

§ 105-164.44K. (Effective for quarters beginning on or after July 1, 2014) Distribution of part of tax on electricity to cities.

(a) Distribution. - The Secretary must distribute to cities forty-four percent (44%) of the net proceeds of the tax collected under G.S. 105-164.4 on electricity, less the cost to the Department of administering the distribution. Each city's share of the amount to be distributed is its franchise tax share calculated under subsection (b) of this section plus its ad valorem share calculated under subsection (c) of this section. If the net proceeds of the tax allocated under this section are not sufficient to distribute the franchise tax share of each city under subsection (b) of this section, the proceeds shall be distributed to each city on a pro rata basis. The Secretary must make the distribution within 75 days after the end of each quarter.

(b) Franchise Tax Share. - The quarterly franchise tax share of a city is the total amount of electricity gross receipts franchise tax distributed to the city under repealed G.S. 105-116.1 or repealed provisions of G.S. 159B-27 for the same related quarter that was the last quarter in which taxes were imposed on electric power companies under repealed G.S. 105-116 or repealed provisions of G.S. 159B-27. The quarterly franchise tax share of a city includes adjustments made for the hold-harmless amounts under repealed G.S. 105-116. If the franchise tax share of a city, including the hold-harmless adjustments, is less than zero, then the amount is zero. The determination made by the Department with respect to a city's franchise tax share is final and is not subject to administrative or judicial review.

The franchise tax share of a city that has dissolved, merged with another city, or divided into two or more cities since it received a distribution under repealed G.S. 105-116.1 or repealed provisions of G.S. 159B-27 is adjusted as follows:

(1) If a city dissolves and is no longer incorporated, the franchise tax share of the city is added to the amount distributed under subsection (c) of this section.

(2) If two or more cities merge or otherwise consolidate, their franchise tax shares are combined.

(3) If a city divides into two or more cities, the franchise tax share of the city that divides is allocated among the new cities in proportion to the total amount of ad valorem taxes levied by each on property having a tax situs in the city.

(c) Ad Valorem Share. - The ad valorem share of a city is its proportionate share of the amount that remains for distribution after determining each city's franchise tax share under subsection (b) of this section. The prohibitions in G.S. 105-472(d) on the receipt of funds by a city apply to the distribution under this subsection.

A city's proportionate share is the amount of ad valorem taxes it levies on property having a tax situs in the city compared to the ad valorem taxes levied by all cities on property having a tax situs in the cities. The ad valorem method set out in G.S. 105-472(b)(2) applies in determining the share of a city under this subsection based on ad valorem taxes, except that the amount of ad valorem taxes levied by a city does not include ad valorem taxes levied on behalf of a taxing district and collected by the city.

(d) Nature. - The General Assembly finds that the revenue distributed under this section is local revenue, not a State expenditure, for the purpose of Section 5(3) of Article III of the North Carolina Constitution. The Governor may not reduce or withhold the distribution. (2013-316, s. 4.3(a); 2013-363, s. 11.2.)

§ 105-164.44L. (Effective for quarters beginning on or after July 1, 2014) Distribution of part of tax on piped natural gas to cities.

(a) Distribution. - The Secretary must distribute to cities twenty percent (20%) of the net proceeds of the tax collected under G.S. 105-164.4 on piped natural gas, less the cost to the Department of administering the distribution. Each city's share of the amount to be distributed is its excise tax share calculated under subsection (b) of this section plus its ad valorem share calculated under subsection (c) of this section. If the net proceeds of the tax allocated under this section are not sufficient to distribute the excise tax share of each city under subsection (b) of this section, the proceeds shall be distributed to each city on a pro rata basis. The Secretary must make the distribution within 75 days after the end of each quarter.

(b) Excise Tax Share. - The quarterly excise tax share of a city that is not a gas city is the amount of piped natural gas excise tax distributed to the city under repealed G.S. 105-187.44 for the same related quarter that was the last quarter in which taxes were imposed on piped natural gas under repealed Article 5E of this Chapter. The Secretary must determine the excise tax share of a gas city and divide that amount by four to calculate the quarterly distribution amount for a gas city. The excise tax share of a gas city is the amount the gas city would have received under repealed G.S. 105-187.44 for the last year in which taxes were imposed under repealed Article 5E of this Chapter if piped natural gas consumed by the city or delivered by the city to a customer had not been exempt from tax under repealed G.S. 105-187.41(c)(1) and (c)(2). A gas city must report the information required by the Secretary to make the distribution under this section in the form, manner, and time required by the Secretary. For purposes of this subsection, the term "gas city" has the same meaning as defined in repealed G.S. 105-187.40. The determination made by the Department with respect to a city's excise tax share is final and is not subject to administrative or judicial review.

The excise tax share of a city that has dissolved, merged with another city, or divided into two or more cities since it received a distribution under repealed G.S. 105-187.44 is adjusted as follows:

(1) If a city dissolves and is no longer incorporated, the excise tax share of the city is added to the amount distributed under subsection (c) of this section.

(2) If two or more cities merge or otherwise consolidate, their excise tax shares are combined.

(3) If a city divides into two or more cities, the excise tax share of the city that divides is allocated among the new cities in proportion to the total amount of ad valorem taxes levied by each on property having a tax situs in the city.

(c) Ad Valorem Share. - The ad valorem share of a city is its proportionate share of the amount that remains for distribution after determining each city's excise tax share under subsection (b) of this section. The prohibitions in G.S. 105-472(d) on the receipt of funds by a city apply to the distribution under this subsection.

A city's proportionate share is the amount of ad valorem taxes it levies on property having a tax situs in the city compared to the ad valorem taxes levied by all cities on property having a tax situs in the cities. The ad valorem method set out in G.S. 105-472(b)(2) applies in determining the share of a city under this section based on ad valorem taxes, except that the amount of ad valorem taxes levied by a city does not include ad valorem taxes levied on behalf of a taxing district and collected by the city.

(d) Nature. - The General Assembly finds that the revenue distributed under this section is local revenue, not a State expenditure, for the purpose of Section 5(3) of Article III of the North Carolina Constitution. The Governor may not reduce or withhold the distribution. (2013-316, s. 4.3(a).)

DIVISION IX. LOCAL OPTION SALES AND USE TAXES.

§§ 105-164.45 through 105-164.58: Repealed by Session Laws 1971, c. 77, s. 1.

§§ 105-165 through 105-176. Repealed by Session Laws 1957, c. 1340, s. 5.

§§ 105-177 through 105-178. Repealed by Session Laws 1951, c. 643, s.5.

§ 105-179. Repealed by Session Laws 1957, c. 1340, s. 5.

§ 105-180. Repealed by Session Laws 1951, c. 643, s. 5.

§ 105-181. Repealed by Session Laws 1957, c. 1340, s. 5.

§ 105-182. Repealed by Session Laws 1955, c. 1350, s. 19.

§§ 105-183 through 105-187: Repealed by Session Laws 1957, c. 1340, s. 5.

Article 5A.

North Carolina Highway Use Tax.

§ 105-187.1. Definitions.

The following definitions and the definitions in G.S. 105-164.3 apply to this Article:

(1)   Commissioner. - The Commissioner of Motor Vehicles.

(2)   Division. - The Division of Motor Vehicles, Department of Transportation.

(3)   Long-term lease or rental. - A lease or rental made under a written agreement to lease or rent property to the same person for a period of at least 365 continuous days.

(4)   Recreational vehicle. - Defined in G.S. 20-4.01.

(5)   Rescue squad. - An organization that provides rescue services, emergency medical services, or both.

(6) Retailer. - A retailer as defined in G.S. 105-164.3 who is engaged in the business of selling, leasing, or renting motor vehicles.

(7) Short-term lease or rental. - A lease or rental that is not a long-term lease or rental. (1989, c. 692, s. 4.1; 1991, c. 79, s. 4; 2000-173, s. 10(a); 2001-424, s. 34.24(e); 2001-497, s. 2(b); 2002-72, s. 19(a).)

§ 105-187.2. Highway use tax imposed.

A tax is imposed on the privilege of using the highways of this State. This tax is in addition to all other taxes and fees imposed. (1989, c. 692, s. 4.1.)

§ 105-187.3. Rate of tax.

(a) (Effective until July 1, 2014) Amount. - The rate of the use tax imposed by this Article is three percent (3%) of the retail value of a motor vehicle for which a certificate of title is issued. The tax is payable as provided in G.S. 105-187.4. The maximum tax is one thousand dollars ($1,000) for each certificate of title issued for a Class A or Class B motor vehicle that is a commercial motor vehicle, as defined in G.S. 20-4.01. The maximum tax is one thousand five hundred dollars ($1,500) for each certificate of title issued for a recreational vehicle that is not subject to the one thousand dollar ($1,000) maximum tax.

(a) (Effective July 1, 2014) Amount. - The rate of the use tax imposed by this Article is three percent (3%) of the sum of the following:

(1) The retail value of a motor vehicle for which a certificate of title is issued.

(2) Any fee regulated by G.S. 20-101.1.

The tax is payable as provided in G.S. 105-187.4. The maximum tax is one thousand dollars ($1,000) for each certificate of title issued for a Class A or Class B motor vehicle that is a commercial motor vehicle, as defined in G.S. 20-4.01. The maximum tax is one thousand five hundred dollars ($1,500) for each certificate of title issued for a recreational vehicle that is not subject to the one thousand dollar ($1,000) maximum tax.

(b) Retail Value. - The retail value of a motor vehicle for which a certificate of title is issued because of a sale of the motor vehicle by a retailer is the sales price of the motor vehicle, including all accessories attached to the vehicle when it is delivered to the purchaser, less the amount of any allowance given by the retailer for a motor vehicle taken in trade as a full or partial payment for the purchased motor vehicle.

The retail value of a motor vehicle for which a certificate of title is issued because of a sale of the motor vehicle by a seller who is not a retailer is the market value of the vehicle, less the amount of any allowance given by the seller for a motor vehicle taken in trade as a full or partial payment for the purchased motor vehicle. A transaction in which two parties exchange motor vehicles is considered a sale regardless of whether either party gives additional consideration as part of the transaction.

The retail value of a motor vehicle for which a certificate of title is issued because of a reason other than the sale of the motor vehicle is the market value of the vehicle. The market value of a vehicle is presumed to be the value of the vehicle set in a schedule of values adopted by the Commissioner.

The retail value of a vehicle for which a certificate of title is issued because of a transfer by a State agency that assists the United States Department of Defense with purchasing, transferring, or titling a vehicle to another State agency, a unit of local government, a volunteer fire department, or a volunteer rescue squad is the sales price paid by the State agency, unit of local government, volunteer fire department, or volunteer rescue squad.

(c) Schedules. - In adopting a schedule of values for motor vehicles, the Commissioner shall adopt a schedule whose values do not exceed the wholesale values of motor vehicles as published in a recognized automotive reference manual. (1989, c. 692, ss. 4.1, 4.2; c. 770, s. 74.13; 1993, c. 467, s. 3; 1995, c. 349, s. 1; c. 390, s. 30; 2001-424, s. 34.24(a); 2001-497, s. 2(a); 2009-550, s. 2(e); 2010-95, s. 5; 2013-360, s. 34.29(a); 2013-363, s. 8.1.)

§ 105-187.4. Payment of tax.

(a) Method. The tax imposed by this Article must be paid to the Commissioner when applying for a certificate of title for a motor vehicle. The Commissioner may not issue a certificate of title for a vehicle until the tax imposed by this Article has been paid. The tax may be paid in cash or by check.

(b) Sale by Retailer. When a certificate of title for a motor vehicle is issued because of a sale of the motor vehicle by a retailer, the applicant for the certificate of title must attach a copy of the bill of sale for the motor vehicle to the application. A retailer who sells a motor vehicle may collect from the purchaser of the vehicle the tax payable upon the issuance of a certificate of title for the vehicle, apply for a certificate of title on behalf of the purchaser, and remit the tax due on behalf of the purchaser. If a check submitted by a retailer in payment of taxes collected under this section is not honored by the financial institution upon which it is drawn because the retailer's account did not have sufficient funds to pay the check or the retailer did not have an account at the institution, the Division may suspend or revoke the license issued to the retailer under Article 12 of Chapter 20 of the General Statutes. (1989, c. 692, s. 4.1; 1991, c. 193, s. 1.)

§ 105-187.5. Alternate tax for those who rent or lease motor vehicles.

(a) Election. - A retailer may elect not to pay the tax imposed by this Article at the rate set in G.S. 105-187.3 when applying for a certificate of title for a motor vehicle purchased by the retailer for lease or rental. A retailer who makes this election shall pay a tax on the gross receipts of the lease or rental of the vehicle. Like the tax imposed by G.S. 105-187.3, this alternate tax is a tax on the privilege of using the highways of this State. The tax is imposed on a retailer, but is to be added to the lease or rental price of a motor vehicle and thereby be paid by the person who leases or rents the vehicle.

(b) Rate. - The tax rate on the gross receipts from the short-term lease or rental of a motor vehicle is eight percent (8%) and the tax rate on the gross receipts from the long-term lease or rental of a motor vehicle is three percent (3%). Gross receipts does not include the amount of any allowance given for a motor vehicle taken in trade as a partial payment on the lease or rental price. The maximum tax in G.S. 105-187.3(a) on certain motor vehicles applies to a continuous lease or rental of such a motor vehicle to the same person.

(c) Method. - A retailer who elects to pay tax on the gross receipts of the lease or rental of a motor vehicle shall make this election when applying for a certificate of title for the vehicle. To make the election, the retailer shall complete a form provided by the Division giving information needed to collect the alternate tax based on gross receipts. Once made, an election is irrevocable.

(d) Administration. - The Division shall notify the Secretary of Revenue of a retailer who makes the election under this section. A retailer who makes this election shall report and remit to the Secretary the tax on the gross receipts of the lease or rental of the motor vehicle. The Secretary shall administer the tax imposed by this section on gross receipts in the same manner as the tax levied under G.S. 105-164.4(a)(2). The administrative provisions and powers of the Secretary that apply to the tax levied under G.S. 105-164.4(a)(2) apply to the tax imposed by this section. In addition, the Division may request the Secretary to audit a retailer who elects to pay tax on gross receipts under this section. When the Secretary conducts an audit at the request of the Division, the Division shall reimburse the Secretary for the cost of the audit, as determined by the Secretary. In conducting an audit of a retailer under this section, the Secretary may audit any sales of motor vehicles made by the retailer. (1989, c. 692, s. 4.1; 1991, c. 79, s. 5; c. 193, s. 3; 1995, c. 410, s. 1; 2000-173, s. 10(b); 2001-424, s. 34.24(b); 2001-497, s. 2(c).)

§ 105-187.6. Exemptions from highway use tax.

(a) Full Exemptions. - The tax imposed by this Article does not apply when a certificate of title is issued as the result of a transfer of a motor vehicle:

(1) To (i) the insurer of the motor vehicle under G.S. 20-109.1 because the vehicle is a salvage vehicle or (ii) a used motor vehicle dealer under G.S. 20-109.1 because the vehicle is a salvage vehicle that was abandoned.

(2) To either a manufacturer, as defined in G.S. 20-286, or a motor vehicle retailer for the purpose of resale.

(3) To the same owner to reflect a change or correction in the owner's name.

(3a) To one or more of the same co-owners to reflect the removal of one or more other co-owners, when there is no consideration for the transfer.

(4) By will or intestacy.

(5) By a gift between a husband and wife, a parent and child, or a stepparent and a stepchild.

(6) By a distribution of marital or divisible property incident to a marital separation or divorce.

(7) Repealed by Session Laws 2009-445, s. 16, effective August 7, 2009.

(8) To a local board of education for use in the driver education program of a public school when the motor vehicle is transferred:

a. By a retailer and is to be transferred back to the retailer within 300 days after the transfer to the local board.

b. By a local board of education.

(9) To a volunteer fire department or volunteer rescue squad that is not part of a unit of local government, has no more than two paid employees, and is exempt from State income tax under G.S. 105-130.11, when the motor vehicle is one of the following:

a. A fire truck, a pump truck, a tanker truck, or a ladder truck used to suppress fire.

b. A four-wheel drive vehicle intended to be mounted with a water tank and hose and used for forest fire fighting.

c. An emergency services vehicle.

(10) To a State agency from a unit of local government, volunteer fire department, or volunteer rescue squad to enable the State agency to transfer the vehicle to another unit of local government, volunteer fire department, or volunteer rescue squad.

(11) To a revocable trust from an owner who is the sole beneficiary of the trust.

(b) Partial Exemptions. - A maximum tax of forty dollars ($40.00) applies when a certificate of title is issued as the result of a transfer of a motor vehicle:

(1)   To a secured party who has a perfected security interest in the motor vehicle.

(2)   To a partnership, limited liability company, corporation, trust, or other person where no gain or loss arises on the transfer of the motor vehicle under section 351 or section 721 of the Code, or because the transfer is treated under the Code as being to an entity that is not a separate entity from its owner or whose separate existence is otherwise disregarded, or to a partnership, limited liability company, or corporation by merger, conversion, or consolidation in accordance with applicable law.

(c)   Out-of-state Vehicles. - A maximum tax of one hundred fifty dollars ($150.00) applies when a certificate of title is issued for a motor vehicle that, at the time of applying for a certificate of title, is and has been titled in another state for at least 90 days. (1989, c. 692, s. 4.1; c. 770, ss. 74.9, 74.10; 1991, c. 193, s. 4; c. 689, s. 323; 1993, c. 467, s. 1; 1995, c. 390, s. 31; 1997-443, s. 11A.118(a); 1998-98, s. 15.1; 1999-369, s. 5.9; 2000-140, s. 68; 2001-387, s. 151; 2001-424, s. 34.24(d); 2001-487, s. 68; 2009-81, s. 2; 2009-445, s. 16; 2010-95, s. 6; 2013-400, s. 6.)

§ 105-187.7. Credits.

(a)   Tax Paid in Another State. - A person who, within 90 days before applying for a certificate of title for a motor vehicle on which the tax imposed by this Article is due, has paid a sales tax, an excise tax, or a tax substantially equivalent to the tax imposed by this Article on the vehicle to a taxing jurisdiction outside this State is allowed a credit against the tax due under this Article for the amount of tax paid to the other jurisdiction.

(b)   Tax Paid Within One Year. - A person who applies for a certificate of title for a motor vehicle that is titled in another state but was formerly titled in this State is allowed a credit against the tax due under this Article for the amount of tax paid under this Article by that person on the same vehicle within one year before the application for a certificate of title. (1989, c. 692, s. 4.1; 1995, c. 390, s. 32; c. 512, s. 1.)

§ 105-187.8. Refund for return of purchased motor vehicle.

When a purchaser of a motor vehicle returns the motor vehicle to the seller of the motor vehicle within 90 days after the purchase and receives a vehicle replacement for the returned vehicle or a refund of the price paid the seller, whether from the seller or the manufacturer of the vehicle, the purchaser may obtain a refund of the privilege tax paid on the certificate of title issued for the returned motor vehicle.

To obtain a refund, the purchaser must apply to the Division for a refund within 30 days after receiving the replacement vehicle or refund of the purchase price. The application must be made on a form prescribed by the Commission and must be supported by documentation from the seller of the returned vehicle. (1989, c. 692, s. 4.1; 1995, c. 390, s. 33.)

§ 105-187.9. Disposition of tax proceeds.

(a)   Distribution. - Taxes collected under this Article at the rate of eight percent (8%) shall be credited to the General Fund. Taxes collected under this Article at the rate of three percent (3%) shall be credited to the North Carolina Highway Trust Fund.

(b)   Repealed by Session Laws 2010-31, s. 28.7(i), and Session Laws 2013-183, s. 4.1, effective July 1, 2013.

(c)   Repealed by Session Laws 2013-183, s. 4.1, effective July 1, 2013. (1989, c. 692, s. 4.1; c. 799, s. 33; 1993, c. 321, s. 164(a); 2001-424, s. 34.24(c); 2001-513, s. 15; 2008-107, s. 25.5(a), (c), (e); 2010-31, s. 28.7(f), (h)-(j); 2011-145, ss. 28.33(c), (d); 2011-391, s. 57; 2012-142, s. 24.8(b); 2013-183, s. 4.1.)

§ 105-187.10. Penalties and remedies.

(a)   Penalties. - The penalty for bad checks in G.S. 105-236(1) applies to a check offered in payment of the tax imposed by this Article. In addition, if a check offered to the Division in payment of the tax imposed by this Article is returned unpaid and the tax for which the check was offered, plus the penalty imposed under G.S. 105-236(1), is not paid within 30 days after the Commissioner demands its payment, the Commissioner may revoke the registration plate of the vehicle for which a certificate of title was issued when the check was offered.

(b)   Unpaid Taxes. - The remedies for collection of taxes in Article 9 of this Chapter apply to the taxes levied by this Article and collected by the Commissioner. In applying these remedies, the Commissioner has the same authority as the Secretary.

(c)   Appeals. - A taxpayer who disagrees with the presumed value of a motor vehicle must pay the tax based on the presumed value, but may appeal the value to the Commissioner. A taxpayer who appeals the value must provide two estimates of the value of the vehicle to the Commissioner. If the Commissioner finds that the value of the vehicle is less than the presumed value of the vehicle, the Commissioner shall refund any overpayment of tax made by the taxpayer with interest at the rate specified in G.S. 105-241.21 from the date of the overpayment. (1989, c. 692, s. 4.1; c. 770, s. 74.8; 2007-491, ss. 21, 44(1)b.)

§ 105-187.11: Repealed by Session Laws 2007-527, s. 30, effective August 31, 2007.

§§ 105-187.12 through 105-187.14. Reserved for future codification purposes.

Article 5B.

Scrap Tire Disposal Tax.

§ 105-187.15. Definitions.

The definitions in G.S. 105-164.3 apply to this Article, except that the term "sale" does not include lease or rental, and the following definitions apply to this Article:

(1)   Scrap tire. - A tire that is no longer suitable for its original, intended purpose because of wear, damage, or defect.

(2)   Tire. - A continuous solid or pneumatic rubber covering encircling a wheel. (1991, c. 221, s. 1.)

§ 105-187.16. Tax imposed.

(a) Levy. A privilege tax is imposed on a tire retailer at a percentage rate of the sales price of each new tire sold at retail by the retailer. A privilege tax is imposed on a tire retailer and on a tire wholesale merchant at a percentage rate of the sales price of each new tire sold by the retailer or wholesale merchant to a wholesale merchant or retailer for placement on a vehicle offered for sale, lease, or rental by the retailer or wholesale merchant. An excise tax is imposed on a new tire purchased for storage, use, or consumption in this State or for placement in this State on a vehicle offered for sale, lease, or rental. This excise tax is a percentage rate of the purchase price of the tire. These taxes are in addition to all other taxes.

(b) Rate. The percentage rate of the taxes imposed by subsection (a) of this section is set by the following table; the rate is based on the bead diameter of the new tire sold or purchased:

Bead Diameter of Tire	Percentage Rate
Less than 20 inches	2%
At least 20 inches	1%.

(1991, c. 221, s. 1; 1993, c. 548, s. 1; 1997-209, s. 1; 2001-414, s. 22; 2002-10, s. 1.)

§ 105-187.17. Administration.

The privilege tax this Article imposes on a tire retailer who sells new tires at retail is an additional State sales tax and the excise tax this Article imposes on the storage, use, or consumption of a new tire in this State is an additional State use tax. Except as otherwise provided in this Article, these taxes shall be collected and administered in the same manner as the State sales and use taxes imposed by Article 5 of this Chapter. As under Article 5 of this Chapter, the additional State sales tax paid when a new tire is sold is a credit against the additional State use tax imposed on the storage, use, or consumption of the same tire.

The privilege tax this Article imposes on a tire retailer and on a tire wholesale merchant who sell new tires for placement in this State on a vehicle offered for sale, lease, or rental is a tax on the wholesale sale of the tires. This tax and the excise tax this Article imposes on a new tire purchased for placement in this State on a vehicle offered for sale, lease, or rental shall, to the extent practical, be collected and administered as if they were additional State sales and use taxes. The privilege tax paid when a new tire is sold for placement on a vehicle offered for sale, lease, or rental is a credit against the use tax imposed on the purchase of the same tire for placement in this State on a vehicle offered for sale, lease, or rental. (1991, c. 221, s. 1.)

§ 105-187.18. Exemptions.

(a) The taxes imposed by this Article do not apply to:

(1) Bicycle tires and other tires for vehicles propelled by human power.

(2) Recapped tires.

(3) Tires sold for placement on newly manufactured vehicles.

(b) Except for the exemption for sales a state cannot constitutionally tax, the exemptions and refunds allowed in Article 5 of this Chapter do not apply to the taxes imposed by this Article. (1991, c. 221, s. 1; 1991 (Reg. Sess., 1992), c. 867, s. 1; 1993, c. 364, s. 2; 2003-416, s. 19(a); 2010-166, s. 3.4.)

§ 105-187.19. Use of tax proceeds.

(a) The Secretary shall distribute the taxes collected under this Article, less the allowance to the Department of Revenue for administrative expenses, in accordance with this section. The Secretary may retain the cost of collection by the Department, not to exceed four hundred twenty-five thousand dollars ($425,000) a year, as reimbursement to the Department.

(b) Each quarter, the Secretary shall credit thirty percent (30%) of the net tax proceeds to the General Fund. The Secretary shall distribute the remaining seventy percent (70%) of the net tax proceeds among the counties on a per capita basis according to the most recent annual population estimates certified to the Secretary by the State Budget Officer.

(c) A county may use funds distributed to it under this section only as provided in G.S. 130A-309.54. A county that receives funds under this section and that has an agreement with another unit of local government under which the other unit of local government provides for the disposal of solid waste for the county shall transfer the amount received under this section to the other unit of local government. A unit of local government to which funds are transferred is subject to the same restrictions on use of the funds as the county. (1991, c. 221, s. 1; 1993, c. 485, s. 13; c. 548, ss. 2, 8; 1997-209, ss. 1, 3; 2004-203, s. 5(h); 2007-153, s. 1; 2007-323, s. 24.2; 2009-451, s. 13.3B(a); 2013-360, s. 14.16(a).)

Article 5C.

White Goods Disposal Tax.

§ 105-187.20. Definitions.

The definitions in G.S. 105-164.3 apply to this Article, except that the term "sale" does not include lease or rental, and the following definition applies to this Article:

(1) Repealed by Session Laws 2005-435, s. 35, effective September 27, 2005.

(2) White goods. - Defined in G.S. 130A-290(a). (1993, c. 471, s. 3; 1998-24, s. 7; 2000-109, s. 9(a); 2005-435, s. 35.)

§ 105-187.21. Tax imposed.

A privilege tax is imposed on a white goods retailer at a flat rate for each new white good that is sold by the retailer. An excise tax is imposed on a new white good purchased outside the State for storage, use, or consumption in this State. The rate of the privilege tax and the excise tax is three dollars ($3.00). These taxes are in addition to all other taxes. (1993, c. 471, s. 3; 1998-24, ss. 1, 7; 2000-109, s. 9(a).)

§ 105-187.22. Administration.

The privilege tax this Article imposes on a white goods retailer is an additional State sales tax and the excise tax this Article imposes on the storage, use, or consumption of a new white good in this State is an additional State use tax. Except as otherwise provided in this Article, these taxes shall be collected and administered in the same manner as the State sales and use taxes imposed by Article 5 of this Chapter. As under Article 5 of this Chapter, the additional State sales tax paid when a new white good is sold at retail is a credit against the additional State use tax imposed on the storage, use, or consumption of the same white good. (1993, c. 471, s. 3; 1998-24, s. 7; 2000-109, s. 9(a).)

§ 105-187.23. Exemptions and refunds.

(a) Exemptions. - Except for the exemption for sales a state cannot constitutionally tax, the exemptions allowed in Article 5 of this Chapter do not apply to the taxes imposed by this Article.

(b) Refunds. - The refunds allowed in Article 5 of this Chapter do not apply to the taxes imposed by this Article. A person who buys at least 50 new white goods of any kind in the same sale or purchase may obtain a refund equal to sixty percent (60%) of the amount of tax imposed by this Article on the white goods when all of the white goods purchased are to be placed in new or remodeled dwelling units that are located in this State and do not contain the kind of white goods purchased. To obtain a refund, a person must file an application for a refund with the Secretary. The application must contain the information required by the Secretary, be signed by the purchaser of the white goods, and be submitted by the date set by the Secretary. (1993, c. 471, s. 3; 1998-24, s. 7; 2000-109, s. 9(a); 2003-416, s. 19(b); 2010-166, s. 3.5.)

§ 105-187.24. Use of tax proceeds.

The Secretary shall distribute the taxes collected under this Article, less the Department of Revenue's allowance for administrative expenses, in accordance with this section. The Secretary may retain the Department's cost of collection, not to exceed four hundred twenty-five thousand dollars ($425,000) a year, as reimbursement to the Department.

Each quarter, the Secretary shall credit twenty-eight percent (28%) of the net tax proceeds to the General Fund. The Secretary shall distribute the remaining seventy-two percent (72%) of the net tax proceeds among the counties on a per capita basis according to the most recent annual population estimates certified to the Secretary by the State Budget Officer. The Department shall not distribute the tax proceeds to a county when notified not to do so by the Department of Environment and Natural Resources under G.S. 130A-309.87. If a county is not entitled to a distribution, the proceeds allocated for that county will be credited to the White Goods Management Account.

A county may use funds distributed to it under this section only as provided in G.S. 130A-309.82. A county that receives funds under this section and that has an interlocal agreement with another unit of local government under which the other unit provides for the disposal of solid waste for the county must transfer the amount received under this section to that other unit. A unit to which funds are transferred is subject to the same restrictions on use of the funds as the county. (1993, c. 471, s. 3; 1993 (Reg. Sess., 1994), c. 769, s. 15.1(b); 1998-24, ss. 2, 7; 2000-109, s. 9(a); 2004-203, s. 5(i); 2007-323, s. 24.1; 2013-360, s. 14.17(a).)

§§ 105-187.25 through 105-187.29. Reserved for future codification purposes.

Article 5D.

Dry-Cleaning Solvent Tax.

(Repealed effective January 1, 2020)

§ 105-187.30. (See note for repeal of Article) Definitions.

The definitions in G.S. 105-164.3 apply to this Article, and the following definitions apply to this Article:

(1) Dry-cleaning facility. - Defined in G.S. 143-215.104B.

(2) Dry-cleaning solvent. - Defined in G.S. 143-215.104B. (1997-392, s. 4; 2009-483, s. 5.)

§ 105-187.31. (See note for repeal of Article) Tax imposed.

A privilege tax is imposed on a dry-cleaning solvent retailer at a flat rate for each gallon of dry-cleaning solvent sold by the retailer to a dry-cleaning facility. An excise tax is imposed on dry-cleaning solvent purchased outside the State for storage, use, or consumption by a dry-cleaning facility in this State. The rate of the privilege tax and the excise tax is ten dollars ($10.00) for each gallon of halogenated hydrocarbon-based dry-cleaning solvent and one dollar and thirty-five cents ($1.35) for each gallon of hydrocarbon-based dry-cleaning solvent. These taxes are in addition to all other taxes. (1997-392, s. 4; 2000-19, s. 1.2; 2001-265, s. 1; 2007-530, s. 13; 2009-483, ss. 5, 6.)

§ 105-187.32. (See note for repeal of Article) Administration.

The privilege tax this Article imposes on a dry-cleaning solvent retailer is an additional State sales tax, and the excise tax this Article imposes on the storage, use, or consumption of dry-cleaning solvent by a dry-cleaning facility in this State is an additional State use tax. Except as otherwise provided in this Article these taxes shall be collected and administered in the same manner as the State sales and use taxes imposed by Article 5 of this Chapter. As under Article 5 of this Chapter, the additional State sales tax paid when dry-cleaning solvent is sold at retail is a credit against the additional State use tax imposed on the storage, use, or consumption of the same dry-cleaning solvent. (1997-392, s. 4; 2009-483, s. 5.)

§ 105-187.33. (See note for repeal of Article) Exemptions and refunds.

Except for the exemption for sales a state cannot constitutionally tax, the exemptions and refunds allowed in Article 5 of this Chapter do not apply to the taxes imposed by this Article. (1997-392, s. 4; 2003-416, s. 19(c); 2009-483, s. 5; 2010-166, s. 3.6.)

§ 105-187.34. (See note for repeal of Article) Use of tax proceeds.

The Secretary must credit the taxes collected under this Article, less the Department of Revenue's allowance for administrative expenses, to the Dry-Cleaning Solvent Cleanup Fund. The Secretary may retain the Department's cost of collection, not to exceed one hundred twenty-five thousand dollars ($125,000) a year, as reimbursement to the Department. (1997-392, s. 4; 2009-483, s. 5.)

§ 105-187.35. Sunset.

This Article is repealed effective January 1, 2020. (2009-483, s. 9.)

§ 105-187.36. Reserved for future codification purposes.

§ 105-187.37. Reserved for future codification purposes.

§ 105-187.38. Reserved for future codification purposes.

§ 105-187.39. Reserved for future codification purposes.

Article 5E.

Piped Natural Gas Tax.

§ 105-187.40. (Repealed effective July 1, 2014) Definitions.

The definitions in G.S. 105-228.90 and the following definitions apply in this Article:

(1) Gas city. - A city in this State that operated a piped natural gas distribution system as of July 1, 1998. These cities are Bessemer City, Greenville, Kings Mountain, Lexington, Monroe, Rocky Mount, Shelby, and Wilson.

(2) Local distribution company. - A natural gas company to whom the North Carolina Utilities Commission has issued a franchise under Chapter 62 of the General Statutes to serve an area of this State.

(3) Premises. - Defined in G.S. 62-110.2. When applying the definition of premises to this Article, electric service is to be construed as piped natural gas service.

(4) Sales customer. - An end-user who does not have direct access to an interstate gas pipeline and whose piped natural gas is delivered by the seller of the gas.

(5) Transportation customer. - An end-user who does not have direct access to an interstate gas pipeline and whose piped natural gas is delivered by a person who is not the seller of the gas. (1998-22, s. 1; 2013-316, 4.1(d).)

§ 105-187.41. (Repealed effective July 1, 2014) Tax imposed on piped natural gas.

(a) Scope. - An excise tax is imposed on piped natural gas received for consumption in this State. This tax is imposed in lieu of a sales and use tax and a percentage gross receipts tax on piped natural gas.

(b) Rate. - The tax rate is set in the table below. The tax rate is based on monthly therm volumes of piped natural gas received by the end-user of the gas. If an end-user receives piped natural gas that is metered through two or more separate measuring devices, the tax is calculated separately on the volume metered through each device rather than on the total volume metered through all measuring devices, unless the devices are located on the same premises and are part of the same billing account. In that circumstance, the tax is calculated on the total volume metered through the two or more separate measuring devices.

Monthly Volume of Therms Received	Rate Per Therm
First 200	$.047

201 to 15,000 .035

15,001 to 60,000 .024

60,001 to 500,000 .015

Over 500,000 .003

(c) Exemptions. - The tax imposed by this section does not apply to any of the following:

(1) Piped natural gas received by a gas city for consumption by that city.

(2) Piped natural gas delivered by a gas city to a sales or transportation customer of the gas city.

(3) Piped natural gas received by a manufacturer for use in connection with the operation of the manufacturing facility. To be eligible for the exemption, a person must have a manufacturer's certificate issued under G.S. 105-164.28A. A person who uses piped natural gas for an unauthorized purpose is liable for any tax due on the gas.

(4) Piped natural gas received by a farmer to be used for any farming purpose other than preparing food, heating dwellings, and other household purposes. To be eligible for the exemption, a person must have a farmer's certificate issued under G.S. 105-164.28A. A person who uses piped natural gas for an unauthorized purpose is liable for any tax due on the gas.

(d) Repealed by Session Laws 2007-397, s. 11(d), effective July 1, 2010.

(1998-22, s. 1; 2007-397, ss. 11(a)-(e); 2013-316, 4.1(d).)

§ 105-187.42. (Repealed effective July 1, 2014) Liability for the tax.

The excise tax imposed by this section on piped natural gas is payable as follows:

(1) For piped natural gas delivered by a local distribution company to a sales or transportation customer, the tax is payable by the local distribution company.

(2) For piped natural gas delivered by a person who is not a local distribution company to a sales or transportation customer, the tax is payable by that person.

(3) For piped natural gas received by a person by means of direct access to an interstate gas pipeline for consumption by that person, the tax is payable by that person. (1998-22, s. 1; 2013-316, s. 4.1(d).)

§ 105-187.43. (Repealed effective July 1, 2014) Payment of the tax.

(a) Payment. - The tax imposed by this Article is payable monthly. A monthly payment is due by the 20th day of the month following the calendar month in which liability for the tax accrues. The tax imposed by this Article on piped natural gas delivered to a sales or transportation customer accrues when the gas is delivered. The tax payable on piped natural gas received by a person who has direct access to an interstate pipeline for consumption by that person accrues when the gas is received.

(b) Prepayment. - A taxpayer who is consistently liable for at least twenty thousand dollars ($20,000) of tax a month must make a monthly prepayment of the next month's tax liability. This requirement applies when the taxpayer meets the threshold and the Secretary notifies the taxpayer to make prepayments. A prepayment is due on the date a monthly payment is due. The prepayment must equal at least sixty five percent (65%) of any of the following:

(1) The amount of tax due for the current month.

(2) The amount of tax due for the same month in the preceding year.

(3) The average monthly amount of tax due in the preceding calendar year.

(c) Return. - A return is due quarterly. A quarterly return covers a calendar quarter and is due by the last day of the month that follows the quarter covered by the return. (1998-22, s. 1; 1999-337, s. 32(a); 2001-427, s. 6(f); 2006-33, s. 13; 2012-79, s. 2.13; 2013-316, s. 4.1(d).)

§ 105-187.44. (Repealed effective July 1, 2014) Distribution of part of tax proceeds to cities.

(a) City Information. - A quarterly return filed under this Article must indicate the amount of tax attributable to the following:

(1) Piped natural gas delivered during the quarter to sales or transportation customers in each city in the State.

(2) Piped natural gas received during the quarter in each city in the State by persons who have direct access to an interstate gas pipeline and who receive the gas for their own consumption.

If a tax return does not state this information, the Secretary must determine how much of the tax proceeds are to be attributed to each city.

(b) Distribution. - Within 75 days after the end of each calendar quarter, the Secretary must distribute to the cities part of the tax proceeds collected under this Article during that quarter. The amount to be distributed to a city is one-half of the amount of tax attributable to that city for that quarter under subsection (a) of this section. The General Assembly finds that the revenue distributed under this section is local revenue, not a State expenditure, for the purpose of Section 5(3) of Article III of the North Carolina Constitution. Therefore, the Governor may not reduce or withhold the distribution. (1998-22, s. 1; 1998-217, s. 32(b); 1999-337, s. 32(b); 2002-120, s. 3; 2013-316, s. 4.1(d).)

§ 105-187.45. (Repealed effective July 1, 2014) Information exchange and information returns.

(a) Utilities Information. - The North Carolina Utilities Commission or the Public Staff of that Commission must give the Secretary a list of the entities that receive piped natural gas from an interstate pipeline and any other information available to the Commission that the Secretary asks for in administering the tax imposed by this Article.

(b) Information Return. - The Secretary may require the operator of an interstate pipeline to report the amount of piped natural gas taken from the pipeline in this State, the persons that received the gas, and the volume received by each person. (1998-22, s. 1; 2013-316, s. 4.1(d).)

§ 105-187.46. (Repealed effective July 1, 2014) Records and audits.

(a) Records. - A person who is required to file a return under this Article must keep a record of all documents used to determine information provided in the return. The records must be kept for three years after the due date of the return to which the records apply.

(b) Audits. - The Secretary may audit a person who is required to file a return under this Article. (1998-22, s. 1; 2013-316, s. 4.1(d).)

§ 105-187.47. Reserved for future codification purposes.

§ 105-187.48. Reserved for future codification purposes.

§ 105-187.49. Reserved for future codification purposes.

Article 5F.

Certain Machinery and Equipment.

§ 105-187.50. Definitions.

The definitions in G.S. 105-164.3 apply in this Article. (2001-347, s. 2.17; 2007-323, s. 31.22(a); 2009-451, s. 27A.3(v); 2010-91, s. 5.)

§ 105-187.51. Tax imposed on mill machinery.

(a) Scope. - A privilege tax is imposed on the following persons:

(1) A manufacturing industry or plant that purchases mill machinery or mill machinery parts or accessories for storage, use, or consumption in this State. A manufacturing industry or plant does not include the following:

a. A delicatessen, cafe, cafeteria, restaurant, or another similar retailer that is principally engaged in the retail sale of foods prepared by it for consumption on or off its premises.

b. A production company.

(2) A contractor or subcontractor that purchases mill machinery or mill machinery parts or accessories for use in the performance of a contract with a manufacturing industry or plant.

(3) A subcontractor that purchases mill machinery or mill machinery parts or accessories for use in the performance of a contract with a general contractor that has a contract with a manufacturing industry or plant.

(b) Rate. - The tax is one percent (1%) of the sales price of the machinery, part, or accessory purchased. The maximum tax is eighty dollars ($80.00) per article. As used in this section, the term "accessories" does not include electricity. (2001-347, s. 2.17; 2005-435, s. 56(a); 2010-147, s. 2.3.)

§ 105-187.51A: Repealed by Session Laws 2007-397, s. 12(d) effective July 1, 2010.

§ 105-187.51B. Tax imposed on certain recyclers, research and development companies, industrial machinery refurbishing companies, and companies located at ports facilities.

(a) Tax. - A privilege tax is imposed on the following:

(1) A major recycling facility that purchases any of the following tangible personal property for use in connection with the facility:

a. Cranes, structural steel crane support systems, and foundations related to the cranes and support systems.

b. Port and dock facilities.

c. Rail equipment.

d. Material handling equipment.

(2) A company primarily engaged at the establishment in research and development activities in the physical, engineering, and life sciences included in industry 54171 of NAICS and that purchases equipment or an attachment or repair part for equipment that meets all of the following requirements:

a. Is capitalized by the company for tax purposes under the Code.

b. Is used by the company at the establishment in the research and development of tangible personal property.

c. Would be considered mill machinery or mill machinery parts or accessories under G.S. 105-187.51 if it were purchased by a manufacturing industry or plant and used in the research and development of tangible personal property manufactured by the industry or plant.

(3) A company primarily engaged at the establishment in software publishing activities included in industry group 5112 of NAICS and that purchases equipment or an attachment or repair part for equipment that meets all of the following requirements:

a. Is capitalized by the company for tax purposes under the Code.

b. Is used by the company at the establishment in the research and development of tangible personal property.

c. Would be considered mill machinery under G.S. 105-187.51 if it were purchased by a manufacturing industry or plant and used in the research and development of tangible personal property manufactured by the industry or plant.

(4) A company primarily engaged at the establishment in industrial machinery refurbishing activities included in industry group 811310 of NAICS and that purchases equipment or an attachment or repair part for equipment that meets all of the following requirements:

a. Is capitalized by the company for tax purposes under the Code.

b. Is used by the company at the establishment in repairing or refurbishing tangible personal property.

c. Would be considered mill machinery under G.S. 105-187.51 if it were purchased by a manufacturing industry or plant and used by the industry or plant to manufacture tangible personal property.

(5) A company located at a ports facility for waterborne commerce that purchases specialized equipment to be used at the facility to unload or process bulk cargo to make it suitable for delivery to and use by manufacturing facilities.

(b) Rate. - The tax is one percent (1%) of the sales price of the equipment or other tangible personal property. The maximum tax is eighty dollars ($80.00) per article. (2005-276, s. 33.21; 2006-66, s. 24.9(a); 2006-196, s. 12; 2007-323, s. 31.7(a); 2007-527, s. 13(a); 2008-107, s. 28.21(a); 2011-302, s. 1; 2013-414, s. 46.)

§ 105-187.51C. (Expiring for sales occurring on or after July 1, 2015) Tax imposed on datacenter machinery and equipment.

(a) Tax. - A privilege tax is imposed on the owner of a datacenter that meets the requirements of subsection (a1) of this section and that purchases machinery or equipment to be located and used at the datacenter that is capitalized for tax purposes under the Code and is used either:

(1) For the provision of datacenter services, including equipment cooling systems for managing the performance of the datacenter property; hardware for distributed and mainframe computers and servers; data storage devices; network connectivity equipment and peripheral components and systems.

(2) For the generation, transformation, transmission, distribution, or management of electricity, including exterior substations and other business personal property used for these purposes.

(a1) Requirements. - The Secretary of Commerce must certify that the datacenter meets all of the following requirements:

(1) The investment requirements of this subdivision. The level of investment required by this subdivision must consist of private funds that have been or will be made in real and tangible personal property for the facility within five years of the date on which the first property investment is made by the owner of the facility.

a. For facilities located in a development tier one area, at least one hundred fifty million dollars ($150,000,000).

b. For facilities located in a development tier two area or a development tier three area, at least two hundred twenty-five million dollars ($225,000,000).

(2) The wage standard requirements of G.S. 105-129.83.

(3) The health insurance requirements of G.S. 105-129.83.

(a2) Second Datacenter. - A privilege tax is imposed on an owner of a datacenter that is subject to tax under subsection (a) of this section, constructs a second datacenter, and purchases machinery or equipment to be located and used at that datacenter. As used in this subsection, the owner of a datacenter includes an entity that is owned by or under common control with the owner of a datacenter subject to tax under subsection (a) of this section. The tax applies only if the second datacenter meets the following requirements and the machinery or equipment that is purchased is capitalized for tax purposes under the Code and is used for one of the purposes listed in subsection (a) of this section:

(1) The Secretary of Commerce certifies that an investment of private funds of at least seventy-five million dollars ($75,000,000) has been or will be made in real and tangible personal property for the facility within five years after the facility subject to tax under subsection (a) of this section is placed into service and that the datacenter meets the requirements in subsection (a1) of this section, other than the minimum investment amount in that subsection.

(2) The two datacenters are linked through a fiber-optic connection or a similar connection.

(3) The datacenters are placed in service within five years of each other.

(a3) Contractor Option. - A contractor or subcontractor that is subject to this subsection may elect to pay tax on its purchases of machinery and equipment described in subsection (a) of this section at the rate set in this section instead of the rate set in Article 5 of this Chapter. To make this election, a contractor or subcontractor must register with the Secretary for payment of tax under this section. The following contractors and subcontractors are subject to this section:

(1) A contractor that purchases the machinery and equipment for use in the performance of a contract with the owner of a datacenter subject to tax under this section.

(2) A subcontractor that purchases the machinery and equipment for use in the performance of a contract with a general contractor that has a contract with the owner of a datacenter subject to tax under this section.

(b) Rate and Scope. - The tax is one percent (1%) of the sales price of the eligible equipment and machinery. The maximum tax is eighty dollars ($80.00) per article. The tax does not apply to equipment and machinery of an eligible Internet datacenter that is exempt from sales tax under G.S. 105-164.13(55).

(c) Forfeiture. - If the required level of investment to qualify as an eligible datacenter is not timely made, then the rate provided under this section is forfeited. If the required level of investment is timely made but any eligible machinery and equipment is not located and used at an eligible datacenter, then the rate provided for that machinery and equipment under this section is forfeited. A taxpayer that forfeits a rate under this section is liable for all past sales and use taxes avoided as a result of the forfeiture, computed at the applicable State and local rates from the date the taxes would otherwise have been due, plus interest at the rate established under G.S. 105-241.21. If the forfeiture is triggered due to the lack of a timely investment required by this section, then interest is computed from the date the sales or use tax would otherwise have been due. For all other forfeitures, interest is computed from the time as of which the machinery or equipment was put to a disqualifying use. A credit is allowed against the State sales or use tax owed as a result of the forfeiture provisions of this subsection for privilege taxes paid pursuant to this section. For purposes of applying this credit, the fact that payment of the privilege tax occurred in a period outside the statute of limitations provided under G.S. 105-241.6 is not considered. The credit reduces the amount forfeited, and interest applies only to the reduced amount. The past taxes and interest are due 30 days after the date of forfeiture. A taxpayer that fails to pay the past taxes and interest by the due date is subject to the provisions of G.S. 105-236.

(d) Sunset. - This section expires for sales occurring on or after July 1, 2015. (2007-323, s. 31.22(b); 2009-445, s. 17; 2010-91, ss. 6, 7; 2011-330, ss. 22, 24.)

§ 105-187.51D. (Effective July 1, 2013 and expiring July 1, 2018) Tax imposed on machinery at large manufacturing and distribution facility.

(a) Definition. - For the purposes of this section, a "large manufacturing and distribution facility" is a facility that is to be used primarily for manufacturing or assembling products and distributing finished products for which the Secretary of Commerce makes a certification that an investment of private funds of at least eighty million dollars ($80,000,000) has been or will be made in real and tangible personal property for the facility within five years after the date on which the first property investment is made and that the facility will achieve an employment level of at least 550 within five years after the date the facility is placed into service and maintain that minimum level of employment throughout its operation.

(b) Tax. - A privilege tax is imposed on a large manufacturing and distribution facility that purchases mill machinery, distribution machinery, or parts or accessories for mill machinery or distribution machinery for storage, use, or consumption in this State. The tax is one percent (1%) of the sales price of the machinery, part, or accessory purchased. The maximum tax is eighty dollars ($80.00) per article. As used in this section, the term "accessories" does not include electricity.

(c) Forfeiture. - If the required level of investment or employment to qualify as [a] large manufacturing and distribution facility is not timely made, achieved, or maintained, then the rate provided under this section is forfeited. If the rate is forfeited due to a failure to timely make the required investment or to timely achieve the minimum required employment level, then the rate provided under this section is forfeited on all purchases. If the rate is forfeited due to a failure to maintain the minimum required employment level once that level has been achieved, then the rate provided under this section is forfeited for those purchases occurring on or after the date the taxpayer fails to maintain the minimum required employment level.

A taxpayer that forfeits a rate under this section is liable for all past sales and use taxes avoided as a result of the forfeiture, computed at the applicable State and local rates from the date the taxes would otherwise have been due, plus interest at the rate established under G.S. 105-241.21. Interest is computed from the date the sales or use tax would otherwise have been due. A credit is allowed against the State sales or use tax owed as a result of the forfeiture provisions of this subsection for privilege taxes paid pursuant to this section. For purposes of applying this credit, the fact that payment of the privilege tax occurred in a period outside the statute of limitations provided under G.S. 105-241.6 is not considered. The credit reduces the amount forfeited, and interest applies only to the reduced amount. The past taxes and interest are due 30 days after the date of forfeiture. A taxpayer that fails to pay the past taxes and interest by the due date is subject to the provisions of G.S. 105-236.

(d) Sunset. - This section expires for sales occurring on or after July 1, 2018. (2011-302, s. 2.)

§ 105-187.52. Administration.

(a) Administration. - The privilege taxes imposed by this Article are in lieu of the State use tax. Except as otherwise provided in this Article, the collection and administration of these taxes is the same as the State use tax imposed by Article 5 of this Chapter.

(b) Credit. - A credit is allowed against the tax imposed by this Article for the amount of a sales or use tax, privilege or excise tax, or substantially equivalent tax due and paid to another state or for the amount of sales and use tax paid to this State. The credit allowed by this subsection does not apply to tax paid to another state that does not grant a similar credit for the privilege tax paid in North Carolina.

(c) Exemption. - State agencies are exempted from the privilege taxes imposed by this Article. (2001-347, s. 2.17; 2005-276, s. 33.22; 2006-162, s. 11; 2007-527, s. 14; 2011-330, s. 25(b); 2013-414, s. 16.)

§ 105-187.53. Commercial logging items.

This Article does not apply to an item that is exempt from sales and use tax under G.S. 105-164.13(4f). (2006-19, s. 2.)

§ 105-187.54. Reserved for future codification purposes.

§ 105-187.55. Reserved for future codification purposes.

§ 105-187.56. Reserved for future codification purposes.

§ 105-187.57. Reserved for future codification purposes.

§ 105-187.58. Reserved for future codification purposes.

§ 105-187.59. Reserved for future codification purposes.

Article 5G.

Solid Waste Disposal Tax.

§ 105-187.60. Definitions.

The definitions set out in G.S. 105-164.3 and G.S. 130A-290 apply to this Article. (2007-550, s. 14(a).)

§ 105-187.61. Tax imposed.

(a) Tax Rate. - An excise tax is imposed on the disposal of municipal solid waste and construction and demolition debris in any landfill permitted pursuant to Article 9 of Chapter 130A of the General Statutes at a rate of two dollars ($2.00) per ton of waste. An excise tax is imposed on the transfer of municipal solid waste and construction and demolition debris to a transfer station permitted pursuant to Article 9 of Chapter 130A of the General Statutes for disposal outside the State at a rate of two dollars ($2.00) per ton of waste.

(b) Tax Liability. - The excise tax imposed by this section is due on municipal solid waste and construction and demolition debris received from third parties and on municipal solid waste and construction and demolition debris disposed of by the owner or operator. The tax is payable by the owner or operator of each landfill and transfer station permitted under Article 9 of Chapter 130A of the General Statutes. (2007-550, s. 14(a).)

§ 105-187.62. Administration.

(a) Collection. - The owner or operator of each landfill and transfer station permitted pursuant to Article 9 of Chapter 130A of the General Statutes must maintain scales designed to determine waste tonnage that are approved by the Department of Agriculture and Consumer Services. Each owner or operator must record waste tonnage disposed of in a landfill or transferred to a station for disposal outside the State and must maintain other records as required by the Secretary of Revenue. An owner or operator may add the amount of the solid waste disposal tax due to the charges made to a third party for disposal of municipal solid waste or construction and demolition debris.

(b) Payment. - The tax imposed by this Article is payable when a return is due. A return and payment are due on a quarterly basis. A quarterly return covers a calendar quarter and is due by the last day of the month following the end of the quarter.

(c) Bad Debt Deduction. - In the event that an owner or operator pays the tax on tonnage received from a customer and the account of that customer is found to be worthless and charged off for income tax purposes, the owner or operator may recover the tax paid on the tonnage it received but for which it was never compensated. The tax shall be recovered by reducing the overall tonnage on which the owner or operator pays tax in a calendar quarter by the tonnage for which it was never compensated from the worthless account. A local government that has paid tax on an account that is subsequently found to be worthless shall recover the tax paid in the same manner, if it meets all the conditions for recovery that would apply if the local government were subject to income tax. If the owner or operator subsequently collects on an account that has been declared worthless, any tax recovered must be repaid in the next calendar quarter. (2007-550, s. 14(a); 2008-207, s. 1.)

§ 105-187.63. Use of tax proceeds.

From the taxes received pursuant to this Article, the Secretary may retain the costs of collection, not to exceed two hundred twenty-five thousand dollars ($225,000) a year, as reimbursement to the Department. The Secretary must credit or distribute taxes received pursuant to this Article, less the cost of collection, on a quarterly basis as follows:

(1) Fifty percent (50%) to the Inactive Hazardous Sites Cleanup Fund established by G.S. 130A-310.11.

(2) Thirty-seven and one-half percent (37.5%) to cities and counties in the State on a per capita basis, using the most recent annual estimate of population certified by the State Budget Officer. One-half of this amount must be distributed to cities, and one-half of this amount must be distributed to counties. For purposes of this distribution, the population of a county does not include the population of a city located in the county.

A city or county is excluded from the distribution under this subdivision if it does not provide solid waste management programs and services and is not responsible by contract for payment for these programs and services. The Department of Environment and Natural Resources must provide the Secretary with a list of the cities and counties that are excluded under this subdivision. The list must be provided by May 15 of each year and applies to distributions made in the fiscal year that begins on July 1 of that year.

Funds distributed under this subdivision must be used by a city or county solely for solid waste management programs and services.

(3) Twelve and one-half percent (12.5%) to the General Fund. (2007-543, s. 2; 2007-550, s. 14(a); 2008-207, s. 2; 2009-484, s. 4; 2013-360, s. 14.18(a).)

§ 105-187.64: Reserved for future codification purposes.

§ 105-187.65: Reserved for future codification purposes.

§ 105-187.66: Reserved for future codification purposes.

§ 105-187.67: Reserved for future codification purposes.

§ 105-187.68: Reserved for future codification purposes.

§ 105-187.69: Reserved for future codification purposes.

Article 5H.

911 Service Charge for Prepaid Wireless Telecommunications Service.

§ 105-187.70. (Effective July 1, 2013) Department to comply with Article 3 of Chapter 62A of the General Statutes.

The Department of Revenue shall comply with the provisions of Article 3 of Chapter 62A of the General Statutes to receive and transfer to the 911 Fund the 911 service charge for prepaid wireless telecommunications service collected on retail transactions occurring in this State. (2011-122, s. 6; 2012-79, s. 1.6.)

Article 6.

Gift Taxes.

§§ 105-188 through 105-197.1: Repealed by Session Laws 2008-107, s. 28.18(a), effective January 1, 2009.

§ 105-191: Repealed by Session Laws 1995 (Regular Session, 1996), c. 646, s. 7.

§ 105-192. Repealed by Session Laws 1959, c. 1259, s. 9.

§§ 105-188 through 105-197.1: Repealed by Session Laws 2008-107, s. 28.18(a), effective January 1, 2009.

§ 105-196: Repealed by Session Laws 1995 (Regular Session, 1996), c. 646, s. 7.

§§ 105-188 through 105-197.1: Repealed by Session Laws 2008-107, s. 28.18(a), effective January 1, 2009.

Article 7.

Schedule H. Intangible Personal Property.

§ 105-198: Repealed by Session Laws 1995, c. 41, s. 1(b).

§§ 105-199 through 105-200: Repealed by Session Laws 1985, c. 656, s. 32.

§§ 105-201 through 105-204: Repealed by Session Laws 1995, c. 41, s. 1(b).

§ 105-205. Repealed by Session Laws 1985, c. 656, s. 32.

§§ 105-206 through 105-207: Repealed by Session Laws 1995, c. 41, s. 1(b).

§ 105-208. Repealed by Session Laws 1959, c. 1259, s. 9.

§ 105-209: Repealed by Session Laws 1995, c. 41, s. 1(b).

§ 105-210: Repealed by Session Laws 1979, c. 179, s. 4.

§§ 105-211 through 105-212: Repealed by Session Laws 1995, c. 41, s. 1(b).

§ 105-213: Repealed by Session Laws 1995, c. 41, s. 1(b).

§ 105-213.1: Recodified as § 105-275.2 by Session Laws 1995.

§§ 105-214 through 105-217: Repealed by Session Laws 1995, c. 41, s. 1(b).

Article 8.

Schedule I. Compensating Use Tax.

§§ 105-218 through 105-228: Repealed by Session Laws 1957, c. 1340, s. 5.

Article 8A.

Gross Earnings Taxes on Freight Line Companies in Lieu of Ad Valorem Taxes.

§ 105-228.1. Defining taxes levied and assessed in this Article.

The purpose of this Article is to levy a fair and equal tax under authority of Section 2(2) of Article V of the North Carolina Constitution and to provide a practical means for ascertaining and collecting it. The taxes levied and assessed in this Article are on gross earnings, as defined in the Article, and are in lieu of ad valorem taxes upon the properties of persons taxed in this Article. (1954, c. 400, s. 8; 1998-98, ss. 64, 109.)

§ 105-228.2. Tax upon freight car line companies.

(a) For purposes of taxation under this section the property of freight line companies as defined is declared to constitute a special class of property. In lieu of all ad valorem taxes by either or both the State government and the respective local taxing jurisdictions, a tax upon gross earnings in the State as elsewhere defined shall be imposed.

(b) Any person or persons, joint-stock association or corporation, wherever organized or incorporated, engaged in the business of operating cars or engaged in the business of furnishing or leasing cars not otherwise listed for taxation in this State, for the transportation of freight (whether such cars be owned by such company or any other person or company), over any railway or lines, in whole or in part, within this State, such line or lines not being owned, leased or operated by such company, whether such cars be termed box, flat, coal, ore, tank, stock, gondola, furniture, or refrigerator car or by some other name, shall be deemed a freight line company.

(c) For the purposes of taxation under this section all cars used exclusively within the State, or used partially within and without the State, and a proportionate part of the intangible values of the business as a going concern, are hereby declared to have situs in this State.

(d) Every freight line company, as hereinbefore defined, shall pay annually a sum in the nature of a tax at three per centum (3%) upon the total gross earnings received from all sources by such freight line companies within the State, which shall be in lieu of all ad valorem taxes in this State of any freight company so paying the same.

(e) The term "gross earnings received from all sources by such freight line companies within the State" as used in this Article is hereby declared and shall be construed to mean all earnings from the operation of freight cars within the

State for all car movements or business beginning and ending within the State and a proportion, based upon the proportion of car mileage within the State to the total car mileage, or earnings on all interstate car movements or business passing through, or into or out of the State.

(f)   Every railroad company using or leasing the cars of any freight line company shall, upon making payment to such freight line company for the use or lease, after June 30, 1943, of such cars withhold so much thereof as is designated in this section. On or before March first of each year such railroad company shall make and file with the Secretary of Revenue a statement showing the amount of such payment for the next preceding 12-month period ending December 31, and of the amounts so withheld by it, and shall remit to the Secretary of Revenue the amounts so withheld. If any railroad company shall fail to make such report or fail to remit the amount of tax herein levied, or shall fail to withhold the part of such payment hereby required to be withheld, such railroad company shall become liable for the amount of the tax herein levied and shall not be entitled to deduct from its gross earnings for purposes of taxation the amounts so paid by it to freight line companies.

It is not the purpose of this subsection to impose an unreasonable burden of accounting on railroad companies operating in this State, and the Secretary of Revenue is hereby authorized, upon the application of any railroad company, to approve any method of accounting which he finds to be reasonably adequate for determining the amount of mileage earnings by any car line company whose equipment is operated within the State by or on the lines of such railroad company. Further, if in the opinion of the Secretary of Revenue the tax imposed by this section can be satisfactorily collected direct from the freight line companies, he is hereby authorized to fix rules and regulations for such direct collection, with the authority to return at any time to the method of collection at source above provided in this subsection.

(g)   Every car line company shall file such additional reports annually, and in such form and as of such date as the Secretary of Revenue may deem necessary to determine the equitable amount of tax levied under this section.

(h)   Upon the filing of such reports it shall be the duty of the Secretary of Revenue to inspect and verify the same and assess the amount of taxes due from freight line companies therein named. Any freight line company against which a tax is assessed under the provisions of this Article may at any time within 15 days after the last day for the filing of reports by railroad companies, appear before the Secretary of Revenue at a hearing to be granted by the

Secretary and offer evidence and argument on any matter bearing upon the validity or correctness of the tax assessed against it, and the Secretary shall review his assessment of such tax and shall make his order confirming or modifying the same as he shall deem just and equitable, and if any overpayment is found to have been made it shall be refunded by the Secretary. Provided, however that such payment if in the amount of three dollars ($3.00) or more shall be refunded to the taxpayer within 60 days of the discovery thereof; if the amount of overpayment is less than three dollars ($3.00) then such overpayment shall be refunded only upon receipt by the Secretary of Revenue of a written demand for such refund from the taxpayer. Provided further, that no overpayment shall be refunded irrespective of whether upon discovery or receipt of written demand if such discovery is not made or such demand is not received within three years from the filing date of the return or within six months of the payment of the tax alleged to be an overpayment, whichever date is the later.

(i)   The provisions of Article 9 of this Chapter apply to this Article.

(j)   The provisions of this Article shall apply to all freight line gross earnings accruing from and after June 30, 1943. (1943, c. 400, s. 8; 1957, c. 1340, s. 14; 1973, c. 476, s. 193; 1998-212, s. 29A.14(j).)

Article 8B.

Taxes Upon Insurance Companies.

§ 105-228.3. Definitions.

The following definitions apply in this Article:

(1)   Article 65 corporation. - A corporation subject to Article 65 of Chapter 58 of the General Statutes, regulating hospital, medical, and dental service corporations.

(1a)   Captive insurance company. - Defined in G.S. 58-10-340.

(2)   Insurer. - An insurer as defined in G.S. 58-1-5 or a group of employers who have pooled their liabilities pursuant to G.S. 97-93 of the Workers' Compensation Act.

(3)   Self-insurer. - An employer that carries its own risk pursuant to G.S. 97-93 of the Workers' Compensation Act. (1945, c. 752, s. 2; 1985 (Reg. Sess., 1986), c. 928, s. 12; 1995, c. 360, s. 1(b); 2013-116, s. 6(a).)

§ 105-228.4: Recodified as § 58-6-7 by Session Laws 1995, c. 360, s. 1(c).

§ 105-228.4A. Tax on captive insurance companies.

(a)   Tax Levied. - A tax is levied in this section on a captive insurance company doing business in this State. In the case of a branch captive insurance company, the tax levied in this section applies only to the branch business of the company. Two or more captive insurance companies under common ownership and control are taxed under this section as a single captive insurance company.

(b)   Other Taxes. - A captive insurance company that is subject to the tax levied by this section is not subject to any of the following:

(1)   Franchise taxes imposed by Article 3 of this Chapter.

(2)   Income taxes imposed by Article 4 of this Chapter.

(3)   Local privilege taxes or local taxes computed on the basis of gross premiums.

(4)   The insurance regulatory charge imposed by G.S. 58-6-25.

(c)   Administration. - The definitions in G.S. 58-10-340 apply in this section. A company subject to this section must file with the Secretary a full and accurate report of the premiums contracted for or collected on policies or contracts of insurance written by the company during the preceding calendar year. In the case of a multiyear policy or contract, the premiums must be prorated among the years covered by the policy or contract. The report is due on or before March 1. The taxes imposed by this section are due to the Secretary with the report.

(d)   Tax on Assumed Reinsurance Premiums. - The tax to be applied to assumed reinsurance premiums is computed at the percentages provided in the table below. The tax does not apply to premiums for risks or portions of risks that are subject to taxation on a direct basis under subsection (e) of this section. The tax is not payable in connection with the receipt of assets in exchange for the assumption of loss reserves and other liabilities of one insurer by another insurer if the two insurers are under common control and the Commissioner of Insurance verifies both of the following: (i) the transaction between the insurers is part of a plan to discontinue the operations of one of the insurers, and (ii) the intent of the insurers is to renew or maintain business with the captive insurance company.

Premiums Collected	Rate of Tax
Up to $20,000,000	.225%
$20,000,000 to $40,000,000	.150%
$40,000,000 to $60,000,000	.050%
$60,000,000 and over	.025%

(e) Tax on Direct Premiums. - The tax to be applied to direct premiums is computed at the percentages provided in the table below. In determining the amount of premiums subject to tax under this subsection, the taxpayer may deduct the amounts paid to policyholders as return premiums. Return premiums include dividends on unabsorbed premiums or premium deposits returned or credited to policyholders.

Premiums Collected	Rate of Tax
Up to $20,000,000	0.4%
$20,000,000 and more	0.3%

(f) Total Tax Liability. - The aggregate amount of tax payable under this section by a protected cell captive insurance company with more than 10 cells may not be less than ten thousand dollars ($10,000) and may not exceed the lesser of (i) one hundred thousand dollars ($100,000) plus five thousand dollars ($5,000) multiplied by the number of cells over 10 and (ii) two hundred thousand dollars ($200,000). The aggregate amount of tax payable under this section for any other captive insurance company may not be less than five thousand dollars ($5,000) and may not exceed one hundred thousand dollars ($100,000).

If a captive insurance company is a special purpose financial captive and if the special purpose financial captive is under common ownership and control with one or more other captive insurance companies, the following provisions apply to the consolidated group of companies that are taxed as a single captive insurance company pursuant to subsection (a) of this section:

(1)   The amount of premium tax payable under this section is allocated to each member of the consolidated group in the same proportion that the premium allocable to the member bears to the total premium of all members.

(2)   The aggregate amount of tax payable under this section by the consolidated group is equal to the greater of the following:

a.   The sum of the premium tax allocated to the members.

b.   Five thousand dollars ($5,000).

(3)   If the total premium tax allocated to all members of a consolidated group that are special purpose financial captives exceeds one hundred thousand dollars ($100,000), then the total premium tax allocated to those members is one hundred thousand dollars ($100,000).

(4)   If the total premium tax allocated to all members of the consolidated group that are not special purpose financial captives exceeds one hundred thousand dollars ($100,000), then the total premium tax allocated to those members is one hundred thousand dollars ($100,000). (2013-116, s. 6(b).)

§ 105-228.5. Taxes measured by gross premiums.

(a)   Tax Levied. – A tax is levied in this section on insurers, Article 65 corporations, health maintenance organizations, and self-insurers. An insurer, health maintenance organization, or Article 65 corporation that is subject to the tax levied by this section is not subject to franchise or income taxes imposed by Articles 3 and 4, respectively, of this Chapter.

(b)   Tax Base. –

(1) Insurers. - The tax imposed by this section on an insurer or a health maintenance organization shall be measured by gross premiums from business done in this State during the preceding calendar year.

(2) Repealed by Session Laws 2006-196, effective for taxable years beginning on or after January 1, 2008.

(3) Article 65 Corporations. - The tax imposed by this section on an Article 65 corporation shall be measured by gross collections from membership dues, exclusive of receipts from cost plus plans, received by the corporation during the preceding calendar year.

(4) Self-insurers. - The tax imposed by this section on a self-insurer shall be measured by the gross premiums that would be charged against the same or most similar industry or business, taken from the manual insurance rate then in force in this State, applied to the self-insurer's payroll for the previous calendar year as determined under Article 2 of Chapter 97 of the General Statutes modified by the self-insurer's approved experience modifier.

(b1) Calculation of Tax Base. - In determining the amount of gross premiums from business in this State, all gross premiums received in this State, credited to policies written or procured in this State, or derived from business written in this State shall be deemed to be for contracts covering persons, property, or risks resident or located in this State unless one of the following applies:

(1) The premiums are properly reported and properly allocated as being received from business done in some other nation, territory, state, or states.

(2) The premiums are from policies written in federal areas for persons in military service who pay premiums by assignment of service pay.

Gross premiums from business done in this State in the case of life insurance contracts, including supplemental contracts providing for disability benefits, accidental death benefits, or other special benefits that are not annuities, means all premiums collected in the calendar year, other than for contracts of reinsurance, for policies the premiums on which are paid by or credited to persons, firms, or corporations resident in this State, or in the case of group policies, for contracts of insurance covering persons resident within this State. The only deductions allowed shall be for premiums refunded on policies rescinded for fraud or other breach of contract and premiums that were paid in advance on life insurance contracts and subsequently refunded to the insured, premium payer, beneficiary or estate. Gross premiums shall be deemed to have been collected for the amounts as provided in the policy contracts for the time in force during the year, whether satisfied by cash payment, notes, loans, automatic premium loans, applied dividend, or by any other means except waiver of premiums by companies under a contract for waiver of premium in case of disability.

Gross premiums from business done in this State for all other health care plans and contracts of insurance, including contracts of insurance required to be carried by the Workers' Compensation Act, means all premiums written during the calendar year, or the equivalent thereof in the case of self-insurers under the Workers' Compensation Act, for contracts covering property or risks in this State, other than for contracts of reinsurance, whether the premiums are designated as premiums, deposits, premium deposits, policy fees, membership fees, or assessments. Gross premiums shall be deemed to have been written for the amounts as provided in the policy contracts, new and renewal, becoming effective during the year irrespective of the time or method of making payment or settlement for the premiums, and with no deduction for dividends whether returned in cash or allowed in payment or reduction of premiums or for additional insurance, and without any other deduction except for return of premiums, deposits, fees, or assessments for adjustment of policy rates or for cancellation or surrender of policies.

(c)   Exclusions. - Every insurer, in computing the premium tax, shall exclude all of the following from the gross amount of premiums, and the gross amount of excluded premiums is exempt from the tax imposed by this section:

(1)   All premiums received on or after July 1, 1973, from policies or contracts issued in connection with the funding of a pension, annuity, or profit-sharing plan qualified or exempt under section 401, 403, 404, 408, 457 or 501 of the Code as defined in G.S. 105-228.90.

(2)   Premiums or considerations received from annuities, as defined in G.S. 58-7-15.

(3)   Funds or considerations received in connection with funding agreements, as defined in G.S. 58-7-16.

(4)   The following premiums, to the extent federal law prohibits their taxation under this Article:

a. Federal Employees Health Benefits Plan premiums.

b. Medicaid or Medicare premiums.

(d) (See Editor's note) Tax Rates; Disposition. -

(1) Workers' Compensation. - The tax rate to be applied to gross premiums, or the equivalent thereof in the case of self-insurers, on contracts applicable to liabilities under the Workers' Compensation Act is two and five-tenths percent (2.5%). The net proceeds shall be credited to the General Fund.

(2) Other Insurance Contracts. - The tax rate to be applied to gross premiums on all other taxable contracts issued by insurers or health maintenance organizations and to be applied to gross premiums and gross collections from membership dues, exclusive of receipts from cost plus plans, received by Article 65 corporations is one and nine-tenths percent (1.9%). The net proceeds shall be credited to the General Fund.

(3) Additional Rate on Property Coverage Contracts. - An additional tax at the rate of seventy-four hundredths percent (0.74%) applies to gross premiums on insurance contracts for property coverage. The tax is imposed on ten percent (10%) of the gross premiums from insurance contracts for automobile physical damage coverage and on one hundred percent (100%) of the gross premiums from all other contracts for property coverage. Twenty-five percent (25%) of the net proceeds of this additional tax must be credited to the Volunteer Fire Department Fund established in Article 87 of Chapter 58 of the General Statutes. Twenty percent (20%) of the net proceeds must be credited to the Department of Insurance for disbursement pursuant to G.S. 58-84-25. Up to twenty percent (20%), as determined in accordance with G.S. 58-87-10(f), must be credited to the Workers' Compensation Fund. The remaining net proceeds must be credited to the General Fund.

The following definitions apply in this subdivision:

a. Automobile physical damage. - The following lines of business identified by the NAIC: private passenger automobile physical damage and commercial automobile physical damage.

b. Property coverage. - The following lines of business identified by the NAIC: fire, farm owners multiple peril, homeowners multiple peril, nonliability portion of commercial multiple peril, ocean marine, inland marine, earthquake, private passenger automobile physical damage, commercial automobile physical damage, aircraft, and boiler and machinery. The term also includes insurance contracts for wind damage.

    c.   NAIC. - National Association of Insurance Commissioners.

(4)   Repealed by Session Laws 2006-196, effective for taxable years beginning on or after January 1, 2008.

(5)   Repealed by Session Laws 2003-284, s. 43.1, effective for taxable years beginning on or after January 1, 2004.

(6)   Repealed by Session Laws 2005-276, s. 38.4(a), effective for taxable years beginning on or after January 1, 2007.

(e)   Report and Payment. - Each taxpayer doing business in this State shall, within the first 15 days of March, file with the Secretary of Revenue a full and accurate report of the total gross premiums as defined in this section, the payroll and other information required by the Secretary in the case of a self-insurer, or the total gross collections from membership dues exclusive of receipts from cost plus plans collected in this State during the preceding calendar year. The taxes imposed by this section shall be remitted to the Secretary with the report.

(f)   Installment Payments Required. - Taxpayers that are subject to the tax imposed by this section and have a premium tax liability of ten thousand dollars ($10,000) or more for business done in North Carolina during the immediately preceding year shall remit three equal quarterly installments with each installment equal to at least thirty-three and one-third percent (33 1/3%) of the premium tax liability incurred in the immediately preceding taxable year. The quarterly installment payments shall be made on or before April 15, June 15, and October 15 of each taxable year. The company shall remit the balance by the following March 15 in the same manner provided in this section for annual returns.

The Secretary may permit an insurance company to pay less than the required estimated payment when the insurer reasonably believes that the total estimated payments made for the current year will exceed the total anticipated tax liability for the year.

An underpayment or an overpayment of an installment payment required by this subsection accrues interest in accordance with G.S. 105-241.21. An overpayment of tax shall be credited to the company and applied against the taxes imposed upon the company under this Article.

(g) Exemptions. - This section does not apply to farmers' mutual assessment fire insurance companies or to fraternal orders or societies that do not operate for a profit and do not issue policies on any person except members. This section does not apply to a captive insurance company taxed under G.S. 105-228.4A. (1945, c. 752, s. 2; 1947, c. 501, s. 8; 1951, c. 643, s. 8; 1955, c. 1313, s. 5; 1957, c. 1340, s. 12; 1959, c. 1211; 1961, c. 783; 1963, c. 1096; 1969, c. 1221; 1973, cc. 142, 1019; 1975, c. 143; c. 559, s. 8; 1979, c. 714, s. 2; 1983, c. 713, s. 81; 1985, c. 119, s. 3; c. 719, ss. 1, 2; 1985 (Reg. Sess., 1986), c. 1031, ss. 1-5; 1987, c. 709, s. 2; c. 814, s. 2; 1989 (Reg. Sess., 1990), c. 814, s. 27; 1991, c. 689, s. 297; 1993 (Reg. Sess., 1994), c. 600, s. 4; 1995, c. 360, s. 1(d); 1995 (Reg. Sess., 1996), c. 747, s. 2; 1998-98, s. 17; 2001-424, s. 34.22(a), (d), (e); 2001-487, s. 69(a); 2001-489, s. 2(a)-(d), (f), (g); 2003-284, s. 43.1; 2005-276, s. 38.4(a); 2005-435, s. 57(a); 2006-196, ss. 1-5; 2007-250, s. 1; 2007-491, s. 23; 2013-116, s. 6(c); 2013-360, s. 20.2(a).)

§ 105-228.5A. Credit against gross premium tax for assessments paid to the Insurance Guaranty Association and the Life and Health Insurance Guaranty Association.

(a) The following definitions apply in this section:

(1) Assessment. - An assessment as described in G.S. 58-48-35 or an assessment as described in G.S. 58-62-41.

(2) Association. - The North Carolina Insurance Guaranty Association created under G.S. 58-48-25 or the North Carolina Life and Health Insurance Guaranty Association created under G.S. 58-62-26.

(3) Repealed by Session Laws 1995, c. 360, s. 1(e).

(4) Member insurer. - A member insurer as defined in G.S. 58-48-20 or a member insurer as defined in G.S. 58-62-16.

(b) A member insurer who pays an assessment is allowed as a credit against the tax imposed under G.S. 105-228.5 an amount equal to twenty percent (20%) of the amount of the assessment in each of the five taxable years following the year in which the assessment was paid. In the event a member insurer ceases doing business, all assessments for which it has not taken a credit under this section may be credited against its premium tax liability for the year in which it ceases doing business. The amount of the credit allowed by this section may not exceed the member insurer's premium tax liability for the taxable year.

(c) Any sums that are acquired by refund, under either G.S. 58-48-35 or G.S. 58-62-41, from the Association by member insurers, and that have previously been offset against premium taxes as provided in subsection (b) of this section, shall be paid by the member insurers to this State in the manner required by the Secretary of Revenue. The Association shall notify the Secretary that the refunds have been made. (1991, c. 689, s. 298; 1991 (Reg. Sess., 1992), c. 1007, s. 8; 1995, c. 360, s. 1(e).)

§ 105-228.5B. Distribution of part of tax proceeds to High Risk Pool.

By November 1 of each year, the State Treasurer must transfer from the General Fund to the North Carolina Health Insurance Risk Pool Fund established in G.S. 58-50-225 an amount equal to thirty percent (30%) of the growth in revenue from the tax applied to gross premiums under G.S. 105-228.5(d)(2). The growth in revenue from this tax is the difference between the amount of revenue collected during the preceding fiscal year on premiums taxed under that subdivision less $475,545,413, which is the amount of revenue collected during fiscal year 2006-2007 on premiums taxed under that subdivision. The Treasurer must draw the amount required under this section from revenue collected on premiums taxed under that subdivision. (2007-532, s. 4(a), (b); 2008-118, s. 3.2(d), (e); 2009-445, s. 10.)

§ 105-228.6. Taxes in case of withdrawal from State.

Any insurance company which for any cause withdraws from this State or ceases to register and transact new business in this State shall be liable for the taxes specified in G.S. 105-228.5 with respect to gross premiums collected in the calendar year in which such withdrawal may occur. In case any company which was formerly licensed or registered in this State and which subsequently ceased to do business therein, may apply to reenter this State, application for reentry or renewal of registration shall be denied unless and until said company shall have paid all taxes, together with any penalties and interest, due as to premiums collected in the year of withdrawal and also taxes as specified in G.S. 105-228.5 for gross premiums collected in the calendar year next preceding the year in which such application for renewal of registration is made. (1945, c. 752, s. 2; 1985 (Reg. Sess., 1986), c. 1031, s. 5.1; 1987, c. 814, s. 4; 1989, c. 346, s. 1.)

§ 105-228.7: Repealed by Session Laws 1987, c. 629, s. 21.

§ 105-228.8. Retaliatory premium taxes.

(a) When the laws of any other state impose, or would impose, any premium taxes, upon North Carolina companies doing business in the other state that are, on an aggregate basis, in excess of the premium taxes directly imposed upon similar companies by the statutes of this State, the Secretary of Revenue shall impose the same premium taxes, on an aggregate basis, upon the companies chartered in the other state doing business or seeking to do business in North Carolina. Any company subject to the retaliatory tax imposed by this section shall report and pay the tax with the annual premium tax return required by G.S. 105-228.5. The retaliatory tax imposed by this section shall be included in the quarterly prepayment rules for premium taxes.

(b) For purposes of this section, the following definitions shall be applied:

(1) "State" includes the District of Columbia and other states, territories, and possessions of the United States, the provinces of Canada, and other nations.

(2) "Companies" includes all entities subject to tax under G.S. 105-228.5.

(c) For purposes of this section, any premium taxes that are, or would be, imposed upon North Carolina companies by any city, county, or other political subdivision or agency of another state shall be deemed to be imposed directly by that state.

(d) In computing the premium taxes that another state imposes, or would impose, upon a North Carolina company doing business in the state, it shall be assumed that North Carolina companies pay the highest rates of premium tax that are generally imposed by the other state on similar companies chartered outside of the state.

(e) This section shall not apply to special purpose obligations or assessments based on premiums imposed in connection with particular kinds of insurance, to the special purpose regulatory charge imposed under G.S. 58-6-25, or to dedicated special purpose taxes based on premiums.

(f) If the laws of another state retaliate against North Carolina companies on other than an aggregate basis, the Secretary of Revenue shall retaliate against companies chartered in that state on the same basis. (1945, c. 752, s. 2; 1987, c. 814, s. 1; 1989 (Reg. Sess., 1990), c. 1069, s. 21; 1991, c. 689, s. 291; 1995, c. 360, s. 1(f); 2011-330, s. 10.)

§ 105-228.9. Commissioner of Insurance to administer portions of Article.

The following taxes relating to insurance are collected by the Commissioner of Insurance:

(1) Surplus lines tax, G.S. 58-21-85.

(2) Tax on risk retention groups not chartered in this State, G.S. 58-22-20(3).

(3) Tax on person procuring insurance directly with an unlicensed insurer, G.S. 58-28-5(b).

The Commissioner of Insurance has the same authority and responsibility in administering those taxes as the Secretary of Revenue has in administering this Article. (1945, c. 752, s. 2; 1955, c. 1350, s. 22; 1973, c. 476, s. 193; 1987, c. 804, s. 9; 1995, c. 360, s. 1(a); 1995 (Reg. Sess., 1996), c. 747, s. 1.)

§ 105-228.10. No additional local taxes.

No city or county may levy on a person subject to the tax levied in this Article a privilege tax or a tax computed on the basis of gross premiums. (1945, c. 752, s. 2; 1998-98, s. 18.)

Article 8C.

Excise Tax on Banks.

§§105-228.11 through 105-228.20. Repealed by Session Laws 1973, c. 1053, s. 1.

§ 105-228.21: Omitted.

Article 8D.

Taxation of Savings and Loan Associations.

§§ 105-228.22 through 105-228.24: Repealed by Session Laws 1998-98, s. 1(a).

§ 105-228.24A: Recodified as § 105-130.43 by Session Laws 1998-98, s. 1(d).

§§ 105-228.25 through 105-228.27: Repealed by Session Laws 1983, c. 26, s. 1.

Article 8E.

Excise Tax on Conveyances.

§ 105-228.28. Scope.

This Article applies to every person conveying an interest in real estate located in North Carolina other than a governmental unit or an instrumentality of a governmental unit. (1967, c. 986, s. 1; 1999-28, s. 1.)

§ 105-228.29. Exemptions.

This Article does not apply to any of the following transfers of an interest in real property:

(1)   By operation of law.

(2)   By lease for a term of years.

(3)   By or pursuant to the provisions of a will.

(4)   By intestacy.

(5)   By gift.

(6)   If no consideration in property or money is due or paid by the transferee to the transferor.

(7)   By merger, conversion, or consolidation.

(8)   By an instrument securing indebtedness. (1967, c. 986, s. 1; 1999-28, s. 1; 1999-369, s. 5.10(a)-(c).)

§ 105-228.30. Imposition of excise tax; distribution of proceeds.

(a)   An excise tax is levied on each instrument by which any interest in real property is conveyed to another person. The tax rate is one dollar ($1.00) on each five hundred dollars ($500.00) or fractional part thereof of the consideration or value of the interest conveyed. The transferor must pay the tax to the register of deeds of the county in which the real estate is located before recording the instrument of conveyance. If the instrument transfers a parcel of real estate lying in two or more counties, however, the tax must be paid to the register of deeds of the county in which the greater part of the real estate with respect to value lies.

The excise tax on instruments imposed by this Article applies to timber deeds and contracts for the sale of standing timber to the same extent as if these deeds and contracts conveyed an interest in real property.

(b)   The register of deeds of each county must remit the proceeds of the tax levied by this section to the county finance officer. The finance officer of each county must credit one-half of the proceeds to the county's general fund and remit the remaining one-half of the proceeds, less taxes refunded and the county's allowance for administrative expenses, to the Department of Revenue on a monthly basis. A county may retain two percent (2%) of the amount of tax proceeds allocated for remittance to the Department of Revenue as compensation for the county's cost in collecting and remitting the State's share of the tax. The Department of Revenue shall credit the funds remitted to the Department of Revenue under this subsection to the General Fund. (1967, c. 986, s. 1; 1991, c. 689, s. 338; 1991 (Reg. Sess., 1992), c. 1019, s. 1; 1993 (Reg. Sess., 1994), c. 772, s. 2; 1995, c. 456, s. 3; 1999-28, s. 1; 2000-16, s. 1; 2001-427, s. 14(a); 2011-330, s. 30(b); 2013-360, s. 14.4(a).)

§ 105-228.31. Repealed by Session Laws 1999-28, s. 1.

§ 105-228.32. Instrument must be marked to reflect tax paid.

A person who presents an instrument for registration must report to the Register of Deeds the amount of tax due. It is the duty of the person presenting the instrument for registration to report the correct amount of tax due. Before the instrument may be recorded, the Register of Deeds must collect the tax due and mark the instrument to indicate that the tax has been paid and the amount of the tax paid. (1967, c. 986, s. 1; 1969, c. 599, s. 1; 1973, c. 476, s. 193; 1999-28, s. 1; 2009-454, s. 2.)

§ 105-228.33. Taxes recoverable by action.

A county may recover unpaid taxes under this Article in an action in the name of the county brought in the superior court of the county. The action may be filed if the taxes remain unpaid more than 30 days after the register of deeds has demanded payment. In such actions, costs of court shall include a fee to the county of twenty-five dollars ($25.00) for expense of collection. (1967, c. 986, s. 1; 1999-28, s. 1.)

§ 105-228.34: Repealed by Session Laws 1999-28, s. 1.

§ 105-228.35. Administrative provisions.

Except as otherwise provided in this Article, the provisions of Article 9 of this Chapter apply to this Article. (1967, c. 986, s. 1; 1999-28, s. 1; 2000-170, s. 1.)

§ 105-228.36: Repealed by Session Laws 1999-28, s. 1.

§ 105-228.37. Refund of overpayment of tax.

(a)   Refund Request. - A taxpayer who pays more tax than is due under this Article may request a refund of the overpayment by filing a written request for a refund with the board of county commissioners of the county where the tax was paid. The request must be filed within six months after the date the tax was paid and must explain why the taxpayer believes a refund is due.

(b)   Hearing by County. - A board of county commissioners must conduct a hearing on a request for refund. Within 60 days after a timely request for a refund has been filed and at least 10 days before the date set for the hearing, the board must notify the taxpayer in writing of the time and place at which the hearing will be conducted. The date set for the hearing must be within 90 days after the timely request for a hearing was filed or at a later date mutually agreed upon by the taxpayer and the board. The board must make a decision on the requested refund within 90 days after conducting a hearing under this subsection.

(c)   Process if Refund Granted. - If the board of commissioners decides that a refund is due, it must refund the overpayment, together with any applicable interest, to the taxpayer and inform the Department of the refund. The Department may assess the taxpayer for the amount of the refund in accordance with G.S. 105-241.9 if the Department disagrees with the board's decision.

(d)   Process if Refund Denied. - If the board of commissioners finds that no refund is due, the written decision of the board must inform the taxpayer that the taxpayer may request a departmental review of the denial of the refund in accordance with the procedures set out in G.S. 105-241.11.

(e) Recording Correct Deed. - Before a tax is refunded, the taxpayer must record a new instrument reflecting the correct amount of tax due. If no tax is due because an instrument was recorded in the wrong county, then the taxpayer must record a document stating that no tax was owed because the instrument being corrected was recorded in the wrong county. The taxpayer must include in the document the names of the grantors and grantees and the deed book and page number of the instrument being corrected.

When a taxpayer records a corrected instrument, the taxpayer must inform the register of deeds that the instrument being recorded is a correcting instrument. The taxpayer must give the register of deeds a copy of the decision granting the refund that shows the correct amount of tax due. The correcting instrument must include the deed book and page number of the instrument being corrected. The register of deeds must notify the county finance officer and the Secretary when the correcting instrument has been recorded.

(f) Interest. - An overpayment of tax bears interest at the rate established in G.S. 105-241.21 from the date that interest begins to accrue. Interest begins to accrue on an overpayment 30 days after the request for a refund is filed by the taxpayer with the board of county commissioners. (2000-170, s. 2; 2007-491, s. 24; 2011-330, s. 30(a).)

§§ 105-228.38 through 105-228.89. Reserved for future codification purposes.

Article 9.

General Administration; Penalties and Remedies.

§ 105-228.90. Scope and definitions.

(a) Scope. - This Article applies to all of the following:

(1) Subchapters I, V, and VIII of this Chapter.

(2) The annual report filing requirements of G.S. 55-16-22.

(3) The primary forest product assessment levied under Article 81 of Chapter 106 of the General Statutes.

(4) The inspection taxes levied under Article 3 of Chapter 119 of the General Statutes.

(5) Chapter 105A of the General Statutes.

(b) Definitions. - The following definitions apply in this Article:

(1) Charter school. - A nonprofit corporation that has a charter under G.S. 115C-238.29D to operate a charter school.

(1a) City. - A city as defined by G.S. 160A-1(2). The term also includes an urban service district defined by the governing board of a consolidated city-county, as defined by G.S. 160B-2(1).

(1b) Code. - The Internal Revenue Code as enacted as of January 2, 2013, including any provisions enacted as of that date that become effective either before or after that date.

(1c) County. - Any one of the counties listed in G.S. 153A-10. The term also includes a consolidated city-county as defined by G.S. 160B-2(1).

(2) Department. - The Department of Revenue.

(3) Electronic Funds Transfer. - A transfer of funds initiated by using an electronic terminal, a telephone, a computer, or magnetic tape to instruct or authorize a financial institution or its agent to credit or debit an account.

(4) Income tax return preparer. - Any person who prepares for compensation, or who employs one or more persons to prepare for compensation, any return of tax imposed by Article 4 of this Chapter or any claim for refund of tax imposed by Article 4 of this Chapter. For purposes of this definition, the completion of a substantial portion of a return or claim for refund is treated as the preparation of the return or claim for refund. The term does not include a person merely because the person (i) furnishes typing, reproducing, or other mechanical assistance, (ii) prepares a return or claim for refund of the employer, or an officer or employee of the employer, by whom the person is regularly and continuously employed, (iii) prepares as a fiduciary a return or claim for refund for any person, or (iv) represents a taxpayer in a hearing regarding a proposed assessment.

(4b) NAICS. - The North American Industry Classification System adopted by the United States Office of Management and Budget as of December 31, 2007.

(4d) Pass-through entity. - An entity or business, including a limited partnership, a general partnership, a joint venture, a Subchapter S Corporation, or a limited liability company, all of which is treated as owned by individuals or other entities under the federal tax laws, in which the owners report their share of the income, losses, and credits from the entity or business on their income tax returns filed with this State. For the purpose of this section, an owner of a pass-through entity is an individual or entity who is treated as an owner under the federal tax laws.

(5) Person. - An individual, a fiduciary, a firm, an association, a partnership, a limited liability company, a corporation, a unit of government, or another group acting as a unit. The term includes an officer or employee of a corporation, a member, a manager, or an employee of a limited liability company, and a member or employee of a partnership who, as officer, employee, member, or manager, is under a duty to perform an act in meeting the requirements of Subchapter I, V, or VIII of this Chapter, of G.S. 55-16-22, of Article 81 of Chapter 106 of the General Statutes, or of Article 3 of Chapter 119 of the General Statutes.

(6) Secretary. - The Secretary of Revenue.

(7) Tax. - A tax levied under Subchapter I, V, or VIII of this Chapter, the primary forest product assessment levied under Article 81 of Chapter 106 of the General Statutes, or an inspection tax levied under Article 3 of Chapter 119 of the General Statutes. Unless the context clearly requires otherwise, the term "tax" includes penalties and interest as well as the principal amount.

(8) Taxpayer. - A person subject to the tax or reporting requirements of Subchapter I, V, or VIII of this Chapter, of Article 81 of Chapter 106 of the General Statutes, or of Article 3 of Chapter 119 of the General Statutes. (1991 (Reg. Sess., 1992), c. 930, s. 13; 1993, c. 12, s. 1; c. 354, s. 18; c. 450, s. 1; 1993 (Reg. Sess., 1994), c. 662, s. 1; c. 745, s. 13; 1995, c. 17, s. 9; c. 461, s. 14; 1995 (Reg. Sess., 1996), c. 664, s. 1; 1997-55, s. 1; 1997-475, s. 6.9; 1998-171, s. 1; 1999-415, s. 1; 2000-72, s. 1; 2000-126, s. 1; 2000-140, s. 69; 2001-414, s. 23; 2001-427, s. 4(a); 2002-106, s. 1; 2002-126, s. 30C.1(a); 2003-25, s. 1; 2003-284, s. 37A.1; 2003-416, s. 4(d); 2004-110, s. 1.1; 2005-276, ss. 35.1(a), (d); 2006-18, s. 1; 2007-323, s. 31.1(a); 2007-491, s. 25; 2008-107, s.

28.1(a); 2009-451, s. 27A.6(a), (b); 2010-31, s. 31.1(a); 2011-5, s. 1; 2011-145, s. 13.25(xx); 2011-330, ss. 11, 31(a), 37; 2012-79, s. 1.7(a); 2013-10, s. 1.)

§ 105-229: Repealed by Session Laws 1995 (Regular Session, 1996), c. 646, s. 9.

§ 105-230. Charter suspended for failure to report.

(a) If a corporation or a limited liability company fails to file any report or return or to pay any tax or fee required by this Subchapter for 90 days after it is due, the Secretary shall inform the Secretary of State of this failure. The Secretary of State shall suspend the articles of incorporation, articles of organization, or certificate of authority, as appropriate, of the corporation or limited liability company. The Secretary of State shall immediately notify by mail every domestic or foreign corporation or limited liability company so suspended of its suspension. The powers, privileges, and franchises conferred upon the corporation or limited liability company by the articles of incorporation, the articles of organization, or the certificate of authority terminate upon suspension.

(b) Any act performed or attempted to be performed during the period of suspension is invalid and of no effect, unless the Secretary of State reinstates the corporation or limited liability company pursuant to G.S. 105-232. (1939, c. 158, ss. 901, 902; 1957, c. 498; 1967, c. 823, s. 31; 1969, c. 965, s. 2; 1973, c. 476, s. 193; 1987, c. 644, s. 1; 1989 (Reg. Sess., 1990), c. 1024, s. 19(a); 1993, c. 354, ss. 19, 20; 1998-212, s. 29A.14(l); 2001-387, s. 152.)

§ 105-231: Recodified as the second paragraph of § 105-230 by S.L. 1998-212, s. 29A.14(k).

§ 105-232. Rights restored; receivership and liquidation.

(a) Any corporation or limited liability company whose articles of incorporation, articles of organization, or certificate of authority to do business in this State has been suspended by the Secretary of State under G.S. 105-230, that complies with all the requirements of this Subchapter and pays all State taxes, fees, or penalties due from it (which total amount due may be computed, for years prior and subsequent to the suspension, in the same manner as if the suspension had not taken place), and pays to the Secretary of Revenue a fee of twenty-five dollars ($25.00) to cover the cost of reinstatement, is entitled to exercise again its rights, privileges, and franchises in this State. The Secretary of Revenue shall notify the Secretary of State of this compliance and the Secretary of State shall reinstate the corporation or limited liability company by appropriate entry upon the records of the office of the Secretary of State. Upon entry of reinstatement, it relates back to and takes effect as of the date of the suspension by the Secretary of State and the corporation or limited liability company resumes carrying on its business as if the suspension had never occurred, subject to the rights of any person who reasonably relied, to that person's prejudice, upon the suspension. The Secretary of State shall immediately notify by mail the corporation or limited liability company of the reinstatement.

(b) When the articles of incorporation, articles of organization, or certificate of authority to do business in this State has been suspended by the Secretary of State under G.S. 105-230, and the corporation or limited liability company has ceased to operate as a going concern, if there remains property held in the name of the corporation or limited liability company or undisposed of at the time of the suspension, or there remain future interests that may accrue to the corporation, the limited liability company, or its successors, members, or stockholders, any interested party may apply to the superior court for the appointment of a receiver. Application for the receiver may be made in a civil action to which all stockholders, members, or their representatives or next of kin shall be made parties. Stockholders or members whose whereabouts are unknown, unknown stockholders or members, unknown heirs and next of kin of deceased stockholders, members, creditors, dealers, and other interested persons may be served by publication. A guardian ad litem may be appointed for any stockholders, members, or their representatives who are infants or incompetent. The receiver shall enter into a bond if the court requires one and shall give notice to creditors by publication or otherwise as the court may prescribe. Any creditor who fails to file a claim with the receiver within the time set shall be barred of the right to participate in the distribution of the assets. The receiver may (i) sell the property interests of the corporation or limited liability company upon such terms and in such manner as the court may order, (ii) apply the proceeds to the payment of any debts of the corporation or limited liability company, and (iii) distribute the remainder among the stockholders, the members, or their representatives in proportion to their interests in the property interests. Shares due to any stockholder or member who is unknown or whose whereabouts are unknown shall be paid into the office of the clerk of the superior court, to be disbursed according to law. In the event the records of the corporation or limited liability company are lost or do not reflect the owners of the property interests, the court shall determine the owners from the best evidence available, and the receiver shall be protected in acting in accordance with the court's finding. This proceeding is authorized for the sole purpose of providing a procedure for disposing of the assets of the corporation or limited liability company by the payment of its debts and by the transfer to its stockholders, its members, or their representatives their proportionate shares of its assets. (1939, c. 158, s. 903; c. 370, s. 1; 1943, c. 400, s. 9; 1947, c. 501, s. 9; 1951, c. 29; 1969, c. 541, s. 10; 1973, c. 476, s. 193; c. 1065; 1987, c. 644, s. 2; 1989 (Reg. Sess., 1990), c. 1024, s. 19(b); 1991, c. 645, s. 21; 1993, c. 354, s. 21; 2001-387, s. 153; 2001-487, s. 62(dd).)

§ 105-233: Repealed by Session Laws 2006-162, s. 12(a), effective July 24, 2006.

§ 105-234: Repealed by Session Laws 2006-162, s. 12(a), effective July 24, 2006.

§ 105-235. Every day's failure a separate offense.

The willful failure, refusal, or neglect to observe and comply with any order, direction, or mandate of the Secretary of Revenue, or to perform any duty enjoined by this Subchapter, by any person, firm, or corporation subject to the provisions of this Subchapter, or any officer, agent, or employee thereof, shall, for each day such failure, refusal, or neglect continues, constitute a separate and distinct offense. (1939, c. 158, s. 906; 1973, c. 476, s. 193.)

§ 105-236. Penalties; situs of violations; penalty disposition.

(a) Penalties. - The following civil penalties and criminal offenses apply:

(1) Penalty for Bad Checks. - When the bank upon which any uncertified check tendered to the Department of Revenue in payment of any obligation due to the Department returns the check because of insufficient funds or the nonexistence of an account of the drawer, the Secretary shall assess a penalty equal to ten percent (10%) of the check, subject to a minimum of one dollar ($1.00) and a maximum of one thousand dollars ($1,000). This penalty does not apply if the Secretary finds that, when the check was presented for payment, the drawer of the check had sufficient funds in an account at a financial institution to

pay the check and, by inadvertence, the drawer of the check failed to draw the check on the account that had sufficient funds.

(1a) Penalty for Bad Electronic Funds Transfer. - When an electronic funds transfer cannot be completed due to insufficient funds or the nonexistence of an account of the transferor, the Secretary shall assess a penalty equal to ten percent (10%) of the amount of the transfer, subject to a minimum of one dollar ($1.00) and a maximum of one thousand dollars ($1,000). This penalty may be waived by the Secretary in accordance with G.S. 105-237.

(1b) Making Payment in Wrong Form. - For making a payment of tax in a form other than the form required by the Secretary pursuant to G.S. 105-241(a), the Secretary shall assess a penalty equal to five percent (5%) of the amount of the tax, subject to a minimum of one dollar ($1.00) and a maximum of one thousand dollars ($1,000). This penalty may be waived by the Secretary in accordance with G.S. 105-237.

(2) Failure to Obtain a License. - For failure to obtain a license before engaging in a business, trade or profession for which a license is required, the Secretary shall assess a penalty equal to five percent (5%) of the amount prescribed for the license per month or fraction thereof until paid, not to exceed twenty-five percent (25%) of the amount so prescribed, but in any event shall not be less than five dollars ($5.00). In cases in which the taxpayer, after written notification by the Department, fails to obtain a license as required under G.S. 105-449.65 or G.S. 105-449.131, the Secretary may assess a penalty of one thousand dollars ($1,000).

(3) (Effective until January 1, 2014) Failure to File Return. - In case of failure to file any return on the date it is due, determined with regard to any extension of time for filing, the Secretary shall assess a penalty equal to five percent (5%) of the amount of the tax if the failure is for not more than one month, with an additional five percent (5%) for each additional month, or fraction thereof, during which the failure continues, not exceeding twenty-five percent (25%) in the aggregate, or five dollars ($5.00), whichever is the greater.

(3) (Effective January 1, 2014) Failure to File Return. - In case of failure to file any return on the date it is due, determined with regard to any extension of time for filing, the Secretary shall assess a penalty equal to five percent (5%) of the amount of the tax if the failure is for not more than one month, with an additional five percent (5%) for each additional month, or fraction thereof, during

which the failure continues, not exceeding twenty-five percent (25%) in aggregate.

(4) (Effective until January 1, 2014) Failure to Pay Tax When Due. - In the case of failure to pay any tax when due, without intent to evade the tax, the Secretary shall assess a penalty equal to ten percent (10%) of the tax, subject to a minimum of five dollars ($5.00). This penalty does not apply in any of the following circumstances:

a. When the amount of tax shown as due on an amended return is paid when the return is filed.

b. When the Secretary proposes an assessment for tax due but not shown on a return and the tax due is paid within 45 days after the later of the following:

1. The date of the notice of proposed assessment of the tax, if the taxpayer does not file a timely request for a Departmental review of the proposed assessment.

2. The date the proposed assessment becomes collectible under one of the circumstances listed in G.S. 105-241.22(3) through (6), if the taxpayer files a timely request for a Departmental review of the proposed assessment.

c. When a taxpayer timely files a consolidated or combined return at the request of the Secretary under Part 1 of Article 4 of this Chapter and the tax due is paid within 45 days after the latest of the following:

1. The date the return is filed.

2. The date of a notice of proposed assessment based on the return, if the taxpayer does not file a timely request for a Departmental review of the proposed assessment.

3. The date the Departmental review of the proposed assessment ends as a result of the occurrence of one of the actions listed in G.S. 105-241.22(3) through (6), if the taxpayer files a timely request for a Departmental review.

(4) (Effective January 1, 2014) Failure to Pay Tax When Due. - In the case of failure to pay any tax when due, without intent to evade the tax, the Secretary shall assess a penalty equal to ten percent (10%) of the tax. This penalty does not apply in any of the following circumstances:

a. When the amount of tax shown as due on an amended return is paid when the return is filed.

b. When the Secretary proposes an assessment for tax due but not shown on a return and the tax due is paid within 45 days after the later of the following:

1. The date of the notice of proposed assessment of the tax, if the taxpayer does not file a timely request for a Departmental review of the proposed assessment.

2. The date the proposed assessment becomes collectible under one of the circumstances listed in G.S. 105-241.22(3) through (6), if the taxpayer files a timely request for a Departmental review of the proposed assessment.

c. When a taxpayer timely files a consolidated or combined return at the request of the Secretary under Part 1 of Article 4 of this Chapter and the tax due is paid within 45 days after the latest of the following:

1. The date the return is filed.

2. The date of a notice of proposed assessment based on the return, if the taxpayer does not file a timely request for a Departmental review of the proposed assessment.

3. The date the Departmental review of the proposed assessment ends as a result of the occurrence of one of the actions listed in G.S. 105-241.22(3) through (6), if the taxpayer files a timely request for a Departmental review.

(5) Negligence. -

a. Finding of negligence. - For negligent failure to comply with any of the provisions to which this Article applies, or rules issued pursuant thereto, without intent to defraud, the Secretary shall assess a penalty equal to ten percent (10%) of the deficiency due to the negligence.

b. Large individual income tax deficiency. - In the case of individual income tax, if a taxpayer understates taxable income, by any means, by an amount equal to twenty-five percent (25%) or more of gross income, the Secretary shall assess a penalty equal to twenty-five percent (25%) of the deficiency. For purposes of this subdivision, "gross income" means gross income as defined in section 61 of the Code.

c. Other large tax deficiency. - In the case of a tax other than individual income tax, if a taxpayer understates tax liability by twenty-five percent (25%) or more, the Secretary shall assess a penalty equal to twenty-five percent (25%) of the deficiency.

d. No double penalty. - If a penalty is assessed under subdivision (6) of this section, no additional penalty for negligence shall be assessed with respect to the same deficiency.

e. Repealed by Session Laws 2013-316, s. 7(c), effective January 1, 2013, and applicable to estates of decedents dying on or after that date.

f. Consolidated or combined return. - The amount of tax shown as due on a consolidated or combined return filed at the request of the Secretary under Part 1 of Article 4 of this Chapter is not considered a deficiency and is not subject to this subdivision unless one or more of the following applies:

1. The return is an amended consolidated or combined return that includes the same corporations as the initial consolidated or combined return filed at the request of the Secretary. In this case the deficiency is the extent to which the amount shown as due on the amended return exceeds the amount shown as due on the initial return.

2. Repealed by Session Laws 2011-390, s. 5, effective January 1, 2012.

3. Pursuant to a written request from a taxpayer, the Secretary has provided written advice to that taxpayer stating that the Secretary will require a consolidated or combined return under the facts and circumstances set out in the request, and the Secretary requires a taxpayer to file a consolidated or combined return under G.S. 105-130.5A because the taxpayer's facts and circumstances meet those described in the written advice.

(5a) Misuse of Exemption Certificate. - For misuse of an exemption certificate by a purchaser, the Secretary shall assess a penalty equal to two hundred fifty dollars ($250.00). An exemption certificate is a certificate issued by the Secretary that authorizes a retailer to sell tangible personal property to the holder of the certificate and either collect tax at a preferential rate or not collect tax on the sale. Examples of an exemption certificate include a certificate of resale, a direct pay certificate, and a farmer's certificate.

(5b) Road Tax Understatement. - If a motor carrier understates its liability for the road tax imposed by Article 36B of this Chapter by twenty-five percent (25%) or more, the Secretary shall assess the motor carrier a penalty in an amount equal to two times the amount of the deficiency.

(6) Fraud. - If there is a deficiency or delinquency in payment of any tax because of fraud with intent to evade the tax, the Secretary shall assess a penalty equal to fifty percent (50%) of the total deficiency.

(7) Attempt to Evade or Defeat Tax. - Any person who willfully attempts, or any person who aids or abets any person to attempt in any manner to evade or defeat a tax or its payment, shall, in addition to other penalties provided by law, be guilty of a Class H felony.

(8) Willful Failure to Collect, Withhold, or Pay Over Tax. - Any person required to collect, withhold, account for, and pay over any tax who willfully fails to collect or truthfully account for and pay over the tax shall, in addition to other penalties provided by law, be guilty of a Class 1 misdemeanor. Notwithstanding any other provision of law, no prosecution for a violation brought under this subdivision shall be barred before the expiration of six years after the date of the violation.

(9) Willful Failure to File Return, Supply Information, or Pay Tax. - Any person required to pay any tax, to file a return, to keep any records, or to supply any information, who willfully fails to pay the tax, file the return, keep the records, or supply the information, at the time or times required by law, or rules issued pursuant thereto, is, in addition to other penalties provided by law, guilty of a Class 1 misdemeanor. Notwithstanding any other provision of law, no prosecution for a violation brought under this subdivision is barred before the expiration of six years after the date of the violation.

(9a) Aid or Assistance. - Any person, pursuant to or in connection with the revenue laws, who willfully aids, assists in, procures, counsels, or advises the preparation, presentation, or filing of a return, affidavit, claim, or any other document that the person knows is fraudulent or false as to any material matter, whether or not the falsity or fraud is with the knowledge or consent of the person authorized or required to present or file the return, affidavit, claim, or other document, is guilty of a felony as follows:

a. If the person who commits an offense under this subdivision is an income tax return preparer and the amount of all taxes fraudulently evaded on returns filed in one taxable year is one hundred thousand dollars ($100,000) or more, the person is guilty of a Class C felony.

b. If the person who commits an offense under this subdivision is an income tax return preparer and the amount of all taxes fraudulently evaded on returns filed in one taxable year is less than one hundred thousand dollars ($100,000), the person is guilty of a Class F felony.

c. If the person who commits an offense under this subdivision is not covered under sub-subdivision a. or b. of this subdivision, the person is guilty of a Class H felony.

(10) Failure to File Informational Returns. -

a. Repealed by Session Laws 1998-212, s. 29A.14(m), effective January 1, 1999.

b. The Secretary may request a person who fails to file timely statements of payment to another person with respect to wages, dividends, rents, or interest paid to that person to file the statements by a certain date. If the payer fails to file the statements by that date, the amounts claimed on the payer's income tax return as deductions for salaries and wages, or rents or interest shall be disallowed to the extent that the payer failed to comply with the Secretary's request with respect to the statements.

c. For failure to file an informational return required by Article 36C or 36D of this Chapter by the date the return is due, there shall be assessed a penalty of fifty dollars ($50.00).

(10a) Filing a Frivolous Return. - If a taxpayer files a frivolous return under Part 2 of Article 4 of this Chapter, the Secretary shall assess a penalty in the amount of up to five hundred dollars ($500.00). A frivolous return is a return that meets both of the following requirements:

a. It fails to provide sufficient information to permit a determination that the return is correct or contains information which positively indicates the return is incorrect, and

b. It evidences an intention to delay, impede or negate the revenue laws of this State or purports to adopt a position that is lacking in seriousness.

(10b)   Misrepresentation Concerning Payment. - A person who receives money from a taxpayer with the understanding that the money is to be remitted to the Secretary for application to the taxpayer's tax liability and who willfully fails to remit the money to the Secretary is guilty of a Class F felony.

(11)   Repealed by Session Laws 2006-162, s. 12(b), effective July 24, 2006.

(12)   Repealed by Session Laws 1991, c. 45, s. 27.

(b)   Situs. - Violation of a tax law is considered an act committed in part at the office of the Secretary in Raleigh. The certificate of the Secretary that a tax has not been paid, a return has not been filed, or information has not been supplied, as required by law, is prima facie evidence that the tax has not been paid, the return has not been filed, or the information has not been supplied.

(c)   Penalty Disposition. - Civil penalties assessed by the Secretary are assessed as an additional tax. The clear proceeds of civil penalties assessed by the Secretary must be credited to the Civil Penalty and Forfeiture Fund established in G.S. 115C-457.1. (1939, c. 158, s. 907; 1953, c. 1302, s. 7; 1959, c. 1259, s. 8; 1963, c. 1169, s. 6; 1967, c. 1110, s. 9; 1973, c. 476, s. 193; c. 1287, s. 13; 1979, c. 156, s. 2; 1985, c. 114, s. 11; 1985 (Reg. Sess., 1986), c. 983; 1987 (Reg. Sess., 1988), c. 1076; 1989, c. 557, ss. 7 to 10; 1989 (Reg. Sess., 1990), c. 1005, s. 9; 1991, c. 45, s. 27; 1991 (Reg. Sess., 1992), c. 914, s. 2; c. 1007, s. 10; 1993, c. 354, s. 22; c. 450, s. 10; c. 539, ss. 709, 710, 1292, 1293; 1994, Ex. Sess., c. 24, s. 14(c); 1995, c. 390, s. 36; 1995 (Reg. Sess., 1996), c. 646, s. 10; c. 647, s. 51; c. 696, s. 1; 1997-6, s. 8; 1997-109, s. 3; 1998-178, ss. 1, 2; 1998-212, s. 29A.14(m); 1999-415, ss. 2, 3; 1999-438, ss. 15, 16; 2000-119, s. 2; 2000-120, s. 7; 2000-140, s. 70; 2002-106, ss. 2, 4; 2005-276, s. 6.37(n); 2005-435, s. 1; 2006-162, s. 12(b); 2007-491, s. 26; 2008-107, s. 28.18(b); 2010-31, s. 31.10(a), (b); 2011-330, s. 32; 2011-390, s. 5; 2011-411, s. 8(b); 2012-79, s. 2.18(a); 2013-316, s. 7(c); 2013-414, s. 1(h).)

§ 105-236.1. Enforcement of revenue laws by revenue law enforcement agents.

(a)   General. - The Secretary may appoint employees of the Unauthorized Substances Tax Section of the Tax Enforcement Division to serve as revenue law enforcement officers having the responsibility and subject-matter jurisdiction to enforce the excise tax on unauthorized substances imposed by Article 2D of this Chapter.

The Secretary may appoint up to 11 employees of the Motor Fuels Investigations Section of the Tax Enforcement Division to serve as revenue law enforcement officers having the responsibility and subject-matter jurisdiction to enforce the taxes on motor fuels imposed by Articles 36B, 36C, and 36D of this Chapter and by Chapter 119 of the General Statutes.

The Secretary may appoint employees of the Criminal Investigations Section of the Tax Enforcement Division to serve as revenue law enforcement officers having the responsibility and subject-matter jurisdiction to enforce the following tax violations and criminal offenses:

(1) The felony and misdemeanor tax violations in G.S. 105-236.

(2) The misdemeanor tax violations in G.S. 105-449.117 and G.S. 105-449.120.

(3) The following criminal offenses when they involve a tax imposed under Chapter 105 of the General Statutes:

a. G.S. 14-91 (Embezzlement of State Property).

b. G.S. 14-92 (Embezzlement of Funds).

c. G.S. 14-100 (Obtaining Property By False Pretenses).

c1. G.S. 14-113.20 (Identity Theft).

c2. G.S. 14-133.20A (Trafficking in Stolen Identities).

d. G.S. 14-119 (Forgery).

e. G.S. 14-120 (Uttering Forged Paper).

f. G.S. 14-401.18 (Sale of Certain Packages of Cigarettes).

(b) Authority. - A revenue law enforcement officer is a State officer with jurisdiction throughout the State within the officer's subject-matter jurisdiction. A revenue law enforcement officer may serve and execute notices, orders, warrants, or demands issued by the Secretary or the General Court of Justice in connection with the enforcement of the officer's subject-matter jurisdiction. A revenue law enforcement officer has the full powers of arrest as provided by G.S. 15A-401 while executing the notices, orders, warrants, or demands.

(c) Qualifications. - To serve as a revenue law enforcement officer, an employee must be certified as a criminal justice officer under Chapter 17C of the General Statutes. The Secretary may administer the oath of office to revenue law enforcement officers appointed pursuant to this section. (1997-503, s. 1; 2000-119, s. 1; 2004-124, s. 23.4; 2013-414, s. 17.)

§ 105-237. Waiver of penalties; installment payments.

(a) Waiver. - The Secretary may, upon making a record of the reasons therefor, reduce or waive any penalties provided for in this Subchapter.

(b) Installment Payments. - After a proposed assessment of a tax becomes final, the Secretary may enter into an agreement with the taxpayer for payment of the tax in installments if the Secretary determines that the agreement will facilitate collection of the tax. The agreement may include a waiver of penalties but may not include a waiver of liability for tax or interest due. The Secretary may modify or terminate the agreement if one or more of the following findings is made:

(1) Information provided by the taxpayer in support of the agreement was inaccurate or incomplete.

(2) Collection of tax to which the agreement applies is in jeopardy.

(3) The taxpayer's financial condition has changed.

(4) The taxpayer has failed to pay an installment when due or to pay another tax when due.

(5) The taxpayer has failed to provide information requested by the Secretary.

The Secretary must give a taxpayer who has entered into an installment agreement at least 30 days' written notice before modifying or terminating the agreement on the grounds that the taxpayer's financial condition has changed unless the taxpayer failed to disclose or concealed assets or income when the agreement was made or the taxpayer has acquired assets since the agreement was made that can satisfy all or part of the tax liability. A notice must specify the basis for the Secretary's finding of a change in the taxpayer's financial condition. (1939, c. 158, s. 908; c. 370, s. 1; 1973, c. 476, s. 193; 1993, c. 532, s. 1; 1999-438, s. 17.)

§ 105-237.1. Compromise of liability.

(a) Authority. - The Secretary may compromise a taxpayer's liability for a tax that is collectible under G.S. 105-241.22 when the Secretary determines that the compromise is in the best interest of the State and makes one or more of the following findings:

(1) There is a reasonable doubt as to the amount of the liability of the taxpayer under the law and the facts.

(2) The taxpayer is insolvent and the Secretary probably could not otherwise collect an amount equal to or in excess of the amount offered in compromise. A taxpayer is considered insolvent only in one of the following circumstances:

a. It is plain and indisputable that the taxpayer is clearly insolvent and will remain so in the reasonable future.

b. The taxpayer has been determined to be insolvent in a judicial proceeding.

(3) Collection of a greater amount than that offered in compromise is improbable, and the funds or a substantial portion of the funds offered in the settlement come from sources from which the Secretary could not otherwise collect.

(4) A federal tax assessment arising out of the same facts has been compromised with the federal government on the same or a similar basis as that proposed to the State and the Secretary could probably not collect an amount equal to or in excess of that offered in compromise.

(5) Collection of a greater amount than that offered in compromise would produce an unjust result under the circumstances.

(6) The taxpayer is a retailer or a person under Article 5 of this Chapter; the assessment is for sales or use tax the retailer failed to collect or the person failed to pay on an item taxable under G.S. 105-164.4(a)(10) and (a)(11), and the retailer or person made a good-faith effort to comply with the sales and use tax laws. This subdivision expires for assessments issued after July 1, 2020.

(b) Written Statement. - When the Secretary compromises a tax liability under this section and the amount of the liability is at least one thousand dollars ($1,000), the Secretary must make a written statement that sets out the amount of the liability, the amount accepted under the compromise, a summary of the facts concerning the liability, and the findings on which the compromise is based. The Secretary must sign the statement and keep a record of the statement. If the compromise settles a dispute that is in litigation, the Secretary must obtain the approval of the Attorney General before accepting the compromise, and the Attorney General must sign the statement describing the compromise. (1957, c. 1340, s. 10; 1959, c. 1259, s. 8; 1973, c. 476, s. 193; 1985, c. 114, s. 11; 1991 (Reg. Sess., 1992), c. 1007, s. 11; 2008-107, s. 28.16(f); 2013-316, s. 9(b).)

§ 105-238. Tax a debt.

Every tax imposed by this Subchapter, and all increases, interest, and penalties thereon, shall become, from the time it is due and payable, a debt from the person, firm, or corporation liable to pay the same to the State of North Carolina. (1939, c. 158, s. 909.)

§ 105-239: Repealed by Session Laws 2007-491, s. 2, effective January 1, 2008.

§ 105-239.1. Transferee liability.

(a) Lien and Liability. - Property transferred for an inadequate consideration to a donee, heir, devisee, distributee, stockholder of a liquidated corporation, or any other person at a time when the transferor is insolvent or is rendered insolvent by reason of the transfer is subject to a lien for any taxes owing by the transferor to the State of North Carolina at the time of the transfer whether or not the amount of the taxes has been ascertained or assessed at the time of the transfer. G.S. 105-241 applies to this tax lien. In the event the transferee has disposed of the property so that it cannot be subjected to the State's tax lien, the transferee is personally liable for the difference between the fair market value of the property at the time of the transfer and the actual consideration, if any, paid to the transferor by the transferee.

(b) Procedure. - The Department may proceed to enforce a lien that arises under this section against property transferred by a taxpayer to another person or to hold that person liable for the tax due by sending the person a notice of proposed assessment in accordance with G.S. 105-241.9. The Department has the burden of establishing that a person to whom property was transferred is liable. The period of limitations for assessment of any liability against a transferee or enforcing the lien against the transferred property expires one year after the expiration of the period of limitations for assessment against the transferor.

(c) Proceeds. - When property transferred by a taxpayer to another person is sold to satisfy the lien that arises under this section, the person is entitled to receive from the proceeds of the sale the amount of consideration, if any, the person paid for the property. The proceeds must be applied for this purpose before they are applied to satisfy the lien.

(d) Repealed by Session Laws 2007-491, s. 27, effective January 1, 2008. (1957, c. 1340, s. 10; 1973, c. 476, s. 193; 1993, c. 450, s. 11; 2007-491, s. 27; 2011-284, s. 69.)

§ 105-240. Tax upon settlement of fiduciary's account.

No final account of a fiduciary shall be allowed by the probate court unless such account shows, and the judge of said court finds, that all taxes imposed by the provisions of this Subchapter upon said fiduciary, which have become payable, have been paid, and that all taxes which may become due are secured by bond, deposit, or otherwise. The certificate of the Secretary of Revenue and the receipt for the amount of tax herein certified shall be conclusive as to the payment of the tax to the extent of said certificate.

For the purpose of facilitating the settlement and distribution of estates held by fiduciaries, the Secretary of Revenue, with the approval of the Attorney General, may, on behalf of the State, agree upon the amount of taxes at any time due or to become due from such fiduciaries under the provisions of this Subchapter, and the payment in accordance with such agreement shall be full satisfaction of the taxes to which the agreement relates. (1939, c. 158, s. 911; 1973, c. 476, s. 193.)

§ 105-240.1. Agreements with respect to domicile.

Whenever reasonably necessary in order to facilitate the collection of any tax, the Secretary of Revenue with the consent and approval of the Attorney General, is authorized to make agreements with the taxing officials of other states of the United States or with taxpayers in cases of disputes as to the domicile of a decedent. (1957, c. 1340, s. 10; 1973, c. 476, s. 193.)

§ 105-241. Where and how taxes payable; tax period; liens.

(a) Form of Payment. - Taxes are payable in the national currency. The Secretary shall prescribe where taxes are to be paid and whether taxes must be paid in cash, by check, by electronic funds transfer, or by another method.

(b) Electronic Funds Transfer. - Payment by electronic funds transfer is required as provided in this subsection.

(1) Corporate estimated taxes. - A corporation that is required under the Code to pay its federal-estimated corporate income tax by electronic funds transfer must pay its State-estimated corporate income tax by electronic funds transfer as provided in G.S. 105-163.40.

(2) Prepayment taxes. - A taxpayer that is required to prepay tax under G.S. 105-116 or G.S. 105-164.16 must pay the tax by electronic funds transfer.

(2a) Motor fuel taxes. - A taxpayer that files an electronic return under Subchapter V of this Chapter or Article 3 of Chapter 119 of the General Statutes must pay the tax by electronic funds transfer.

(3) Large tax payments. - Except as otherwise provided in this subsection, the Secretary shall not require a taxpayer to pay a tax by electronic funds transfer unless, during the applicable period for that tax, the average amount of the taxpayer's required payments of the tax was at least twenty thousand dollars ($20,000) a month. The twenty thousand dollar ($20,000) threshold applies separately to each tax. The applicable period for a tax is a 12-month period, designated by the Secretary, preceding the imposition or review of the payment requirement. The requirement that a taxpayer pay a tax by electronic funds transfer remains in effect until suspended by the Secretary. Every 12 months after requiring a taxpayer to pay a tax by electronic funds transfer, the Secretary must determine whether, during the applicable period for that tax, the average amount of the taxpayer's required payments of the tax was at least twenty thousand dollars ($20,000) a month. If it was not, the Secretary must suspend the requirement that the taxpayer pay the tax by electronic funds transfer and must notify the taxpayer in writing that the requirement has been suspended.

(c) Tax Period. - Except as otherwise provided in this Chapter, taxes are levied for the fiscal year of the state in which they became due.

(d) Lien. - This subsection applies except when another Article of this Chapter contains contrary provisions with respect to a lien for a tax levied in that Article. The lien of a tax attaches to all real and personal property of a taxpayer on the date a tax owed by the taxpayer becomes due. The lien continues until the tax and any interest, penalty, and costs associated with the tax are paid. A tax lien is not extinguished by the sale of the taxpayer's property. A tax lien, however, is not enforceable against a bona fide purchaser for value or the holder of a duly recorded lien unless:

(1) In the case of real property, a certificate of tax liability or a judgment was first docketed in the office of the clerk of superior court of the county in which the real property is located.

(2) In the case of personal property, there has already been a levy on the property under an execution or a tax warrant.

The priority of these claims and liens is determined by the date and time of recording, docketing, levy, or bona fide purchase.

If a taxpayer executes an assignment for the benefit of creditors or if insolvency proceedings are instituted against a taxpayer who owes a tax, the tax lien attaches to all real and personal property of the taxpayer as of the date and time the taxpayer executes the assignment for the benefit of creditors or the date and time the insolvency proceedings are instituted. In these cases, the tax lien is subject only to a prior recorded specific lien and the reasonable costs of administering the assignment or the insolvency proceedings. (1939, c. 158, s. 912; 1949, c. 392, s. 6; 1957, c. 1340, s. 5; 1993, c. 450, s. 2; 1999-389, s. 8; 2001-427, s. 6(b); 2005-435, s. 2; 2007-527, s. 31; 2010-95, s. 25; 2012-79, s. 2.15.)

§ 105-241.1: Repealed by Session Laws 2007-491, s. 2, effective January 1, 2008.

§ 105-241.2: Repealed by Session Laws 2007-491, s. 2, effective January 1, 2008.

§ 105-241.3: Repealed by Session Laws 2007-491, s. 2, effective January 1, 2008.

§ 105-241.4: Repealed by Session Laws 2007-491, s. 2, effective January 1, 2008.

§ 105-241.5: Repealed by Session Laws 2007-491, s. 2, effective January 1, 2008.

§ 105-241.6. Statute of limitations for refunds.

(a)   General. - The general statute of limitations for obtaining a refund of an overpayment applies unless a different period applies under subsection (b) of this section. The general statute of limitations for obtaining a refund of an overpayment is the later of the following:

(1)   Three years after the due date of the return.

(2)   Two years after payment of the tax.

(b)   Exceptions. - The exceptions to the general statute of limitations for obtaining a refund of an overpayment are as follows:

(1)   Federal Determination. - If a taxpayer files a return reflecting a federal determination and the return is filed within the time required by this Subchapter,

the period for requesting a refund is one year after the return reflecting the federal determination is filed or three years after the original return was filed or due to be filed, whichever is later.

(2)   Waiver. - A taxpayer's waiver of the statute of limitations for making a proposed assessment extends the period in which the taxpayer can obtain a refund to the end of the period extended by the waiver.

(3)   Worthless Debts or Securities. - Section 6511(d)(1) of the Code applies to an overpayment of the tax levied in Part 2 or 3 of Article 4 of this Chapter to the extent the overpayment is attributable to either of the following:

a.   The deductibility by the taxpayer under section 166 of the Code of a debt that becomes worthless, or under section 165(g) of the Code of a loss from a security that becomes worthless.

b.   The effect of the deductibility of a debt or loss described in subpart a. of this subdivision on the application of a carryover to the taxpayer.

(4)   Capital Loss and Net Operating Loss Carrybacks. - Section 6511(d)(2) of the Code applies to an overpayment of the tax levied in Part 2 or 3 of Article 4 of this Chapter to the extent the overpayment is attributable to a capital loss carryback under section 1212(c) of the Code or to a net operating loss carryback under section 172 of the Code.

(5)   (Effective January 1, 2014) Contingent Event. -

a.   If a taxpayer is subject to a contingent event and files notice with the Secretary, the period to request a refund of an overpayment is six months after the contingent event concludes.

b.   For purposes of this subdivision, "contingent event" means litigation or a State tax audit initiated prior to the expiration of the statute of limitations under subsection (a) of this section, the pendency of which prevents the taxpayer from possessing the information necessary to file an accurate and definite request for a refund of an overpayment under this Chapter.

c.   For purposes of this subdivision, "notice to the Secretary" means written notice filed with the Secretary prior to expiration of the statute of limitations under subsection (a) of this section for a return or payment in which a contingent event prevents a taxpayer from filing a definite request for a refund of an overpayment. The notice must identify and describe the contingent event, identify the type of tax, list the return or payment affected by the contingent event, and state in clear terms the basis for and an estimated amount of the overpayment.

d.   A taxpayer who contends that an event or condition other than litigation or a State tax audit has occurred that prevents the taxpayer from filing an accurate and definite request for a refund of an overpayment within the period under subsection (a) of this section may submit a written request to the Secretary seeking an extension of the statute of limitations allowed under this subdivision. The request must establish by clear, convincing proof that the event or condition is beyond the taxpayer's control and that it prevents the taxpayer's timely filing of an accurate and definite request for a refund of an overpayment. The request must be filed within the period under subsection (a) of this section. The Secretary's decision on the request is final and is not subject to administrative or judicial review. (2007-491, s. 1; 2013-414, s. 47(a).)

§ 105-241.7. Procedure for obtaining a refund.

(a)   Initiated by Department. - The Department must refund an overpayment made by a taxpayer if the Department discovers the overpayment before the expiration of the statute of limitations for obtaining a refund. Discovery occurs in any of the following circumstances:

(1)   The automated processing of a return indicates the return requires further review.

(2)   A review of a return by an employee of the Department indicates an overpayment.

(3)   An audit of a taxpayer by an employee of the Department indicates an overpayment.

(b)   (Effective until January 1, 2014) Initiated by Taxpayer. - A taxpayer may request a refund of an overpayment made by the taxpayer by taking one of the following actions within the statute of limitations for obtaining a refund:

(1)   Filing an amended return reflecting an overpayment due the taxpayer.

(2) Filing a claim for refund. The claim must identify the taxpayer, the type and amount of tax overpaid, the filing period to which the overpayment applies, and the basis for the claim. The taxpayer's statement of the basis of the claim does not limit the taxpayer from changing the basis.

(b) (Effective January 1, 2014) Initiated by Taxpayer. - A taxpayer may request a refund of an overpayment made by the taxpayer by taking one of the actions listed in this subsection within the statute of limitations for obtaining a refund. A taxpayer may not request a refund of an overpayment based on a contingent event as defined in G.S. 105-241.6(b)(5) until the event is finalized and an accurate and definite request for refund of an overpayment may be determined. The actions are:

(1) Filing an amended return reflecting an overpayment due the taxpayer.

(2) Filing a claim for refund. The claim must identify the taxpayer, the type and amount of tax overpaid, the filing period to which the overpayment applies, and the basis for the claim. The taxpayer's statement of the basis of the claim does not limit the taxpayer from changing the basis.

(c) Action on Request. - When a taxpayer files an amended return or a claim for refund, the Department must take one of the actions listed in this subsection within six months after the date the amended return or claim for refund is filed. If the Department does not take one of these actions within this time limit, the inaction is considered a proposed denial of the requested refund.

(1) Send the taxpayer a refund of the amount shown due on the amended return or claim for refund.

(2) Adjust the amount of the requested refund by increasing or decreasing the amount shown due on the amended return or claim for refund and send the taxpayer a refund of the adjusted amount. If the adjusted amount is less than the amount shown due on the amended return or claim for refund, the adjusted refund must include a reason for the adjustment. The adjusted refund is considered a notice of proposed denial for the amount of the requested refund that is not included in the adjusted refund.

(3) Deny the refund and send the taxpayer a notice of proposed denial.

(4) Send the taxpayer a letter requesting additional information concerning the requested refund. If a taxpayer does not respond to a request for

information, the Department may deny the refund and send the taxpayer a notice of proposed denial. If a taxpayer provides the requested information, the Department must take one of the actions listed in this subsection within the later of the following:

 a. The remainder of the six-month period.

 b. 30 days after receiving the information.

 c. A time period mutually agreed upon by the Department and the taxpayer.

(d) Notice. - A notice of a proposed denial of a request for refund must contain the following information:

(1) The basis for the proposed denial. The statement of the basis of the denial does not limit the Department from changing the basis.

(2) The circumstances under which the proposed denial will become final.

(e) Restrictions. - The Department may not refund any of the following:

(1) Until a taxpayer files a final return for a tax period, an amount paid before the final return is filed.

(2) An overpayment setoff under Chapter 105A, the Setoff Debt Collection Act, or under another setoff debt collection program authorized by law.

(3) An income tax overpayment the taxpayer has elected to apply to another purpose as provided in this Article.

(4) An individual income tax overpayment of less than one dollar ($1.00) or another tax overpayment of less than three dollars ($3.00), unless the taxpayer files a written claim for the refund.

(f) Effect of Denial or Refund. - A proposed denial of a refund by the Secretary is presumed to be correct. A refund does not absolve a taxpayer of a tax liability that may in fact exist. The Secretary may propose an assessment for any deficiency as provided in this Article. (2007-491, s. 1; 2011-4, s. 1; 2013-414, s. 47(b).)

§ 105-241.8. Statute of limitations for assessments.

(a) General. - The general statute of limitations for proposing an assessment applies unless a different period applies under subsection (b) of this section. The general statute of limitations for proposing an assessment is the later of the following:

(1) Three years after the due date of the return.

(2) Three years after the taxpayer filed the return.

(b) Exceptions. - The exceptions to the general statute of limitations for proposing an assessment are as follows:

(1) Federal determination. - If a taxpayer files a return reflecting a federal determination and the return is filed within the time required by this Subchapter, the period for proposing an assessment of any tax due is one year after the return is filed or three years after the original return was filed or due to be filed, whichever is later. If there is a federal determination and the taxpayer does not file the return within the required time, the period for proposing an assessment of any tax due is three years after the date the Secretary received the final report of the federal determination.

(2) Failure to file or filing false return. - There is no statute of limitations and the Secretary may propose an assessment of tax due from a taxpayer at any time if any of the following applies:

a. The taxpayer did not file a return.

b. The taxpayer filed a fraudulent return.

c. The taxpayer attempted in any manner to fraudulently evade or defeat the tax.

(3) Tax forfeiture. - If a taxpayer forfeits a tax credit or tax benefit pursuant to forfeiture provisions of this Chapter, the period for proposing an assessment of any tax due as a result of the forfeiture is three years after the date of the forfeiture.

(4) Nonrecognition of gain. - If a taxpayer elects under section 1033(a)(2)(A) of the Code not to recognize gain from involuntary conversion of

property into money, the period for proposing an assessment of any tax due as a result of the conversion or election is the applicable period provided under section 1033(a)(2)(C) or section 1033(a)(2)(D) of the Code. (2007-491, s. 1.)

§ 105-241.9. Procedure for proposing an assessment.

(a) Authority. - The Secretary may propose an assessment against a taxpayer for tax due from the taxpayer. The Secretary must base a proposed assessment on the best information available. A proposed assessment of the Secretary is presumed to be correct.

(b) Time Limit. - The Secretary must propose an assessment within the statute of limitations for proposed assessments unless the taxpayer waives the limitations period before it expires by agreeing in writing to extend the period. A taxpayer may waive the limitations period for either a definite or an indefinite time. If the taxpayer waives the limitations period, the Secretary may propose an assessment at any time within the time extended by the waiver.

(c) Notice. - The Secretary must give a taxpayer written notice of a proposed assessment. The notice of a proposed assessment must contain the following information:

(1) The basis for the proposed assessment. The statement of the basis for the proposed assessment does not limit the Department from changing the basis.

(2) The amount of tax, interest, and penalties included in the proposed assessment. The amount for each of these must be stated separately.

(2a) The date a failure to pay penalty will apply to the proposed assessment if the proposed assessment is not paid by that date and the amount of the penalty. If the proposed assessment is not paid by the specified date, the failure to pay penalty is considered to be assessed and applies to the proposed assessment without further notice.

(3) The circumstances under which the proposed assessment will become final and collectible. (2007-491, s. 1; 2010-95, s. 8(a); 2011-330, s. 34.)

§ 105-241.10. Limit on refunds and assessments after a federal determination.

The limitations in this section apply when a taxpayer files a timely return reflecting a federal determination that affects the amount of State tax payable and the general statute of limitations for requesting a refund or proposing an assessment of the State tax has expired. A federal determination is a correction or final determination by the federal government of the amount of a federal tax due. A return reflecting a federal determination is timely if it is filed within the time required by G.S. 105-130.20, 105-159, 105-160.8, or 105-163.6A, as appropriate. The limitations are:

(1)   Refund. - A taxpayer is allowed a refund only if the refund is the result of adjustments related to the federal determination.

(2)   Assessment. - A taxpayer is liable for additional tax only if the additional tax is the result of adjustments related to the federal determination. A proposed assessment may not include an amount that is outside the scope of this liability. (2007-491, s. 1; 2008-107, s. 28.18(d); 2013-316, s. 7(b).)

§ 105-241.11. Requesting review of proposed denial of refund or proposed assessment.

(a)   Procedure. - A taxpayer who objects to a proposed denial of a refund or a proposed assessment of tax may request a Departmental review of the proposed action by filing a request for review. The request must be filed with the Department as follows:

(1)   Within 45 days of the date the notice of the proposed denial of the refund or proposed assessment was mailed to the taxpayer, if the notice was delivered by mail.

(2)   Within 45 days of the date the notice of the proposed denial of the refund or proposed assessment was delivered to the taxpayer, if the notice was delivered in person.

(3)   At any time between the date that inaction by the Department on a request for refund is considered a proposed denial of the refund and the date the time periods set in the other subdivisions of this subsection expire.

(b) Filing. - A request for a Departmental review of a proposed denial of a refund or a proposed assessment is considered filed on the following dates:

(1) For a request that is delivered in person, the date it is delivered.

(2) For a request that is mailed, the date determined in accordance with G.S. 105-263.

(3) For a request delivered by another method, the date the Department receives it.

(c) FTP Penalty. - A request for a Departmental review of a proposed assessment is considered a request for a Departmental review of a failure to pay penalty that is based on the assessment. A taxpayer who does not request a Departmental review of a proposed assessment may not request a Departmental review of a failure to pay penalty that is based on the assessment. (2007-491, s. 1; 2008-134, s. 5(a); 2010-95, ss. 8(b), 10(b).)

§ 105-241.12. Result when taxpayer does not request a review.

(a) Refund. - If a taxpayer does not file a timely request for a Departmental review of a proposed denial of a refund, the proposed denial is final and is not subject to further administrative or judicial review. A taxpayer whose proposed denial becomes final may not file another amended return or claim for refund to obtain the denied refund.

(b) Assessment. - If a taxpayer does not file a timely request for a Departmental review of a proposed assessment, the proposed assessment is final and is not subject to further administrative or judicial review. Upon payment of the tax, the taxpayer may request a refund of the tax.

Before the Department collects a proposed assessment that becomes final when the taxpayer does not file a timely request for a Departmental review, the Department must send the taxpayer a notice of collection. A notice of collection must contain the following information:

(1) A statement that the proposed assessment is final and collectible.

(2) The amount of tax, interest, and penalties payable by the taxpayer.

(3) An explanation of the collection options available to the Department if the taxpayer does not pay the amount shown due on the notice and any remedies available to the taxpayer concerning these collection options. (2007-491, s. 1.)

§ 105-241.13. Action on request for review.

(a) Action on Request. - If a taxpayer files a timely request for a Departmental review of a proposed denial of a refund or a proposed assessment, the Department must conduct a review of the proposed denial or proposed assessment and take one of the following actions:

(1) Grant the refund or remove the assessment.

(2) Schedule a conference with the taxpayer.

(3) Request additional information from the taxpayer concerning the requested refund or proposed assessment.

(b) Conference. - When the Department reviews a proposed denial of a refund or a proposed assessment and does not grant the refund or remove the assessment, the Department must schedule a conference with the taxpayer. The Department must set the time and place for the conference, which may include a conference by telephone, and must send the taxpayer notice of the designated time and place. The Department must send the notice at least 30 days before the date of the conference or, if the Department and the taxpayer agree, within a shorter period.

The conference is an informal proceeding at which the taxpayer and the Department must attempt to resolve the case. Testimony under oath is not taken, and the rules of evidence do not apply. A taxpayer may designate a representative to act on the taxpayer's behalf. The taxpayer may present any objections to the proposed denial of refund or proposed assessment at the conference.

(c) After Conference. - One of the following must occur after the Department conducts a conference on a proposed denial of a refund or a proposed assessment:

(1) The Department and the taxpayer agree on a settlement.

(2) The Department and the taxpayer agree that additional time is needed to resolve the taxpayer's objection to the proposed denial of the refund or proposed assessment.

(3) The Department and the taxpayer are unable to resolve the taxpayer's objection to the proposed denial of the refund or proposed assessment. If a taxpayer fails to attend a scheduled conference on the proposed denial of a refund or a proposed assessment without prior notice to the Department, the Department and the taxpayer are considered to be unable to resolve the taxpayer's objection. (2007-491, s. 1.)

§ 105-241.14. Final determination after Departmental review.

(a) Refund. - If a taxpayer files a timely request for a Departmental review of a proposed denial of a refund and the Department and the taxpayer are unable to resolve the taxpayer's objection to the proposed denial, the Department must send the taxpayer a notice of final determination concerning the refund. The notice of final determination must state the basis for the determination and inform the taxpayer of the procedure for contesting the determination. The statement of the basis for the determination does not limit the Department from changing the basis.

(b) Assessment. - If a taxpayer files a timely request for a Departmental review of a proposed assessment and the Department and the taxpayer are unable to resolve the taxpayer's objection to the proposed assessment, the Department must send the taxpayer a notice of final determination concerning the assessment. A notice of final determination concerning an assessment must contain the following information:

(1) The basis for the determination. This information may be stated on the notice or be set out in a separate document. The statement of the basis for the determination does not limit the Department from changing the basis.

(2) The amount of tax, interest, and penalties payable by the taxpayer.

(3) The procedure the taxpayer must follow to contest the final determination.

(4)   A statement that the amount payable stated on the notice is collectible by the Department unless the taxpayer contests the final determination.

(5)   An explanation of the collection options available to the Department if the taxpayer does not pay the amount shown due on the notice and any remedies available to the taxpayer concerning these collection options.

(c)   Time Limit. - The process set out in G.S. 105-241.13 for reviewing and attempting to resolve a proposed denial of a refund or a proposed assessment must conclude, and a final determination must be issued within nine months after the date the taxpayer files a request for review. The Department and the taxpayer may extend this time limit by mutual agreement. Failure to issue a notice of final determination within the required time does not affect the validity of a proposed denial of a refund or proposed assessment. (2007-491, s. 1; 2008-134, s. 6(a).)

§ 105-241.15. Contested case hearing on final determination.

A taxpayer who disagrees with a notice of final determination issued by the Department may contest the determination by filing a petition for a contested case hearing at the Office of Administrative Hearings in accordance with Article 3 of Chapter 150B of the General Statutes. A taxpayer may file a petition for a contested case hearing only if the taxpayer has exhausted the prehearing remedy. A taxpayer's prehearing remedy is exhausted when the Department issues a final determination after conducting a review and a conference. (2007-491, s. 1.)

§ 105-241.16. Judicial review of decision after contested case hearing.

A taxpayer aggrieved by the final decision in a contested case commenced at the Office of Administrative Hearings may seek judicial review of the decision in accordance with Article 4 of Chapter 150B of the General Statutes. Notwithstanding G.S. 150B-45, a petition for judicial review must be filed in the Superior Court of Wake County and in accordance with the procedures for a mandatory business case set forth in G.S. 7A-45.4(b) through (f). Before filing a petition for judicial review, a taxpayer must pay the amount of tax, penalties, and interest the final decision states is due. A taxpayer may appeal a decision of the

Business Court to the appellate division in accordance with G.S. 150B-52. (2007-491, s. 1; 2010-95, s. 9.)

§ 105-241.17. Civil action challenging statute as unconstitutional.

A taxpayer who claims that a tax statute is unconstitutional may bring a civil action in the Superior Court of Wake County to determine the taxpayer's liability under that statute if all of the conditions in this section are met. In filing an action under this section, a taxpayer must follow the procedures for a mandatory business case set forth in G.S. 7A-45.4(b) through (f). The conditions for filing a civil action are:

(1) The taxpayer exhausted the prehearing remedy by receiving a final determination after a review and a conference.

(2) The taxpayer commenced a contested case at the Office of Administrative Hearings.

(3) The Office of Administrative Hearings dismissed the contested case petition for lack of jurisdiction because the sole issue is the constitutionality of a statute and not the application of a statute.

(4) The taxpayer has paid the amount of tax, penalties, and interest the final determination states is due.

(5) The civil action is filed within two years of the dismissal. (2007-491, s. 1.)

§ 105-241.18. Class actions.

(a) Authority. - A class action against the State for the refund of a tax paid may be maintained only on the grounds of an alleged unconstitutional statute and only if the requirements of Rule 23 of the North Carolina Rules of Civil Procedure and the requirements of this section are met. For purposes of this section, a class action commences upon the later of the following:

(1) The date a complaint is filed in accordance with G.S. 105-241.17 alleging the existence of a class pursuant to Rule 23 of the North Carolina Rules of Civil Procedure.

(2) The date a complaint filed in accordance with G.S. 105-241.17 is amended to allege the existence of a class.

(b) Class. - To serve as a class representative of a class action brought under this section, a taxpayer must comply with all of the conditions in G.S. 105-241.17 and the taxpayer's claims must be typical of the claims of the class members. A taxpayer who is not a class representative is eligible to become a member of a class if the taxpayer could have filed a claim for refund under G.S. 105-241.7 as of the date the class action commenced or as of a subsequent date set by the court, whether or not the taxpayer actually filed a claim for refund as of that date. An eligible class member who is not a class representative and who indicates a desire to be included in the class in accordance with the procedure approved by the court under subsection (c) of this section is not required to follow the procedures in G.S. 105-241.11 through G.S. 105-241.17 for the administrative and judicial review of a request for refund or a proposed denial of a request for refund.

(c) Procedure. - To become a member of a class action brought under this section, an eligible taxpayer must affirmatively indicate a desire to be included in the class in response to a notice of the class action. If the court so orders, the Department must provide to a class representative a list of names and last known addresses of all taxpayers who are readily determinable by the Department and who are eligible to become a member of the class. The court must approve the content of a notice of a class action, the method for distributing the notice, and the procedure by which an eligible taxpayer affirmatively indicates a desire to be included in the class. The class representative must advance the costs of notifying eligible taxpayers of the class action.

(d) Statute of Limitations. - The statute of limitations for filing a claim for refund of tax paid due to an alleged unconstitutional statute is tolled for a taxpayer who is eligible to become a member of a class action. The tolling begins on the date the class action is commenced. For a taxpayer who does not join the class, the tolling ends when the taxpayer does not affirmatively indicate a desire to be included in the class within the time and in accordance with the procedure approved by the court under subsection (c) of this section. For a taxpayer who joins the class, the tolling ends when a court enters any of the following in the class action:

(1) A final order denying certification of the class.

(2) A final order decertifying the class.

(3) A final order dismissing the class action without an adjudication on the merits.

(4) A final judgment on the merits.

(e) Effect on Nonparticipating Taxpayers. - A taxpayer who does not become a member of a class may file and prosecute a claim for refund, if the statute of limitations has not otherwise expired for filing the claim, or may contest a pending assessment in accordance with the procedures in G.S. 105-241.11 through G.S. 105-241.17. Except as otherwise provided in this subsection, the effect of an adjudication in a class action on a nonparticipating taxpayer's claim for refund or contest of an assessment is governed by the normal rules relating to claim preclusion and issue preclusion.

If a final judgment on the merits is entered in a class action in favor of the class, the following applies to an eligible taxpayer who did not become a member of the class:

(1) The taxpayer is not entitled to receive any monetary relief awarded to the class on account of taxes previously paid by the taxpayer.

(2) If the taxpayer has been assessed for failure to pay the tax at issue in the class action and the taxpayer has not paid the assessment, then the assessment is abated.

(3) The taxpayer is relieved of any future liability for the tax that is the subject of the class action. (2008-107, s. 28.28(b).)

§ 105-241.19. Declaratory judgments, injunctions, and other actions prohibited.

The remedies in G.S. 105-241.11 through G.S. 105-241.18 set out the exclusive remedies for disputing the denial of a requested refund, a taxpayer's liability for a tax, or the constitutionality of a tax statute. Any other action is barred. Neither an action for declaratory judgment, an action for an injunction to prevent the collection of a tax, nor any other action is allowed. (2007-491, s. 1; 2008-107, s. 28.28(c).)

§ 105-241.20. Delivery of notice to the taxpayer.

(a) Scope. - This section applies to the following notices:

(1) A proposed denial of a refund.

(2) A proposed assessment.

(3) A notice of collection.

(4) A final determination.

(b) Method. - The Secretary must deliver a notice listed in subsection (a) of this section to a taxpayer either in person or by United States mail sent to the taxpayer's last known address. A notice mailed to a taxpayer is presumed to have been received by the taxpayer unless the taxpayer makes an affidavit to the contrary within 90 days after the notice was mailed. If the taxpayer makes this affidavit, the notice is considered to have been delivered on the date the taxpayer makes the affidavit, and any time limit affected by the notice is extended to the date the taxpayer makes the affidavit. (2007-491, s. 1.)

§ 105-241.21. Interest on taxes.

(a) Rate. - The interest rate set by the Secretary applies to interest that accrues on overpayments and assessments of tax. On or before June 1 and December 1 of each year, the Secretary must establish the interest rate to be in effect during the six-month period beginning on the next succeeding July 1 and January 1, respectively. In determining the interest rate, the Secretary must give due consideration to current market conditions and to the rate that will be in effect on that date pursuant to the Code. If no new rate is established, the rate in effect during the preceding six-month period continues in effect. The rate established by the Secretary may not be less than five percent (5%) per year and may not exceed sixteen percent (16%) per year.

(b) Accrual on Underpayments. - Interest accrues on an underpayment of tax from the date set by statute for payment of the tax until the tax is paid. Interest accrues only on the principal of the tax and does not accrue on any penalty.

(c) Accrual on Refund. - Interest accrues on an overpayment of tax from the time set in the following subdivisions until the refund is paid.

(1) Franchise, income, and gross premiums. - Interest on an overpayment of a tax levied under Article 3 of this Chapter and payable on an annual basis or of a tax levied under Article 4 or 8B of this Chapter accrues from a date 45 days after the latest of the following dates:

a. The date the final return was filed.

b. The date the final return was due to be filed.

c. The date of the overpayment. The date of an overpayment of a tax levied under Article 4 or Article 8B of this Chapter is determined in accordance with section 6611(d), (f), (g), and (h) of the Code.

(2) All other taxes. - Interest on an overpayment of a tax that is not included in subdivision (1) of this subsection accrues from a date that is 90 days after the date the tax was paid.

(d) When Refund Is Paid. - A refund sent to a taxpayer is considered paid on a date determined by the Secretary that is no sooner than five days after a refund check is mailed. A refund set off against a debt pursuant to Chapter 105A of the General Statutes is considered paid five days after the Department mails the taxpayer a notice of the setoff, unless G.S. 105A-5 or G.S. 105A-8 requires the agency that requested the setoff to return the refund to the taxpayer. In this circumstance, the refund that was set off is not considered paid until five days after the agency that requested the refund mails the taxpayer a check for the refund. (2007-491, s. 1.)

§ 105-241.22. Collection of tax.

The Department may collect a tax in the following circumstances:

(1) When a taxpayer files a return showing an amount due with the return and does not pay the amount shown due. This subdivision does not apply to a consolidated or combined return filed at the request of the Secretary under Part 1 of Article 4 of this Chapter.

(2) When the Department sends a notice of collection after a taxpayer does not file a timely request for a Departmental review of a proposed assessment of tax.

(3) When a taxpayer and the Department agree on a settlement concerning the amount of tax due.

(4) When the Department sends a notice of final determination concerning an assessment of tax and the taxpayer does not file a timely petition for a contested case hearing on the assessment.

(5) When a final decision is issued on a proposed assessment of tax after a contested case hearing.

(6) When the Office of Administrative Hearings dismisses a petition for a contested case for lack of jurisdiction because the sole issue is the constitutionality of a statute and not the application of a statute. (2007-491, s. 1; 2008-134, s. 7(a); 2010-31, s. 31.10(c).)

§ 105-241.23. Jeopardy assessment and collection.

(a) Action. - The Secretary may at any time within the statute of limitations immediately assess and collect any tax the Secretary finds is due from a taxpayer if the Secretary determines that collection of the tax is in jeopardy and immediate assessment and collection are necessary in order to protect the interest of the State. In making a jeopardy collection, the Secretary may use any of the collection remedies in G.S. 105-242 and is not required to wait any period of time before using these remedies. Within 30 days after initiating a jeopardy collection, the Secretary must give the taxpayer the notice of proposed assessment required by G.S. 105-241.9.

(b) Review by Department. - Within five days after initiating a jeopardy collection that is not the result of a criminal investigation or of a liability for a tax imposed under Article 2D of this Chapter, the Secretary must provide the taxpayer with a written statement of the information upon which the Secretary relied in initiating the jeopardy collection. Within 30 days after receipt of this written statement or, if no statement is received, within 30 days after the statement was due, the taxpayer may request the Secretary to review the action taken. After receipt of this request, the Secretary must determine whether initiating the jeopardy collection was reasonable under all the circumstances and whether the amount assessed and collected was reasonable under all the circumstances. The Secretary must give the taxpayer written notice of this determination within 30 days after the request.

(c) Judicial Review. - Within 90 days after the earlier of the date a taxpayer received or should have received a determination of the Secretary concerning a jeopardy collection under subsection (b) of this section, the taxpayer may bring a civil action seeking review of the jeopardy collection. The taxpayer may bring the action in the Superior Court of Wake County or in the county in North Carolina in which the taxpayer resides. Within 20 days after the action is filed, the court must determine whether the initiation of the jeopardy collection was reasonable under the circumstances. If the court determines that an action of the Secretary was unreasonable or inappropriate, the court may order the Secretary to take any action the court finds appropriate. If the taxpayer shows reasonable grounds why the 20-day limit on the court should be extended, the court may grant an extension of not more than 40 additional days. (2007-491, s. 1.)

§ 105-242. Warrants for collection of taxes; garnishment and attachment; certificate or judgment for taxes.

(a) Levy and Sale. - If a taxpayer does not pay a tax within 30 days after it is collectible under G.S. 105-241.22, the Secretary may take either of the following actions to collect the tax:

(1) Issue a warrant directing the sheriff of any county of the State to levy upon and sell the real and personal property of the taxpayer found within the county for the payment of the tax and the cost of executing the warrant and to return to the Secretary the money collected, within a time to be specified in the warrant but not less than 60 days from the date of the warrant. The procedure for executions issued against property upon judgments of a court apply to executions under a warrant.

(2) Issue a warrant to any revenue officer or other employee of the Department charged with the duty to collect taxes, commanding the officer or employee to levy upon and sell the taxpayer's personal property found within the State for the payment of the tax. Except as otherwise provided in this subdivision, the levy upon and sale of personal property by an officer or

employee of the Department is subject to and must be conducted in accordance with the laws governing the sale of property levied upon under execution. The Secretary may sell the property levied upon in any county and may advertise the sale in any reasonable manner and for any reasonable period of time to produce an adequate bid for the property. Levy and sale fees, plus actual advertising costs, must be added to and collected in the same manner as taxes. The Secretary is not required to file a report of sale with the clerk of superior court, if the sale is otherwise publicly reported.

(b) Attachment and Garnishment. - Intangible property that belongs to a taxpayer, is owed to a taxpayer, or has been transferred by a taxpayer under circumstances that would permit it to be levied upon if it were tangible property is subject to attachment and garnishment in payment of a tax that is due from the taxpayer and is collectible under G.S. 105-241.22. Intangible personal property includes bank deposits, rent, salaries, wages, property held in the Escheat Fund, and any other property incapable of manual levy or delivery. G.S. 105-242.1 sets out the procedure for attachment and garnishment of intangible property.

A person who is in possession of intangible property that is subject to attachment and garnishment is the garnishee and is liable for the amount the taxpayer owes. The liability applies only to the amount of the taxpayer's property in the garnishee's possession, reduced by any amount the taxpayer owes the garnishee.

The Secretary may submit to a financial institution, as defined in G.S. 53B-2, information that identifies a taxpayer who owes a tax debt that is collectible under G.S. 105-241.22 and the amount of the debt. The Secretary may submit the information on a quarterly basis or, with the agreement of the financial institution, on a more frequent basis. A financial institution that receives the information must determine the amount, if any, of intangible property it holds that belongs to the taxpayer and must inform the Secretary of its determination. The Secretary must reimburse a financial institution for its costs in providing the information, not to exceed the amount payable to the financial institution under G.S. 110-139 for providing information for use in locating a noncustodial parent.

No more than ten percent (10%) of a taxpayer's wages or salary is subject to attachment and garnishment. The wages or salary of an employee of the United States, the State, or a political subdivision of the State are subject to attachment and garnishment.

(c) Certificate of Tax Liability. - The Department may file a certificate of tax liability to collect a tax that is owed by a taxpayer and is collectible under G.S. 105-241.22. A certificate of tax liability must state the taxpayer's name and the type and amount of tax owed. If the taxpayer resides in this State or has property in this State, the Department must file the certificate of tax liability with the clerk of the superior court of a county in which the taxpayer resides or has property. If the taxpayer does not reside in this State or have property in this State, the Department must file the certificate of tax liability in Wake County.

The clerk of court must record a certificate of tax liability in the same manner as a judgment. A recorded certificate of tax liability is considered a judgment and is enforceable in the same manner as other judgments. The legal rate of interest set in G.S. 24-1 applies to the principal amount of tax stated on the certificate of tax liability. The tax stated on a certificate of tax liability is a lien on real and personal property from the date the certificate is recorded.

A certificate of tax liability is enforceable for a period of 10 years from the date it is recorded. If the certificate is not satisfied within this period, the remaining liability of the taxpayer is abated and the Department must cancel the certificate. An execution sale initiated before the end of the 10-year period may be completed after the end of this period, regardless of whether resales are required because of the posting of increased bids. The Secretary may accept tax payments made after a certificate has expired, regardless of whether any collection actions were taken before the certificate expired. A taxpayer may waive the 10-year period for enforcement of the certificate for either a definite or an indefinite time.

The 10-year period in which a certificate of tax liability is enforceable is tolled during the following periods:

(1) While the taxpayer is absent from the State. The period is tolled during the taxpayer's absence plus one year after the taxpayer returns.

(2) Upon the death of the taxpayer. The period is tolled while the taxpayer's estate is administered plus one year after the estate is closed.

(3) While an action is pending to set aside a conveyance made by the taxpayer as a fraudulent conveyance.

(4) While an insolvency proceeding against the taxpayer is pending.

(5) During the period of any statutory or judicial bar to the enforcement of the certificate.

(6) The period for which a taxpayer has waived the 10-year period.

(c1) Release of Lien. - The Secretary shall release the State tax lien on a taxpayer's property if the liability for which the lien attached has been satisfied. The Secretary may release the State tax lien on all or part of a taxpayer's property if one or more of the following findings is made:

(1) The liability for which the lien attached has become unenforceable due to lapse of time.

(2) The lien is creating an economic hardship due to the financial condition of the taxpayer.

(3) The fair market value of the property exceeds the tax liability and release of the lien on part of the property would not hinder collection of the liability.

(4) Release of the lien will probably facilitate, expedite, or enhance the State's chances for ultimately collecting a tax due the State.

If the Secretary of Revenue shall find that it will be for the best interest of the State in that it will probably facilitate, expedite or enhance the State's chances for ultimately collecting a tax due the State, he may authorize a deputy or agent to release the lien of a State tax judgment or certificate of tax liability upon a specified parcel or parcels of real estate by noting such release upon the judgment docket where such certificate of tax liability is recorded. Such release shall be signed by the deputy or agent and witnessed by the clerk of court or his deputy or assistant and shall be in substantially the following form: "The lien of this judgment upon (insert here a short description of the property to be released sufficient to identify it, such as reference to a particular tract described in a recorded instrument) is hereby released, but this judgment shall continue in full force and effect as to other real property to which it has heretofore attached or may hereafter attach. This __ day of ___, ____

_____

Revenue Officer, N.C. Department of Revenue

WITNESS:

_____42
C.S.C."

The release shall be noted on the judgment docket only upon conditions prescribed by the Secretary and shall have effect only as to the real estate described therein and shall not affect any other rights of the State under said judgment.

(d)   Remedies Cumulative. - The remedies herein given are cumulative and in addition to all other remedies provided by law for the collection of said taxes.

(e)   Exempt Property. - Only the following property is exempt from levy, attachment, and garnishment under this Article:

(1)   The taxpayer's principal residence, unless the Secretary approves of the levy in writing or the Secretary finds that collection of the tax is in jeopardy.

(2)   Tangible personal property that is exempt from federal levy as provided in section 6334 of the Code.

(3)   Intangible personal property that is exempt from federal levy under section 6334 of the Code.

(4)   Ninety percent (90%) of the taxpayer's salary or wages per month.

(f)   Uneconomical Levy. - The Secretary shall not levy against any property if the Secretary estimates before levy that the expenses the Department would incur in levying against the property would exceed the fair market value of the property.

(g)   Erroneous Lien. - A taxpayer may appeal to the Secretary after a certificate is filed under subsection (c) of this section if the taxpayer alleges an error in the filing of the lien. The Secretary shall make a determination of such an appeal as quickly as possible. If the Secretary finds that the filing of the certificate was erroneous, the Secretary shall issue a certificate of release of the lien as quickly as possible. (1939, c. 158, s. 913; 1941, c. 50, s. 10; 1949, c. 392, s. 6; 1951, c. 643, s. 9; 1955, c. 1285; c. 1350, s. 23; 1957, c. 1340, s. 10;

1959, c. 368; 1963, c. 1169, s. 6; 1969, c. 1071, s. 1; 1973, c. 476, s. 193; c. 1287, s. 13; 1979, c. 103, ss. 1, 2; c. 179, s. 5; 1979, 2nd Sess., c. 1085, s. 1; 1989, c. 37, s. 6; c. 580; 1991, c. 228, s. 1; 1991 (Reg. Sess., 1992), c. 1007, ss. 12, 13; 1993, c. 532, s. 5; 1997-121, s. 1; 1999-456, s. 59; 2003-349, s. 2; 2007-491, ss. 28, 29, 31; 2010-31, s. 31.8(h).)

§ 105-242.1. Procedure for attachment and garnishment.

(a) Notice. - G.S. 105-242 specifies when intangible property is subject to attachment and garnishment. Before the Department attaches and garnishes intangible property in payment of a tax, the Department must send the garnishee a notice of garnishment. The notice must be sent in accordance with the methods authorized in G.S. 105-241.20 or, with the agreement of the garnishee, by electronic means. The notice must contain all of the following information, unless the notice is an electronic notice subject to subsection (a1) of this section:

(1) The taxpayer's name.

(2) The taxpayer's social security number or federal identification number.

(3) The amount of tax, interest, and penalties the taxpayer owes.

(4) An explanation of the liability of a garnishee for tax owed by a taxpayer.

(5) An explanation of the garnishee's responsibility concerning the notice.

(a1) Electronic Notice. - Before the Department sends an electronic notice of garnishment to a garnishee, the Department and the garnishee must have an agreement that establishes the protocol for transmitting the notice and provides the information required under subdivisions (4) and (5) of subsection (a) of this section. An electronic notice must contain the information required under subdivisions (1), (2), and (3) of subsection (a) of this section.

(b) Action. - A garnishee must comply with a notice of garnishment or file a written response to the notice within the time set in this subsection. A garnishee that is a financial institution must comply or file a response within 20 days after receiving a notice of garnishment. All other garnishees must comply or file a response within 30 days after receiving a notice of garnishment. A written response must explain why the garnishee is not subject to garnishment and attachment.

Upon receipt of a written response, the Department must contact the garnishee and schedule a conference to discuss the response or inform the garnishee of the Department's position concerning the response. If the Department does not agree with the garnishee on the garnishee's liability, the Department may proceed to enforce the garnishee's liability for the tax by sending the garnishee a notice of proposed assessment in accordance with G.S. 105-241.9.

(c) Release. - A notice of garnishment sent to a financial institution is released when the financial institution complies with the notice. A notice of garnishment sent to all other garnishees is released when the Department sends the garnishee a notice of release. A notice of release must state the name and social security number or federal identification number of the taxpayer to whom the release applies.

(d) Financial Institution. - As used in this section, the term "financial institution" has the same meaning as in G.S. 53B-2. (2007-491, s. 30; 2010-31, s. 31.8(i).)

§ 105-242.2. Personal liability when certain taxes not paid.

(a) Definitions. - The following definitions apply in this section:

(1) Business entity. - A corporation, a limited liability company, or a partnership.

(2) Responsible person. - Any of the following:

a. The president, treasurer, or chief financial officer of a corporation.

b. A manager of a limited liability company or a partnership.

c. An officer of a corporation, a member of a limited liability company, or a partner in a partnership who has a duty to deduct, account for, or pay taxes listed in subsection (b) of this section.

d. A partner who is liable for the debts and obligations of a partnership under G.S. 59-45 or G.S. 59-403.

(b) Responsible Person. - Each responsible person in a business entity is personally and individually liable for the principal amount of taxes that are owed by the business entity and are listed in this subsection. If a business entity does not pay the amount it owes after the amount becomes collectible under G.S. 105-241.22, the Secretary may enforce the responsible person's liability for the amount by sending the responsible person a notice of proposed assessment in accordance with G.S. 105-241.9. This subsection applies to the following:

(1) All sales and use taxes collected by the business entity upon its taxable transactions.

(2) All sales and use taxes due upon taxable transactions of the business entity but upon which it failed to collect the tax, but only if the person knew, or in the exercise of reasonable care should have known, that the tax was not being collected.

(3) All taxes due from the business entity pursuant to the provisions of Articles 36C and 36D of Subchapter V of this Chapter and all taxes payable under those Articles by it to a supplier for remittance to this State or another state.

(4) All income taxes required to be withheld from the wages of employees of the business entity.

(c) Repealed by Session Laws 1991 (Regular Session, 1992), c. 1007, s. 15.

(d) Distributions. - An officer, partner, trustee, or receiver of a business entity required to file a report with the Secretary who has custody of funds of the entity and who allows the funds to be paid out or distributed to the owners of the entity without having remitted to the Secretary any State taxes that are due is personally liable for the payment of the tax. The Secretary may enforce an individual's liability under this subsection by sending the individual a notice of proposed assessment in accordance with G.S. 105-241.9.

(e) Statute of Limitations. - The period of limitations for assessing a responsible person for unpaid taxes under this section expires one year after the expiration of the period of limitations for assessing the business entity.

(1939, c. 158, s. 923; 1941, c. 50, s. 10; 1955, c. 1350, s. 23; 1973, c. 476, s. 193; c. 1287, s. 13; 1983, c. 220, s. 1; 1991, c. 690, s. 7; 1991 (Reg. Sess., 1992), c. 1007, s. 15; 1995, c. 390, s. 15; 1995 (Reg. Sess., 1996), c. 647, s. 52; 1997-6, s. 9; 1998-212, s. 29A.14(p); 1999-337, s. 34; 2007-491, s. 34; 2008-134, s. 10(a); 2013-414, s. 56(a).)

§ 105-243. Taxes recoverable by action.

When requested by the Secretary, the Attorney General must bring an action to recover the amount of tax that is due from a taxpayer and is collectible under G.S. 105-241.22. In the action, the taxpayer may not challenge the liability for the tax. A judgment in the action has the same priority as a tax lien. The judgment is not subject to a claim for a homestead exemption. The action must be brought in one of the following:

(1) The Superior Court of Wake County.

(2) The taxpayer's county of residence.

(3) A county where the taxpayer owns real property.

(4) The county in which the taxpayer has its principal place of business.

(5) A court of competent jurisdiction of another state. (1939, c. 158, s. 914; 1973, c. 476, s. 193; 2007-491, s. 32.)

§ 105-243.1. Collection of tax debts.

(a) Definitions. - The following definitions apply in this section:

(1) Overdue tax debt. - Any part of a tax debt that remains unpaid 90 days or more after it becomes collectible under G.S. 105-241.22. The term does not include a tax debt for which the taxpayer entered into an installment agreement for the tax debt under G.S. 105-237 within 90 days after the tax debt became collectible, if the taxpayer has not failed to make any payments due under the installment agreement.

(2) Tax debt. - The total amount of tax, penalty, and interest collectible under G.S. 105-241.22.

(b)   Outsourcing. - The Secretary may contract for the collection of tax debts owed by nonresidents and foreign entities. At least 30 days before the Department submits a tax debt to a contractor for collection, the Department must notify the taxpayer by mail that the debt may be submitted for collection if payment is not received within 30 days after the notice was mailed.

(b1)   [Outsourcing Limitation. -] In determining the liability of any person for a tax, the Secretary may not employ an agent who is compensated in whole or in part by the State for services rendered on a contingent basis or any other basis related to the amount of tax, interest, or penalty assessed against or collected from the person.

(c)   Secrecy. - A contract for the collection of tax debts is conditioned on compliance with G.S. 105-259. If a contractor violates G.S. 105-259, the contract is terminated, and the Secretary must notify the contractor of the termination. A contractor whose contract is terminated for violation of G.S. 105-259 is not eligible for an award of another contract under this section for a period of five years from the termination. These sanctions are in addition to the criminal penalties set out in G.S. 105-259.

(d)   Fee. - A collection assistance fee is imposed on an overdue tax debt that remains unpaid 30 days or more after the fee notice required by this subsection is mailed to the taxpayer. In order to impose a collection assistance fee on a tax debt, the Department must notify the taxpayer that the fee will be imposed if the tax debt is not paid in full within 30 days after the date the fee notice was mailed to the taxpayer. The Department may not mail the fee notice earlier than 60 days after the tax debt becomes collectible under G.S. 105-241.22. The fee is collectible as part of the debt. The Secretary may waive the fee pursuant to G.S. 105-237 to the same extent as if it were a penalty.

The amount of the collection assistance fee is twenty percent (20%) of the amount of the overdue tax debt. If a taxpayer pays only part of an overdue tax debt, the payment is credited proportionally to fee revenue and tax revenue.

(e)   Use. - The fee is a receipt of the Department and must be applied to the costs of collecting overdue tax debts. The proceeds of the fee must be credited to a special account within the Department and may be expended only as provided in this subsection. The proceeds of the fee may not be used for any purpose that is not directly and primarily related to collecting overdue tax debts. The Department may apply the proceeds of the fee for the purposes listed in this subsection. The remaining proceeds of the fee may be spent only pursuant to appropriation by the General Assembly. The fee proceeds do not revert but remain in the special account until spent for the costs of collecting overdue tax debts. The Department and the Office of State Budget and Management must account for all expenditures using accounting procedures that clearly distinguish costs allocable to collecting overdue tax debts from costs allocable to other purposes and must demonstrate that none of the fee proceeds are used for any purpose other than collecting overdue tax debts.

The Department may apply the fee proceeds for the following purposes:

(1) To pay contractors for collecting overdue tax debts under subsection (b) of this section.

(2) To pay the fee the United States Department of the Treasury charges for setoff to recover tax owed to North Carolina.

(3) To pay for taxpayer locater services, not to exceed one hundred fifty thousand dollars ($150,000) a year.

(4) To pay for postage or other delivery charges for correspondence directly and primarily relating to collecting overdue tax debts, not to exceed five hundred thousand dollars ($500,000) a year.

(5) To pay for operating expenses for Project Collection Tax and the Taxpayer Assistance Call Center.

(6) To pay for expenses of the Examination and Collection Division directly and primarily relating to collecting overdue tax debts.

(f) Reports. - The report of Department activities required by G.S. 105-256 contains information on the Department's efforts to collect tax debts and its use of the proceeds of the collection assistance fee. (2001-380, ss. 2, 8; 2002-126, s. 22.2; 2003-349, s. 3; 2004-124, ss. 23.2(a), 23.3(c); 2004-170, s. 22.5; 2005-276, ss. 22.1(a), 22.1(b), 22.6(a); 2006-66, ss. 19.2, 19.3(a); 2007-323, s. 6.9(a); 2007-491, s. 33; 2012-152, s. 1; 2012-194, s. 61.5(b).)

§ 105-244: Repealed by Session Laws 1998-212, s. 29A.14(o).

§ 105-244.1. Cancellation of certain assessments.

The Secretary of Revenue is hereby authorized, empowered and directed to cancel and abate all assessments made after October 16, 1940, for or on account of any tax owing to the State of North Carolina and which is payable to the Department of Revenue against any person who was killed while a member of the Armed Forces of the United States or who has a service connected disability as a result of which the United States is paying him disability compensation. This provision shall apply only to assessments made after October 16, 1940, for taxes which were due prior to the time the taxpayer was inducted into the Armed Forces of the United States. If any such assessment is or has been paid, the Secretary of Revenue may refund the amount paid but shall not add thereto any interest. (1949, c. 392, s. 6; 1973, c. 476, s. 193; 2011-183, s. 73.)

§ 105-244.2: Expired pursuant to its own terms, effective January 1, 2010.

§ 105-245. Failure of sheriff to execute order.

If any sheriff of this State shall willfully fail, refuse, or neglect to execute any order directed to him by the Secretary of Revenue and within the time provided in this Subchapter, the official bond of such sheriff shall be liable for the tax, penalty, interest, and cost due by the taxpayer. (1939, c. 158, s. 916; 1973, c. 476, s. 193.)

§ 105-246. Actions, when tried.

All actions or processes brought in any of the superior courts of this State, under provisions of this Subchapter, shall have precedence over any other civil causes pending in such courts, and the courts shall always be deemed open for trial of any such action or proceeding brought therein. (1939, c. 158, s. 917.)

§ 105-247. Municipalities not to levy income and inheritance tax.

No city, town, township, or county shall levy any tax on income or inheritance. (1939, c. 158, s. 918.)

§ 105-248. Purpose of State taxes.

The taxes levied in this Subchapter are for the expenses of the State government, the appropriations to its educational, charitable, and penal institutions, the interest on the debt of the State, the public schools, and other specific appropriations made by law, and shall be collected and paid into the General Fund. (1939, c. 158, s. 919; 1981, c. 3; 1993 (Reg. Sess., 1994), c. 745, s. 17.)

§ 105-248.1: Repealed by Session Laws 2007-527, s. 32, effective August 31, 2007.

§ 105-249: Repealed by Session Laws 1998-95, s. 27.

§ 105-249.1: Repealed by Session Laws 1998-95, s. 28.

§ 105-249.2. Due date extended and penalties waived for certain military personnel or persons affected by a presidentially declared disaster.

(a) Combat. - The Secretary may not assess interest or a penalty against a taxpayer for any period that is disregarded under section 7508 of the Code in determining the taxpayer's liability for a federal tax. A taxpayer is granted an extension of time to file a return or take another action concerning a State tax for any period during which the Secretary may not assess interest or a penalty under this section.

(b) Disaster. - The penalties in G.S. 105-236(a)(2), (3), and (4) may not be assessed for any period in which the time for filing a federal return or report or for paying a federal tax is extended under section 7508A of the Code because of a presidentially declared disaster. For the purpose of this section, "presidentially declared disaster" has the same meaning as in section 1033(h)(3) of the Code. (1967, c. 706, s. 1; 1991, c. 439, s. 1; 1991 (Reg. Sess., 1992), c. 922, s. 10; 2001-87, s. 1; 2001-414, s. 24; 2006-162, s. 18; 2008-187, s. 16.)

§ 105-249.3: Repealed by Session Laws 1998-98, s. 19.

§ 105-250. Law applicable to foreign corporations.

All foreign corporations, and the officers and agents thereof, doing business in this State, shall be subject to all the liabilities and restrictions that are or may be imposed upon corporations of like character, organized under the laws of this State, and shall have no other or greater powers. (1939, c. 158, s. 920.)

§ 105-250.1. Repealed by Session Laws 1981 (Regular Session, 1982), c. 1209.

§ 105-251. Information required of taxpayer and corrections based on information.

(a) Scope of Information. - A taxpayer must give information to the Secretary when the Secretary requests the information. The Secretary may request a taxpayer to provide only the following kinds of information on a return, a report, or otherwise:

(1) Information that identifies the taxpayer.

(2) Information needed to determine the liability of the taxpayer for a tax.

(3) Information needed to determine whether an item is subject to a tax.

(4) Information that enables the Secretary to collect a tax.

(5) Other information the law requires a taxpayer to provide or the Secretary needs to perform a duty a law requires the Secretary to perform.

(b) Correction of Liability. - When a taxpayer provides information to the Secretary within the statute of limitations and the information establishes that an assessment against the taxpayer is incorrect or that the taxpayer is allowed a refund, the Secretary must adjust the assessment or issue the refund in accordance with the information. This action is a correction of an error by the Department or by the taxpayer and is not part of the process for the administrative or judicial review of a proposed assessment or a claim for refund. (1939, c. 158, s. 921; 1973, c. 476, s. 193; 1993 (Reg. Sess., 1994), c. 661, s. 2; 2008-134, s. 71.)

§ 105-251.1: Repealed by Session Laws 1991 (Regular Session, 1992), c. 1007, s. 14.

§ 105-252. Returns required.

A person who receives from the Secretary any form requiring information shall fill the form out properly and answer each question fully and correctly. If unable to answer a question, the person shall explain why in writing. The person shall return the form to the Secretary at the time and place required by the Secretary. The person shall also furnish an oath or affirmation verifying the return; the oath or affirmation shall be in the form required by the Secretary. (1939, c. 158, s. 922; 1973, c. 476, s. 193; 1991 (Reg. Sess., 1992), c. 930, s. 5.)

§ 105-253: Recodified as G.S. 105-242.2 by Session Laws 2008-134, s. 10(a), effective July 1, 2008, and applicable to taxes that become collectible on or after that date.

§ 105-254. Secretary to furnish forms.

The Secretary shall prepare forms suitable for carrying out the duties delegated to the Secretary. Upon request, the Secretary shall provide forms to any person subject to the laws administered by the Secretary. Failure to receive or secure a form does not relieve a person from a duty to file a return or a report. (1939, c. 158, s. 924; 1973, c. 476, s. 193; 1991 (Reg. Sess., 1992), c. 930, s. 6.)

§ 105-255. Secretary of Revenue to keep records.

The Secretary of Revenue shall keep books of account and records of collections of taxes as may be prescribed by the Director of the Budget; shall keep an assessment roll for the taxes levied, assessed, and collected under this Subchapter, showing in same the name of each taxpayer, the amount of tax assessed against each, when assessed, the increase or decrease in such assessment; the penalties imposed and collected, and the total tax paid; and shall make monthly reports to the Director of the Budget and to the Auditor and/or State Treasurer of all collections of taxes on such forms as prescribed by the Director of the Budget. (1939, c. 158, s. 925; 1973, c. 476, s. 193.)

§ 105-256. Publications prepared by Secretary of Revenue.

(a) Publications. - The Secretary shall prepare and publish the following:

(1) At least every two years, statistics concerning taxes imposed by this Chapter, including amounts collected, classifications of taxpayers, geographic distribution of taxes, and other facts considered pertinent and valuable.

(2) At least every two years, a tax expenditure report that lists the tax expenditures made by a provision in this Chapter, other than a provision in Subchapter II, and gives an estimate of the amount by which revenue is reduced by each tax expenditure. A "tax expenditure" is an exemption, an exclusion, a deduction, an allowance, a credit, a refund, a preferential tax rate, or another device that reduces the amount of tax revenue that would otherwise be available to the State. An estimate of the amount by which revenue is reduced by a tax expenditure may be stated as ranging between two amounts if the Department does not have sufficient data to make a more specific estimate.

(2a) By May 1 of each year, an economic incentives report that contains information on tax credits and tax refunds, itemized by credit or refund and by taxpayer, for the previous calendar year.

(3) As often as required, a report that is not listed in this subsection but is required by another law.

(4) As often as the Secretary determines is needed, other reports concerning taxes imposed by this Chapter.

(5) At least once a year, a statement of the taxpayer's bill of rights, which sets forth in simple and nontechnical terms the following:

a. The taxpayer's right to have the taxpayer's tax information kept confidential.

b. The rights of a taxpayer and the obligations of the Department during an audit.

c. The procedure for a taxpayer to appeal an adverse decision of the Department at each level of determination.

d. The procedure for a taxpayer to claim a refund for an alleged overpayment.

e. The procedure for a taxpayer to request information, assistance, and interpretations or to make complaints.

f. Penalties and interest that may apply and the basis for requesting waiver of a penalty.

g. The procedures the Department may use to enforce the collection of a tax, including assessment, jeopardy assessment, enforcement of liens, and garnishment and attachment.

(6) On an annual basis, a report on the quality of services provided to taxpayers through the Taxpayer Assistance Call Center, walk-in assistance, and taxpayer education. The report must be submitted to the Joint Legislative Commission on Governmental Operations.

(7) Repealed by Session Laws 2011-330, s. 35, effective June 27, 2011.

(8) By January 1 and July 1 of each year, a semiannual report on the Department's activities listed in this subdivision. The report must be submitted to the Joint Legislative Commission on Governmental Operations and to the Revenue Laws Study Committee.

a. Its efforts to increase compliance with the tax laws. The report must describe the Department's existing initiatives in this area as of July 1, 2006, and must estimate, by tax type and amount, the revenue expected in the fiscal year by the initiative. The report must describe any new initiative implemented since July 1, 2006, and estimate, by tax type and amount, the revenue expected in the fiscal year by the initiative.

b. Its efforts to identify and address fraud and other abuses of the voluntary tax compliance system that result in unreported and underreported tax. The report must describe the Department's long-term plan for achieving greater voluntary compliance and must summarize the steps taken since the last report and their results.

c. Its efforts to collect tax debts. The report must include a breakdown of the amount and age of tax debts collected through warning letters and by other means, must itemize collections by type of tax, must describe the Department's long-term collection plan, and must summarize the steps taken since the last report and their results.

d. Its use of the proceeds of the collection assistance fee imposed by G.S. 105-243.1.

(9) Repealed by Session Laws 2013-416, s. 18(a), effective August 23, 2013.

(b) Information. - The Secretary may require a unit of State or local government to furnish the Secretary statistical information the Secretary needs to prepare a report under this section. Upon request of the Secretary, a unit of government shall submit statistical information on one or more forms provided by the Secretary.

(c) Distribution. - The Secretary shall distribute reports prepared by the Secretary as follows without charge:

(1) Five copies to the Division of State Library of the Department of Cultural Resources, as required by G.S. 125-11.7.

(2) Five copies to the Legislative Services Commission for the use of the General Assembly.

(3) Upon request, one copy to each entity and official to which a copy of the reports of the Appellate Division of the General Court of Justice is furnished under G.S. 7A-343.1.

(4) One copy of the tax expenditure report to each member of the General Assembly and, upon request, one copy of any other report to each member of the General Assembly.

(5) One copy of the taxpayer's bill of rights to each taxpayer the Department contacts regarding determination or collection of a tax, other than by providing a tax form.

(6) Upon request, one copy of the taxpayer's bill of rights to each taxpayer.

The Secretary may charge a person not listed in this subsection a fee for a report prepared by the Secretary in an amount that covers publication or copying costs and mailing costs.

(d) Other Requirements. - The following requirements apply to the Secretary:

(1) Repealed by Session Laws 2006-6, s. 10, effective July 1, 2007.

(2) Escheats. - G.S. 116B-60(g) requires the Secretary to furnish information to the Escheat Fund on October 1 of each year.

(e) Repealed by Session Laws 2004-124, s. 23.3(b), effective July 1, 2004. (1939, c. 158, s. 926; 1955, c. 1350, s. 8; 1973, c. 476, s. 193; 1991, c. 10, s. 1; 1991 (Reg. Sess., 1992), c. 1007, s. 16; 1993, c. 433, s. 1; c. 532, s. 6; 2001-414, ss. 25, 26; 2002-87, s. 8; 2002-126, s. 22.5; 2004-124, s. 23.3(b); 2006-6, s. 10; 2006-66, s. 19.3(b); 2007-491, ss. 35, 36; 2010-166, s. 1.21; 2011-330, ss. 33(a), 35; 2013-414, s. 18(a).)

§ 105-256.1. Corporate annual report.

A corporation that files its annual report with the Secretary must pay the amount provided in G.S. 55-1-22 when it files the report. Amounts collected under this section shall be credited to the General Fund as tax revenue. The Secretary must transmit an annual report filed with the Secretary in accordance with G.S. 55-16-22 to the Secretary of State. (1997-475, s. 6.10.)

§ 105-257. Department may charge fee for report or other document.

The Secretary of Revenue may charge a fee for a report or another document in an amount that covers copying or publication costs and mailing costs. (1933, c. 88, s. 2; 1955, c. 1350, s. 9; 1973, c. 476, s. 193; 1991, c. 10, s. 2.)

§ 105-258. Powers of Secretary of Revenue; who may sign and verify legal documents; who may serve civil papers.

(a) Secretary May Examine Data and Summon Persons. - The Secretary of Revenue is authorized to do any of the following for the purpose of ascertaining the correctness of any return, filing a return where none has been filed, or determining the liability of any person for a tax, or collecting any tax:

(1)	Examine, personally, or by an agent designated by him, any books, papers, records, or other data that may be relevant or material to the inquiry.

(2)	Summon any of the following persons to appear at a time and place named in the summons, to produce such books, papers, records, or other data, and to give such testimony under oath as may be relevant or material to the inquiry:

a.	Any person liable for the tax or required to perform the act, or any officer or employee of such person.

b.	Any person having possession, custody, care or control of books of account containing entries relevant or material to the income and expenditures of the person liable for the tax or required to perform the act, or any other person having knowledge in the premises.

(3)	Administer oaths to the persons listed in this subsection.

(4)	Apply to the Superior Court of Wake County for an order requiring any person who refuses to obey the summons or to give testimony when summoned. Failure to comply with the court order shall be punished as for contempt.

(b)	Department Employees May Sign and Verify Legal Documents. - In a matter to which the Secretary of Revenue is a party or in which the Secretary has an interest, all legal documents may be signed and verified on behalf of the Secretary by (i) a Deputy or Assistant Secretary; (ii) any director or assistant director of any division of the Department of Revenue; or (iii) any other agent or employee of the Department so authorized by the Secretary of Revenue.

(c)	Department Employees May Serve Civil Papers. - In a civil matter to which the Secretary of Revenue is a party or in which the Secretary has an interest, any agent or employee of the Department of Revenue may serve summonses and other legal documents lawfully issued when so authorized by the Secretary of Revenue. (1939, c. 158, s. 927; 1943, c. 400, s. 9; 1955, c. 435; 1959, c. 1259, s. 8A; 1973, c. 476, s. 193; 1987 (Reg. Sess., 1988), c. 1044, s. 1; 1991, c. 157, s. 1; 2007-527, s. 15; 2013-414, s. 1(i).)

§ 105-258.1. Taxpayer interviews.

(a) Scope. - This section applies to in-person interviews between a taxpayer and an officer or employee of the Department relating to the determination or collection of a tax, other than an in-person interview concerning any of the following:

(1) A criminal investigation.

(2) The determination or collection of a tax imposed by Article 2D of this Chapter.

(3) Repealed by Session Laws 2007-491, s. 37, effective January 1, 2008.

(4) A jeopardy assessment and collection.

(b) Recording of Interview. - The Department shall allow a taxpayer to make an audio recording of an interview at the taxpayer's expense and using the taxpayer's equipment. The Department may make an audio recording of an interview at its own expense and using its own equipment. The Department shall, upon request of the taxpayer, provide the taxpayer a transcript of an interview recorded by the Department; the Department may charge the taxpayer for the cost of the requested transcription and reproduction of the transcript.

(c) Disclosure of Procedure. - At or before an initial interview relating to the determination of a tax, the Department shall provide the taxpayer a written explanation of the audit process and the taxpayer's rights in the process. At or before an initial interview relating to the collection of a tax, the Department shall provide the taxpayer a written explanation of the collection process and the taxpayer's rights in the process.

(d) Right of Consultation. - A taxpayer may authorize a person to represent the taxpayer in an interview if the person has a written power of attorney executed by the taxpayer. The Department may not require a taxpayer to accompany the taxpayer's representative to the interview unless the Secretary has summoned the taxpayer pursuant to G.S. 105-258.

(e) Suspension of Interview. - The Department shall suspend an interview relating to the determination of a tax if the taxpayer is not accompanied by a representative and, at any time during the interview, expresses the desire to consult with another person. (1993, c. 532, s. 7; 1993 (Reg. Sess., 1994), c. 745, s. 18; 2007-491, s. 37.)

§ 105-258.2. Taxpayer conversations.

(a) Scope. - This section applies to a conversation that is conducted by telephone or in person, is between a taxpayer and an employee of the Department, and occurs at an office of the Department if the conversation is in person. It does not apply to a conversation that occurs at a presentation, a conference, or another forum.

(b) Documentation. - The Secretary must document advice given to a taxpayer in a conversation with that taxpayer when the taxpayer gives the Secretary the taxpayer's identifying information, asks the Secretary about the application of a tax to the taxpayer in specific circumstances, and requests that the Secretary document the advice in the taxpayer's records. The documentation may be an entry in the account record of the taxpayer or by another method determined by the Secretary. The documentation must set out the date of the conversation, the question asked, and the advice given.

(c) Sales Tax Inquiries. - The Secretary must document advice given in a conversation with a person who is not registered as a retailer or a wholesale merchant under Article 5 of this Chapter when the person gives the Secretary the person's name and address, describes a business in which the person is engaged, asks if the person is required to be registered under Article 5 of this Chapter, and requests that the Secretary document the advice. The Secretary must keep a record of the person's inquiry that sets out the date of the conversation, the person making the inquiry, the business described in the conversation, and the advice given. (2008-107, s. 28.16(c), (d).)

§ 105-259. Secrecy required of officials; penalty for violation.

(a) Definitions. - The following definitions apply in this section:

(1) Employee or officer. - The term includes a former employee, a former officer, and a current or former member of a State board or commission.

(2) Tax information. - Any information from any source concerning the liability of a taxpayer for a tax, as defined in G.S. 105-228.90. The term includes the following:

a. Information contained on a tax return, a tax report, or an application for a license for which a tax is imposed.

b. Information obtained through an audit of a taxpayer or by correspondence with a taxpayer.

c. Information on whether a taxpayer has filed a tax return or a tax report.

d. A list or other compilation of the names, addresses, social security numbers, or similar information concerning taxpayers.

The term does not include (i) statistics classified so that information about specific taxpayers cannot be identified, (ii) an annual report required to be filed under G.S. 55-16-22 or (iii) the amount of tax refunds paid to a governmental entity listed in G.S. 105-164.14(c) or to a State agency.

(b) Disclosure Prohibited. - An officer, an employee, or an agent of the State who has access to tax information in the course of service to or employment by the State may not disclose the information to any other person except as provided in this subsection. Standards used or to be used for the selection of returns for examination and data used or to be used for determining the standards may not be disclosed for any purpose. All other tax information may be disclosed only if the disclosure is made for one of the following purposes:

(1) To comply with a court order, an administrative law judge's order in a contested tax case, or a law.

(2) Review by the Attorney General or a representative of the Attorney General.

(3) To exchange the following types of information with a tax official of another jurisdiction if the laws of the other jurisdiction allow it to provide similar tax information to a representative of this State:

a. Information to aid the jurisdiction in collecting a tax imposed by this State or the other jurisdiction.

b. Information needed for statistical reports and revenue estimates.

(4) To provide a governmental agency or an officer of an organized association of taxpayers with a list of taxpayers who have paid a privilege license tax under Article 2 of this Chapter.

(5) To furnish to the chair of a board of county commissioners information on the county sales and use tax.

(5a) Reserved.

(5b) To furnish to the finance officials of a city a list of the utility taxable gross receipts and piped natural gas tax revenues attributable to the city under G.S. 105-116.1 and G.S. 105-187.44 or under former G.S. 105-116 and G.S. 105-120.

(5c) To provide the following information to a regional public transportation authority or a regional transportation authority created pursuant to Article 26 or Article 27 of Chapter 160A of the General Statutes on an annual basis, when the information is needed to enable the authority to administer its tax laws:

a. The name, address, and identification number of retailers who collect the tax on leased vehicles imposed by G.S. 105-187.5.

b. The name, address, and identification number of a retailer audited by the Department of Revenue regarding the tax on leased vehicles imposed by G.S. 105-187.5, when the Department determines that the audit results may be of interest to the authority.

(5d) To provide the following information to a county or city on an annual basis, when the county or city needs the information for the administration of its local prepared food and beverages tax, room occupancy tax, vehicle rental tax, or heavy equipment rental tax:

a. The name, address, and identification number of retailers who collect the sales and use taxes imposed under Article 5 of this Chapter and may be engaged in a business subject to one or more of these local taxes.

b. The name, address, and identification number of a retailer audited by the Department regarding the sales and use taxes imposed under Article 5 of this

Chapter, when the Department determines that the audit results may be of interest to the county or city in the administration of one or more of these local taxes.

(6) To sort, process, or deliver tax information on behalf of the Department of Revenue.

(6a) To furnish the county or city official designated under G.S. 105-164.29B a list of claimants that have received a refund of the county sales or use tax to the extent authorized in that statute.

(7) To exchange information with the State Highway Patrol Section of the Department of Public Safety, the Division of Motor Vehicles of the Department of Transportation, the International Fuel Tax Association, Inc., or the Joint Operations Center for National Fuel Tax Compliance when the information is needed to fulfill a duty imposed on the Department of Revenue, the State Highway Patrol Section of the Department of Public Safety, or the Division of Motor Vehicles of the Department of Transportation.

(7a) To furnish the name and identifying information of motor carriers whose licenses have been revoked to the administrator of a national criminal justice system database that makes the information available only to criminal justice agencies and public safety organizations.

(8) To furnish to the Department of State Treasurer, upon request, the name, address, and account and identification numbers of a taxpayer who may be entitled to property held in the Escheat Fund.

(9) To furnish to the Division of Employment Security the name, address, and account and identification numbers of a taxpayer when the information is requested by the Division in order to fulfill a duty imposed under Article 2 of Chapter 96 of the General Statutes.

(9a) To furnish information to the Division of Employment Security to the extent required for its NC WORKS study of the working poor pursuant to G.S. 108A-29(r). The Division of Employment Security shall use information furnished to it under this subdivision only in a nonidentifying form for statistical and analytical purposes related to its NC WORKS study. The information that may be furnished under this subdivision is the following with respect to individual income taxpayers, as shown on the North Carolina income tax forms:

a. Name, social security number, spouse's name, spouse's social security number, and county of residence.

b. Filing status and federal personal exemptions.

c. Federal taxable income, additions to federal taxable income, and total of federal taxable income plus additional income.

d. Income while a North Carolina resident, total income from North Carolina sources while a nonresident, and total income from all sources.

e. Exemption for children, nonresidents' and part-year residents' exemption for children, and credit for children.

f. Expenses for child and dependent care, portion of expenses paid while a resident of North Carolina, portion of expenses paid while a resident of North Carolina that was incurred for dependents who were under the age of seven and dependents who were physically or mentally incapable of caring for themselves, credit for child and dependent care expenses, other qualifying expenses, credit for other qualifying expenses, total credit for child and dependent care expenses.

(10) Review by the State Auditor to the extent authorized in G.S. 147-64.7.

(11) To give a spouse who elects to file a joint tax return a copy of the return or information contained on the return.

(11a) To provide a copy of a return to the taxpayer who filed the return.

(11b) In the case of a return filed by a corporation, a partnership, a trust, or an estate, to provide a copy of the return or information on the return to a person who has a material interest in the return if, under the circumstances, section 6103(e)(1) of the Code would require disclosure to that person of any corresponding federal return or information.

(11c) In the case of a return of an individual who is legally incompetent or deceased, to provide a copy of the return to the legal representative of the estate of the incompetent individual or decedent.

(12) To contract with a financial institution for the receipt of withheld income tax payments under G.S. 105-163.6 or for the transmittal of payments by electronic funds transfer.

(13) To furnish the following to the Fiscal Research Division of the General Assembly, upon request:

a. A sample, suitable in character, composition, and size for statistical analyses, of tax returns or other tax information from which taxpayers' names and identification numbers have been removed.

b. An analysis of the fiscal impact of proposed legislation.

(14) To exchange information concerning a tax imposed by Subchapter V of this Chapter with the Standards Division of the Department of Agriculture and Consumer Services when the information is needed to administer the Gasoline and Oil Inspection Act, Article 3 of Chapter 119 of the General Statutes.

(15) To exchange information concerning a tax imposed by Articles 2A, 2C, or 2D of this Chapter with one of the following agencies when the information is needed to fulfill a duty imposed on the Department or the agency:

a. The North Carolina Alcoholic Beverage Control Commission.

b. The Alcohol Law Enforcement Section of the Department of Public Safety.

c. The Bureau of Alcohol, Tobacco, and Firearms of the United States Department of Justice.

d. Law enforcement agencies.

e. The Section of Community Corrections of the Division of Adult Correction of the Department of Public Safety.

(15a) To furnish to the appropriate local, State, or federal law enforcement agency, including a prosecutorial agency, information concerning the commission of an offense under the jurisdiction of that agency when the Department has initiated a criminal investigation of the taxpayer.

(16) To furnish to the Department of Secretary of State the name, address, tax year end, and account and identification numbers of a corporation liable for corporate income or franchise taxes or of a limited liability company liable for a corporate or a partnership tax return to enable the Secretary of State to notify the corporation or the limited liability company of the annual report filing requirement or that its articles of incorporation or articles of organization or its certificate of authority has been suspended.

(16a) To provide the North Carolina Self-Insurance Security Association information on self-insurers' premiums as determined under G.S. 105-228.5(b), (b1), and (c) for the purpose of collecting the assessments authorized in G.S. 97-133(a).

(17) To inform the Business License Information Office of the Department of Commerce of the status of an application for a license for which a tax is imposed and of any information needed to process the application.

(18) To furnish to the Office of the State Controller information needed by the State Controller to implement the setoff debt collection program established under G.S. 147-86.25, verify statewide vendor files, or track debtors of the State.

(19) To furnish to the North Carolina Industrial Commission information concerning workers' compensation reported to the Secretary under G.S. 105-163.7.

(20) (See note for expiration date) To furnish to the Environmental Management Commission information concerning whether a person who is requesting certification of a dry-cleaning facility or wholesale distribution facility from the Commission is liable for privilege tax under Article 5D of this Chapter. This subdivision is repealed when Part 6 of Article 21A of Chapter 143 of the General Statutes expires.

(21) To exchange information concerning the tax on piped natural gas imposed by Article 5E of this Chapter with the North Carolina Utilities Commission or the Public Staff of that Commission.

(22) To provide the Secretary of Administration pursuant to G.S. 143-59.1 a list of vendors and their affiliates who meet one or more of the conditions of G.S. 105-164.8(b) but refuse to collect the use tax levied under Article 5 of this Chapter on their sales delivered to North Carolina.

(23) To provide public access to a database containing the names and account numbers of taxpayers who are not required to pay sales and use taxes under Article 5 of this Chapter to a retailer because of an exemption or because they are authorized to pay the tax directly to the Department of Revenue.

(24) To furnish the Department of Commerce and the Division of Employment Security a copy of the qualifying information required in G.S. 105-129.7(b) or G.S. 105-129.86(b).

(25) To provide public access to a database containing the names and registration numbers of retailers who are registered to collect sales and use taxes under Article 5 of this Chapter.

(26) To contract for the collection of tax debts pursuant to G.S. 105-243.1.

(27) To provide a publication required under this Chapter.

(28) To exchange information concerning a tax credit claimed under Article 3E of this Chapter with the North Carolina Housing Finance Agency.

(29) To provide to the Economic Investment Committee established pursuant to G.S. 143B-437.54 information necessary to implement economic development programs under the responsibility of the Committee.

(30) To prove that a business does not meet the definition of "small business" under Article 3F of this Chapter because the annual receipts of the business, combined with the annual receipts of all related persons, exceeds the applicable amount.

(31) Repealed by Session Laws 2010-166, s. 3.7, effective July 1, 2010.

(32) Repealed by Session Laws 2006-162, s. 4(c), as amended by Session Laws 2007-527, s. 24, effective July 24, 2006.

(33) To provide to the North Carolina State Lottery Commission the information required under G.S. 18C-141.

(34) To exchange information concerning a tax credit claimed under G.S. 105-130.47 or G.S. 105-151.29 with the North Carolina Film Office of the Department of Commerce and with the regional film commissions.

(35) Repealed by Session Laws 2010-166, s. 3.7, effective July 1, 2010.

(36) To furnish to a taxpayer claiming a credit under G.S. 105-130.47 or G.S. 105-151.29 information used by the Secretary to adjust the amount of the credit claimed by the taxpayer.

(37) To furnish the Department of Commerce with the information needed to complete the study required under G.S. 105-129.82.

(38) To verify with a nonprofit organization or a unit of State or local government information relating to eligibility for a credit under G.S. 105-129.16H.

(39) To furnish the Department of State Treasurer with information it requests about whether a unit of local government has timely filed a withholding report, has been charged a penalty, or has paid a penalty, as such information may be helpful in auditing local government accounts pursuant to G.S. 159-34 and determining compliance with the Local Government Finance Act.

(40) To furnish a nonparticipating manufacturer, as defined in G.S. 66-292, the amount of the manufacturer's tobacco products that a taxpayer sells in this State and that the Secretary reports to the Attorney General under G.S. 105-113.4C.

(41) To furnish the North Carolina Forest Service of the Department of Agriculture and Consumer Services pertinent contact and financial information concerning companies that are involved in the primary processing of timber products so that the Commissioner of Agriculture is able to comply with G.S. 106-1029 under the Primary Forest Product Assessment Act.

(42) To furnish to a taxpayer claiming a credit under G.S. 105-129.16A information used by the Secretary to adjust the amount of the credit claimed by the taxpayer.

(43) To furnish requested workforce data to the North Carolina Longitudinal Data System, as required by G.S. 116E-6. Information furnished to the North Carolina Longitudinal Data System shall be provided in a nonidentifying form for statistical and analytical purposes to facilitate and enable the linkage of student data and workforce data and shall not include information allowing the identification of specific taxpayers.

(44) To furnish the State Budget Director or the Director's designee a sample of tax returns or other tax information from which taxpayers' names and identification numbers have been removed that is suitable in character, composition, and size for statistical analyses by the Office of State Budget and Management.

(45) To furnish tax information to the Office of the State Controller under G.S. 143B-426.38A. The use and reporting of individual data may be restricted to only those activities specifically allowed by law when potential fraud or other illegal activity is indicated.

(c) Punishment. - A person who violates this section is guilty of a Class 1 misdemeanor. If the person committing the violation is an officer or employee, that person shall be dismissed from public office or public employment and may not hold any public office or public employment in this State for five years after the violation. (1939, c. 158, s. 928; 1951, c. 190, s. 2; 1973, c. 476, s. 193; c. 903, s. 4; c. 1287, s. 13; 1975, c. 19, s. 29; c. 275, s. 7; 1977, c. 657, s. 6; 1979, c. 495; 1983, c. 7; 1983 (Reg. Sess., 1984), c. 1004, s. 3; c. 1034, s. 125; 1987, c. 440, s. 4; 1989, c. 628; c. 728, s. 1.47; 1989 (Reg. Sess., 1990), c. 945, s. 15; 1993, c. 485, s. 31; c. 539, s. 712; 1994, Ex. Sess., c. 14, s. 51; c. 24, s. 14(c); 1993 (Reg. Sess., 1994), c. 679, s. 8.4; 1995, c. 17, s. 11; c. 21, s. 2; 1997-118, s. 6; 1997-261, s. 14; 1997-340, s. 2; 1997-392, s. 4.1; 1997-475, s. 6.11; 1998-22, ss. 10, 11; 1998-98, ss. 13.1(b), 20; 1998-139, s. 1; 1998-212, s. 12.27A(o); 1999-219, s. 7.1; 1999-340, s. 8; 1999-341, s. 8; 1999-360, s. 2.1; 1999-438, s. 18; 1999-452, s. 28.1; 2000-120, s. 8; 2000-173, s. 11; 2001-205, s. 1; 2001-380, s. 5; 2001-476, s. 8(b); 2001-487, ss. 47(d), 123; 2002-87, s. 7; 2002-106, s. 5; 2002-172, s. 2.3; 2003-349, s. 4; 2003-416, s. 2; 2004-124, s. 32D.3; 2004-170, s. 23; 2004-204, 1st Ex. Sess., s. 4; 2005-276, ss. 31.1(cc), 39.1(c), 7.27(b); 2005-400, s. 20; 2005-429, s. 2.13; 2005-435, ss. 32(b), 32(c), 37, 48; 2006-162, s. 4(c); 2006-196, s. 11; 2006-252, s. 2.21; 2007-397, s. 13(d); 2007-491, s. 38; 2007-527, ss. 24, 33, 34, 35, 36; 2008-107, s. 28.25(d); 2008-144, s. 4; 2009-283, s. 1; 2009-445, s. 39; 2009-483, ss. 5, 10; 2010-31, ss. 13.15, 31.8(g); 2010-95, s. 11; 2010-166, s. 3.7; 2010-167, s. 2(c); 2011-145, ss. 19.1(g), (h), (k), (n), (p), 13.25(nn), (xx); 2011-330, s. 33(b); 2011-401, ss. 3.9, 5.1; 2012-83, s. 35; 2012-133, s. 1(b); 2013-155, s. 6; 2013-360, ss. 6.9, 7.10(c); 2013-414, s. 19.)

§ 105-260. Evaluation of Department personnel.

The Secretary may not use records of tax enforcement results, or production goals based on these records, as the sole criteria in evaluating employees of the Department who are directly involved in tax collection activities or in evaluating the immediate supervisors of these employees. The Secretary must consider records of taxpayer complaints that named an employee as discourteous, unresponsive, or incompetent in evaluating the employee. (1939, c. 158, s. 929; 1973, c. 476, s. 193; 1981, c. 859, s. 79; c. 1127, s. 53; 1993, c. 532, s. 8.)

§ 105-260.1. Delegation of authority to hold hearings.

The Secretary of Revenue may delegate to a Deputy or Assistant Secretary of Revenue the authority to hold any hearing required or allowed under this Chapter. (1985, c. 258.)

§ 105-261. Secretary and deputies to administer oaths.

The Secretary of Revenue and such deputies as he may designate shall have the power to administer an oath to any person or to take the acknowledgment of any person in respect to any return or report required by this Subchapter or under the rules and regulations of the Secretary of Revenue, and shall have access to all the books and records of any person, firm, corporation, county, or municipality in this State. (1939, c. 158, s. 930; 1973, c. 476, s. 193.)

§ 105-262. Rules.

(a) Authority. - The Secretary of Revenue may adopt rules needed to administer a tax collected by the Secretary or to fulfill another duty delegated to the Secretary. G.S. 150B-1 and Article 2A of Chapter 150B of the General Statutes set out the procedure for the adoption of rules by the Secretary.

(b) Repealed by Session Laws 2012-43, s. 1, effective June 20, 2012, and Session Laws 2012-79, s. 1.14(d), effective June 26, 2012.

(c) Fiscal Note. - The Secretary must ask the Office of State Budget and Management to prepare a fiscal note for a proposed new rule or a proposed change to a rule that has a substantial economic impact, as defined in G.S. 150B-21.4(b1). The Secretary shall not take final action on a proposed rule change that has a substantial economic impact until at least 60 days after the fiscal note has been prepared. (1939, c. 158, s. 931; 1955, c. 1350, s. 2; 1973, c. 476, s. 193; 1981, c. 859, s. 80; c. 1127, s. 53; 1991, c. 45, s. 28; c. 477, s. 7; 1995, c. 507, s. 27.8(p); 2000-140, s. 93.1(a); 2001-424, s. 12.2(b); 2007-491, s. 39; 2010-31, s. 31.10(f); 2012-43, s. 1; 2012-79, s. 1.14(d).)

§ 105-262.1. Rules to exercise authority under G.S. 105-130.5A.

(a) Purpose and Scope. - It is the policy of the State to provide necessary guidance on a timely basis to corporate taxpayers subject under G.S. 105-130.5A to have their net income adjusted or to be required to file a combined return. Except for a voluntary redetermination as allowed under G.S. 105-130.5A(c), the Secretary may not redetermine the State net income of a corporation properly attributable to its business carried on in the State under G.S. 105-130.5A until a rule adopted by the Secretary in accordance with this section becomes effective. This section provides an expedited procedure for the adoption of rules needed to administer G.S. 105-130.5A. The Secretary may not interpret G.S. 105-130.5A in the form of a bulletin or directive under G.S. 105-264.

The Secretary is exempt from G.S. 150B-21.1 through G.S. 150B-21.4 of Part 2 of Article 2A of Chapter 150B of the General Statutes but is subject to the expedited procedure for the adoption of rules as established by this section. The Secretary is exempt from Part 3 of Article 2A of Chapter 150B of the General Statutes but is subject to the expedited review procedure as established by this section.

(b) Definitions. - The definitions in G.S. 150B-2 apply in this section.

(c) Fiscal Note. - The Secretary must prepare a fiscal note for a proposed new rule or a proposed change to a rule that has a substantial economic impact. The fiscal note must be submitted with the proposed rule when the rule is submitted to the Codifier of Rules, and the Codifier of Rules must publish the fiscal note with the proposed rule on the Internet. The Secretary must accept a written comment on the fiscal note in the same manner the Secretary accepts written comments on the proposed rule. The Secretary is not subject to the fiscal note requirement under G.S. 105-262(c). For purposes of this section, a "substantial economic impact" has the same meaning as defined in G.S. 150B-21.4(b1).

(d) Adoption. - The Secretary may adopt a rule under this section by using the procedure for adoption of a temporary rule set forth in G.S. 150B-21.1(a3). The Secretary must provide electronic notification of the adoption of a rule to persons on the mailing list maintained in accordance with G.S. 150B-21.2(d) and any other interested parties, including those originally given notice of the rule making and those who provided comment on the rule. If the Secretary receives written comment objecting to the rule and requesting review by the Commission, the rule must be reviewed in accordance with subsections (e) through (i) of this section. A person may object to the rule and request review by the Commission at any point following the agency's adoption of the rule and by 5:00 P.M. on the third business day following electronic notification from the Secretary of the adoption of a rule. If the Secretary receives no written comment objecting to the rule and requesting review by the Commission, the Secretary must deliver the rule to the Codifier of Rules. The Codifier of Rules must enter the rule into the North Carolina Administrative Code upon receipt of the rule.

(e) Review. - If the Secretary receives written comment objecting to the rule and requesting review by the Commission, the Secretary must submit the rule to the Commission for review. The Commission may not consider questions relating to the quality or efficacy of the rule but must restrict its review to a determination of whether the rule meets all of the following criteria:

(1) It is within the authority delegated to the agency by the General Assembly.

(2) It is clear and unambiguous.

(3) It is reasonably necessary to implement or interpret an enactment of the General Assembly, or of Congress, or a regulation of a federal agency. The Commission must consider the cumulative effect of all rules adopted by the agency related to the specific purpose for which the rule is proposed.

(4) It was adopted in accordance with this section.

(f) Manner of Review. - When the Commission reviews a rule under this section, the time limits in subsections (b) and (b1) of G.S. 150B-21.1 apply. The

Commission must review the rule to determine whether the rule meets the standards in subsection (e) of this section. The Commission must direct a member of its staff who is an attorney licensed to practice law in North Carolina to review the rule. The staff member must make a recommendation to the Commission or its designee. The Commission's designee must be a panel of at least three members of the Commission. The staff member, Commission's designee, or the Commission may also request technical changes as allowed in G.S. 150B-21.10. In reviewing the rule, the Commission may consider any information submitted by the Secretary or another person.

(g)   Objection. - If the Commission or its designee finds that the rule does not meet the standards in subsection (e) of this section and objects to the rule, the Commission or its designee must send the Secretary a written statement of the objection and the reason for the objection within one business day. The Secretary must take one of the following actions:

(1)   Change the rule to satisfy the Commission's objection and submit the revised rule to the Commission.

(2)   Submit a written response to the Commission indicating that the Secretary has decided not to change the rule.

(h)   Changes. - When the Secretary changes a rule in response to an objection by the Commission, the Commission must determine whether the change satisfies the Commission's objection. If it does, the Commission must approve the rule. If it does not, the Commission must send the Secretary a written statement of the Commission's continued objection and the reason for the continued objection.

(i)   Approval. - If the Commission or its designee finds that the rule meets the standards in subsection (e) of this section, the Commission or its designee must approve the rule and deliver the rule to the Codifier of Rules. The Codifier of Rules must enter the rule into the North Carolina Administrative Code upon receipt from the Commission or its designee.

(j)   Return of Rule. - A rule to which the Commission has objected remains under review by the Commission until the Secretary decides not to satisfy the Commission's objection and makes a written request to the Commission to return the rule to the Secretary. When the Commission returns a rule to the Secretary in accordance with this section, the Secretary may file an action for declaratory judgment in Wake County Superior Court pursuant to Article 26 of Chapter 1 of the General Statutes.

(k) Effective Date. - G.S. 150B-21.3 does not apply to a rule adopted under this section. A rule adopted under this section becomes effective on the last day of the month the Codifier of Rules enters the rule in the North Carolina Administrative Code. (2012-43, s. 2; 2013-414, s. 48.)

§ 105-263. Timely filing of mailed documents and requests for extensions.

(a) Mailed Document. - Sections 7502 and 7503 of the Code govern when a return, report, payment, or any other document that is mailed to the Department is timely filed.

(b) Extension. - The Secretary may extend the time in which a person must file a return with the Secretary. To obtain an extension of time for filing a return, a person must comply with any application requirement set by the Secretary. An extension of time for filing a franchise tax return or an income tax return does not extend the time for paying the tax due or the time when a penalty attaches for failure to pay the tax. An extension of time for filing any return other than a franchise tax return or an income tax return extends the time for paying the tax due and the time when a penalty attaches for failure to pay the tax. When an extension of time for filing a return extends the time for paying the tax expected to be due with the return, interest, at the rate established pursuant to G.S. 105-241.21, accrues on the tax due from the original due date of the return to the date the tax is paid. (1939, c. 158, s. 932; 1973, c. 476, s. 193; 1977, c. 1114, s. 2; 1989 (Reg. Sess., 1990), c. 984, s. 14; 1991 (Reg. Sess., 1992), c. 930, s. 11; 1997-300, s. 1; 2007-491, s. 44(1)a; 2008-107, s. 28.18(c); 2010-95, s. 10(a); 2012-79, s. 1.8; 2013-414, s. 1(j).)

§ 105-264. Effect of Secretary's interpretation of revenue laws.

(a) Interpretation. - It is the duty of the Secretary to interpret all laws administered by the Secretary. The Secretary's interpretation of these laws shall be consistent with the applicable rules. An interpretation by the Secretary is prima facie correct. When the Secretary interprets a law by adopting a rule or publishing a bulletin or directive on the law, the interpretation is a protection to the officers and taxpayers affected by the interpretation, and taxpayers are entitled to rely upon the interpretation. If the Secretary changes an interpretation, a taxpayer who relied on it before it was changed is not liable for any penalty or additional assessment on any tax that accrued before the interpretation was changed and was not paid by reason of reliance upon the interpretation.

(b) Advice. - If a taxpayer requests specific advice from the Department and receives erroneous advice in response, the taxpayer is not liable for any penalty or additional assessment attributable to the erroneous advice furnished by the Department to the extent that the following conditions are all satisfied:

(1) The advice was reasonably relied upon by the taxpayer.

(2) The penalty or additional assessment did not result from the taxpayer's failure to provide adequate or accurate information.

(3) The Department provided the advice in writing or the Department's records establish that the Department provided erroneous verbal advice.

(c) Revised Interpretations. - This section does not prevent the Secretary from changing an interpretation, and it does not prevent a change in an interpretation from applying on and after the effective date of the change. An interpretation that revises a prior interpretation by expanding the scope of a tax or otherwise increasing the amount of tax due may not become effective sooner than the following:

(1) For a tax that is payable on a monthly or quarterly basis, the first day of a month that is at least 90 days after the date the revised interpretation is issued.

(2) For a tax that is payable on an annual basis, the first day of a tax year that begins after the date the revised interpretation is issued.

(d) Fee. - The Secretary may charge a fee for providing specific written advice at the request of a taxpayer. The fee is a receipt of the Department and must be applied to the costs of providing the specific advice. The proceeds of the fee must be credited to a special account within the Department and do not revert but remain in the special account until spent by the Department for the costs of providing the specific advice. The Secretary may adopt a tiered fee structure based on the taxpayer's income or gross receipts, the relative complexity of the advice requested, or the tax schedule for which advice is requested. The fee shall not be less than one hundred dollars ($100.00) or more than five thousand dollars ($5,000). The fee may be waived by the Secretary. (1939, c. 158, s. 933; 1955, c. 1350, s. 4; 1957, c. 1340, s. 14; 1973, c. 476, s. 193; 1991, c. 45, s. 29; 1993, c. 532, s. 9; 1998-98, s. 21; 2008-107, s. 28.16(e); 2010-31, s. 31.7A(a); 2011-390, s. 6.)

§ 105-264.1. Secretary's interpretation applies to local taxes that are based on State taxes.

An interpretation by the Secretary of a law administered by the Secretary applies to a local law administered by a unit of local government when the local law refers to the State law to determine the application of the local law. A person who is subject to the local law or the unit of local government that administers the local law may ask the Secretary for an interpretation of the State law that determines the application of the local law. An interpretation by the Secretary of a State law that determines the application of a local law provides the same protections against liability under the local law that it provides under the State law. (2008-134, s. 12(a).)

§ 105-265: Repealed by Session Laws 1991, c. 45, s. 19.

§ 105-266: Repealed by Session Laws 2007-491, s. 2, effective January 1, 2008.

§ 105-266.1: Repealed by Session Laws 2007-491, s. 2, effective January 1, 2008.

§ 105-266.2. Refund of tax paid on substantial income later restored.

This section applies to a taxpayer who is subject to the alternative tax under § 1341(a)(5) of the Code for the current taxable year because the taxpayer restored an item of income that had been included in the taxpayer's gross income for an earlier taxable year. For the purpose of Article 4 of this Chapter, the taxpayer is considered to have made a payment of tax for the current taxable year on the later of the date the return for the current taxable year was filed or the date the return was due to be filed. The amount of this payment of tax is (i) the amount the taxpayer's tax under Article 4 for the earlier taxable year was increased because the item of income was included in gross income for that year minus (ii) the amount the taxpayer's tax under Article 4 for the current taxable year was decreased because the item was deductible for that year. To the extent this payment of tax creates an overpayment, the overpayment is refundable in accordance with G.S. 105-241.21. (1997-213, s. 1; 2007-491, s. 44(1)c.)

§ 105-267: Repealed by Session Laws 2007-491, s. 2, effective January 1, 2008.

§ 105-267.1: Repealed by Session Laws 1991, c. 45, s. 30.

§ 105-268. Reciprocal comity.

The courts of this State shall recognize and enforce liabilities for taxes lawfully imposed by other states which extend a like comity to this State. (1939, c. 158, s. 938.)

§ 105-268.1. Agreements to coordinate the administration and collection of taxes.

The Secretary of Revenue is hereby authorized, with the approval of the Governor and Council of State, to enter into agreements with the United States government or any department or agency thereof, or with a state or any political subdivision thereof, for the purpose of coordinating the administration and collection of taxes imposed by this State and administered and collected by said Secretary with taxes imposed by the United States or by any other state or political subdivision thereof. (1943, c. 747, s. 1; 1971, c. 806, s. 2; 1973, c. 476, s. 193.)

§ 105-268.2. Expenditures and commitments authorized to effectuate agreements.

The Secretary of Revenue with the approval of the Governor and Council of State is authorized and empowered to undertake such commitments and make such expenditures, within the appropriations provided by law, as may be necessary to effectuate such agreements. (1943, c. 747, s. 2; 1971, c. 806, s. 2; 1973, c. 476, s. 193.)

§ 105-268.3. Returns to be filed and taxes paid pursuant to agreements.

Notwithstanding any other provision of law, returns shall be filed and taxes paid in accordance with the provisions of any agreement entered into pursuant to this Article. (1943, c. 747, s. 3; 1971, c. 806, s. 2.)

§ 105-269. Extraterritorial authority to enforce payment.

(a)   The Secretary, with the assistance of the Attorney General, is authorized to bring suits in the courts of other states to collect taxes legally due this State. The officials of other states that extend a like comity to this State are empowered to sue for the collection of taxes in the courts of this State. A certificate by the Secretary of State, under the Great Seal of the State, that these officers have authority to collect the tax is conclusive evidence of this authority. Whenever the Secretary considers it expedient to employ local counsel to assist in bringing suit in an out-of-state court, the Secretary, with the concurrence of the Attorney General, may employ local counsel on the basis of a negotiated retainer or in accordance with prevailing commercial law league rates.

(b)   Repealed by Session Laws 2001-380, s. 4, effective August 20, 2001, and applicable to tax debts that remain unpaid on or after that date. (1939, c. 158, s. 939; 1963, c. 1169, s. 6; 1973, c. 476, s. 193; 1983 (Reg. Sess., 1984), c. 1005; 2001-380, s. 4.)

§ 105-269.1. Local authorities authorized to furnish office space.

Boards of county commissioners and governing boards of cities and towns are hereby fully authorized and empowered to furnish adequate and suitable office space for field representatives of the Department of Revenue upon request of the Secretary of Revenue, and are hereby authorized and empowered to make necessary expenditures therefor. (1951, c. 643, s. 9; 1973, c. 476, s. 193.)

§ 105-269.2: Repealed by Session Laws 2007-491, s. 2, effective January 1, 2008.

§ 105-269.3. Enforcement of Subchapter V and fuel inspection tax.

The State Highway Patrol and law enforcement officers and other appropriate personnel in the Department of Public Safety may assist the Department of Revenue in enforcing Subchapter V of this Chapter and Article 3 of Chapter 119 of the General Statutes. The State Highway Patrol and law enforcement officers of the Department of Public Safety have the power of peace officers in matters concerning the enforcement of Subchapter V of this Chapter and Article 3 of Chapter 119 of the General Statutes. (1963, c. 1169, s. 6; 1991, c. 42, s. 16; 1991 (Reg. Sess., 1992), c. 1007, s. 17; 1993, c. 485, s. 15; 1993 (Reg. Sess., 1994), c. 745, s. 19; 2002-159, s. 31.5(b); 2002-190, s. 2; 2011-145, s. 19.1(g).)

§ 105-269.4. Election to apply income tax refund to following year's tax.

Any taxpayer required to file an income tax return under Article 4 of this Subchapter whose return shows that the taxpayer is entitled to a refund may elect to apply part or all of the refund to that taxpayer's estimated income tax liability for the following year. The Secretary of Revenue shall amend the income tax returns to permit the election authorized by this section. (1983, c. 663, s. 1; 1989 (Reg. Sess., 1990), c. 814, s. 28.)

§ 105-269.5. Contribution of income tax refund to Wildlife Conservation Account.

Any taxpayer entitled to a refund of income taxes under Article 4 of this Chapter may elect to contribute all or part of the refund to the Wildlife Conservation Account established under G.S. 143-247.2 to be used for the management, protection, and preservation of wildlife in accordance with that statute. The Secretary shall provide appropriate language and space on the income tax form in which to make the election. The taxpayer's election becomes irrevocable upon filing the taxpayer's income tax return for the taxable year. The Secretary shall transmit the contributions made pursuant to this section to the State Treasurer for credit to the Wildlife Conservation Account. (1983, c. 865, s. 2; 1991, c. 45, s. 20; 1993, c. 543, s. 6.)

§ 105-269.6: Repealed by Session Laws 2002-158, s. 6(a), effective for taxable years beginning on or after January 1, 2003.

§§ 105-269.7 through 105-269.12. Reserved for future codification purposes.

§ 105-269.13. Debts not collectible under North Carolina law.

(a) Debts Not Collectible. - The following debts are not collectible and are not subject to execution under Article 28 of Chapter 1 of the General Statutes or any other provision of law:

(1) A loan made by a person who does not comply with G.S. 105-88.

(2) A debt owed to a retailer described in subsection (b) of this section as the result of the purchase of tangible personal property.

(b) Retailer. - A debt owed to a retailer is subject to this section if all of the following applies to the retailer:

(1) The retailer meets one or more of the conditions in G.S. 105-164.8(b).

(2) The retailer is not registered to collect the use tax due under Article 5 of this Chapter on its sales delivered to an address in North Carolina.

(3) The retailer reported gross sales of at least five million dollars ($5,000,000) on its most recent federal income tax return.

(c) Assignment. - An assignment to a person of a debt listed in subsection (a) of this section is subject to the collection restrictions imposed by this section. (2000-120, s. 9.)

§ 105-269.14. Payment of use tax with individual income tax.

(a) Requirement. - An individual who owes use tax that is payable on an annual basis pursuant to G.S. 105-164.16(d) and who is required to file an individual income tax return under Part 2 of Article 4 of this Chapter must pay the use tax with the individual income tax return for the taxable year. The Secretary must provide appropriate space and information on the individual income tax form and instructions. The information must include the following:

(1) An explanation of an individual's obligation to pay use tax on items purchased from mail order, Internet, or other sellers that do not collect State and local sales and use taxes on the items.

(2) A method to help an individual determine the amount of use tax the individual owes. The method must list categories of items, such as personal computers and clothing, that are commonly sold by mail order or Internet and must include a table that gives the average amounts of use tax payable by taxpayers in various income ranges.

(b) Distribution. - The Secretary must distribute a portion of the net use tax proceeds collected under this section to counties and cities. The portion to be distributed to all counties and cities is the total net use tax proceeds collected under this section multiplied by a fraction. The numerator of the fraction is the local use tax proceeds collected under this section. The denominator of the fraction is the total use tax proceeds collected under this section. The Secretary must distribute this portion to the counties and cities in proportion to their total distributions under Articles 39, 40, 42, and 43 of this Chapter and Chapter 1096 of the 1967 Session Laws for the most recent period for which data are available. The provisions of G.S. 105-472, 105-486, and 105-501 do not apply to tax proceeds distributed under this section. (1999-341, s. 2; 2000-120, s. 10; 2002-72, s. 20; 2003-284, s. 44.1; 2005-276, s. 33.24; 2007-323, s. 31.16.3(i); 2009-451, s. 27A.3(b), (c); 2010-95, s. 42.)

§ 105-269.15. Income tax credits of partnerships.

(a) Qualification. - A partnership that engages in an activity that is eligible for a tax credit qualifies for the credit as an entity and then passes through to each of its partners the partner's distributive share of the credit for which the partnership entity qualifies. Maximum dollar limits and other limitations that apply in determining the amount of a tax credit available to a taxpayer apply to the same extent in determining the amount of a tax credit for which the partnership entity qualifies, with one exception. The exception is a limitation that the tax credit cannot exceed the amount of tax imposed on the taxpayer.

(b) Allowance of Credit to Partner. - A partner's distributive share of an income tax credit passed through by a partnership is allowed to the partner only to the extent the partner would have qualified for the credit if the partner stood in the position of the partnership. All limitations on an income tax credit apply to each partner to the extent of the partner's distributive share of the credit, except that a corporate partner's distributive share of an individual income tax credit is allowed as a corporation income tax credit to the extent the corporate partner could have qualified for a corporation income tax credit if it stood in the position of the partnership. All limitations on an income tax credit apply to the sum of the credit passed through to the partner plus the credit for which the partner qualifies directly.

(c) Determination of Distributive Share. - A partner's distributive share of an income tax credit shall be determined in accordance with sections 702 and 704 of the Code. (1993 (Reg. Sess., 1994), c. 674, s. 3; 2001-335, s. 1.)

Article 10.

Liability for Failure to Levy Taxes.

§ 105-270. Repeal of laws imposing liability upon governing bodies of local units.

All laws and clauses of laws, statutes and parts of statutes, imposing civil or criminal liability upon the governing bodies, of local units, or the members of such governing bodies, for failure to levy or to vote for the levy of any particular tax or rate of tax for any particular purpose, are hereby repealed, and said governing bodies and any and all members thereof are hereby freed and released from any civil or criminal liability heretofore imposed by any law or statute for failure to levy or to vote for the levy of any particular tax or tax rate for any particular purpose. (1933, c. 418.)

SUBCHAPTER II. LISTING, APPRAISAL, AND ASSESSMENT OF PROPERTY AND COLLECTION OF TAXES ON PROPERTY.

Article 11.

Short Title, Purpose, and Definitions.

§ 105-271. Official title.

This Subchapter may be cited as the Machinery Act. (1939, c. 310, s. 1; 1971, c. 806. s. 1.)

§ 105-272. Purpose of Subchapter.

The purpose of this Subchapter is to provide the machinery for the listing, appraisal, and assessment of property and the levy and collection of taxes on property by counties and municipalities. It is the intent of the General Assembly to make the provisions of this Subchapter uniformly applicable throughout the State, and to assure this objective no local act to become effective on or after July 1, 1971, shall be construed to repeal or amend any section of this Subchapter in whole or in part unless it shall expressly so provide by specific reference to the section to be repealed or amended. As used in this section, the term "local act" means any act of the General Assembly that applies to one or more counties by name, to one or more municipalities by name, or to all municipalities within one or more named counties. (1939, c. 310, s. 1802; 1971, c. 806, s. 1; 1991, c. 11, s. 1.)

§ 105-273. Definitions.

The following definitions apply in this Subchapter:

(1)   Abstract. - The document on which the property of a taxpayer is listed for ad valorem taxation and on which the appraised and assessed values of the property are recorded.

(2)   Appraisal. - The true value of property or the process by which true value is ascertained.

(3)   Assessment. - The tax value of property or the process by which the assessment is determined.

(3a)   (Effective for taxes imposed for taxable years beginning on or after July 1, 2010. See note for repeal.) "Builder" means a taxpayer licensed as a general contractor under G.S. 87-1 and engaged in the business of buying real property, making improvements to it, and then reselling it.

(4)   Repealed by Session Laws 1973, c. 695, s. 15, effective January 1, 1974.

(4a)   Code. - Defined in G.S. 105-228.90.

(5) Collector or tax collector. - A person charged with the duty of collecting taxes for a county or municipality.

(5a) Construction contractor. - A taxpayer who is regularly engaged in building, installing, repairing, or improving real property.

(6) Corporation. - An organization having capital stock represented by shares or an incorporated, nonprofit organization.

(6a) Discovered property. - Any of the following:

a. Property that was not listed during a listing period.

b. Property that was listed but the listing included a substantial understatement.

c. Property that has been granted an exemption or exclusion and does not qualify for the exemption or exclusion.

(6b) Discover property. - Determine any of the following:

a. Property has not been listed during a listing period.

b. A taxpayer made a substantial understatement of listed property.

c. Property was granted an exemption or exclusion and the property does not qualify for an exemption or exclusion.

(7) Document. - A book, paper, record, statement, account, map, plat, film, picture, tape, object, instrument, or any other thing conveying information.

(7a) Failure to list property. - Any of the following:

a. Failure to list property during a listing period.

b. A substantial understatement of listed property.

c. Failure to notify the assessor that property granted an exemption or exclusion under an application for exemption or exclusion does not qualify for the exemption or exclusion.

(8) Intangible personal property. - Patents, copyrights, secret processes, formulae, good will, trademarks, trade brands, franchises, stocks, bonds, cash, bank deposits, notes, evidences of debt, leasehold interests in exempted real property, bills and accounts receivable, or other like property.

(8a) Inventories. - Any of the following:

a. Goods held for sale in the regular course of business by manufacturers, retail and wholesale merchants, and construction contractors. As to retail and wholesale merchants and construction contractors, the term includes packaging materials that accompany and become a part of the goods sold.

b. Goods held by construction contractors to be furnished in the course of building, installing, repairing, or improving real property.

c. As to manufacturers, raw materials, goods in process, finished goods, or other materials or supplies that are consumed in manufacturing or processing or that accompany and become a part of the sale of the property being sold. The term does not include fuel used in manufacturing or processing and materials or supplies not used directly in manufacturing or processing.

d. A modular home as defined in G.S. 105-164.3(21b) that is used exclusively as a display model and held for eventual sale at the retail merchant's place of business.

e. Crops, livestock, poultry, feed used in the production of livestock and poultry, or other agricultural or horticultural products held for sale, whether in process or ready for sale.

(9) List or listing. - An abstract, when the term is used as a noun.

(10) Repealed by Session Laws 1987, c. 43, s. 1.

(10a) Local tax official. - A county assessor, an assistant county assessor, a member of a county board of commissioners, a member of a county board of equalization and review, a county tax collector, or the municipal equivalent of one of these officials.

(10b) Manufacturer. - A taxpayer who is regularly engaged in the mechanical or chemical conversion or transformation of materials or substances into new products for sale or in the growth, breeding, raising, or other production of new products for sale. The term does not include delicatessens, cafes, cafeterias, restaurants, and other similar retailers that are principally engaged in the retail sale of foods prepared by them for consumption on or off their premises.

(11) Municipal corporation or municipality. - A city, town, incorporated village, sanitary district, rural fire protection district, rural recreation district, mosquito control district, hospital district, metropolitan sewerage district, watershed improvement district, a consolidated city-county as defined by G.S. 160B-2, or another district or unit of local government by or for which ad valorem taxes are levied.

(12) Person. - An individual, a trustee, an executor, an administrator, another fiduciary, a corporation, a limited liability company, an unincorporated association, a partnership, a sole proprietorship, a company, a firm, or another legal entity.

(13) Real property, real estate, or land. - Any of the following:

a. The land itself.

b. Buildings, structures, improvements, or permanent fixtures on land.

c. All rights and privileges belonging or in any way appertaining to the property.

d. A manufactured home as defined in G.S. 143-143.9(6), unless it is considered tangible personal property for failure to meet all of the following requirements:

1. It is a residential structure.

2. It has the moving hitch, wheels, and axles removed.

3. It is placed upon a permanent foundation either on land owned by the owner of the manufactured home or on land in which the owner of the manufactured home has a leasehold interest pursuant to a lease with a primary term of at least 20 years and the lease expressly provides for disposition of the manufactured home upon termination of the lease.

(13a) Retail merchant. - A taxpayer who is regularly engaged in the sale of tangible personal property, acquired by a means other than manufacture, processing, or producing by the merchant, to users or consumers.

(13b) Substantial understatement. - The omission of a material portion of the value, quantity, or other measurement of taxable property. The determination of materiality in each case shall be made by the assessor, subject to the taxpayer's right to review of the determination by the county board of equalization and review or board of commissioners and appeal to the Property Tax Commission.

(14) Tangible personal property. - All personal property that is not intangible and that is not permanently affixed to real property.

(15) Tax or taxes. - The principal amount of any property tax or dog license tax and costs, penalties, and interest.

(16) Taxing unit. - A county or municipality authorized to levy ad valorem property taxes.

(17) Taxpayer. - A person whose property is subject to ad valorem property taxation by any county or municipality and any person who, under the terms of this Subchapter, has a duty to list property for taxation.

(18) Valuation. - Appraisal and assessment.

(19) Wholesale merchant. - A taxpayer who is regularly engaged in the sale of tangible personal property, acquired by a means other than manufacture, processing, or producing by the merchant, to other retail or wholesale merchants for resale or to manufacturers for use as ingredient or component parts of articles being manufactured for sale. (1939, c. 310, s. 2; 1971, c. 806, s. 1; 1973, c. 695, ss. 14, 15; 1985, c. 656, s. 20; 1985 (Reg. Sess., 1986), c. 947, ss. 3, 4; 1987, c. 43, s. 1; c. 440, s. 2; c. 805, s. 3; c. 813, ss. 1-4; 1991, c. 34, s. 3; 1991 (Reg. Sess., 1992), c. 975, s. 1; c. 1004, s. 1; 1993, c. 354, s. 23; c. 459, s. 1; 1995, c. 461, s. 15; 1998-212, s. 29A.18(c); 2001-506, s. 1; 2002-156, s. 4; 2003-400, s. 4; 2006-106, ss. 1, 8; 2008-35, s. 1.1; 2009-308, s. 1; 2009-445, s. 20.)

Article 12.

Property Subject to Taxation.

§ 105-274. Property subject to taxation.

(a)   All property, real and personal, within the jurisdiction of the State shall be subject to taxation unless it is:

(1)   Excluded from the tax base by a statute of statewide application enacted under the classification power accorded the General Assembly by Article V, § 2(2), of the North Carolina Constitution, or

(2)   Exempted from taxation by the Constitution or by a statute of statewide application enacted under the authority granted the General Assembly by Article V, § 2(3), of the North Carolina Constitution.

(b)   No provision of this Subchapter shall be construed to exempt from taxation any property situated in this State belonging to any foreign corporation unless the context of the provision clearly indicates a legislative intent to grant such an exemption. (1939, c. 310, ss. 303, 1800; 1961, c. 1169, s. 8; 1967, c. 1185; 1971, c. 806, s. 1.)

§ 105-275. Property classified and excluded from the tax base.

The following classes of property are designated special classes under Article V, Sec. 2(2), of the North Carolina Constitution and are excluded from tax:

(1)   Repealed by Session Laws 1987, c. 813, s. 5.

(2)   Tangible personal property that has been imported from a foreign country through a North Carolina seaport terminal and which is stored at such a terminal while awaiting further shipment for the first 12 months of such storage. (The purpose of this classification is to encourage the development of the ports of this State.)

(3)   Real and personal property owned by nonprofit water or nonprofit sewer associations or corporations.

(4)   Repealed by Session Laws 1987, c. 813, s. 5.

(5)   Vehicles that the United States government gives to veterans on account of disabilities they suffered in World War II, the Korean Conflict, or the Vietnam Era so long as they are owned by:

a.   A person to whom a vehicle has been given by the United States government or

b.   Another person who is entitled to receive such a gift under Title 38, section 252, United States Code Annotated.

(5a)   A motor vehicle owned by a disabled veteran that is altered with special equipment to accommodate a service-connected disability. As used in this section, disabled veteran means a person as defined in 38 U.S.C. § 101(2) who is entitled to special automotive equipment for a service-connected disability, as provided in 38 U.S.C. § 3901.

(6)   Special nuclear materials held for or in the process of manufacture, processing, or delivery by the manufacturer or processor thereof, regardless whether the manufacturer or processor owns the special nuclear materials. The terms "manufacture" and "processing" do not include the use of special nuclear materials as fuel. The term "special nuclear materials" includes (i) uranium 233, uranium enriched in the isotope 233 or in the isotope 235; and (ii) any material artificially enriched by any of the foregoing, but not including source material. "Source material" means any material except special nuclear material which contains by weight one twentieth of one percent (0.05%) or more of (i) uranium, (ii) thorium, or (iii) any combination thereof. Provided however, that to qualify for this exemption no such nuclear materials shall be discharged into any river, creek or stream in North Carolina. The classification and exclusion provided for herein shall be denied to any manufacturer, fabricator or processor who permits burial of such material in North Carolina or who permits the discharge of such nuclear materials into the air or into any river, creek or stream in North Carolina if such discharge would contravene in any way the applicable health and safety standards established and enforced by the Department of Environment and Natural Resources or the Nuclear Regulatory Commission. The most stringent of these standards shall govern.

(7)   Real and personal property that is:

a.   Owned either by a nonprofit corporation formed under the provisions of Chapter 55A of the General Statutes or by a bona fide charitable organization, and either operated by such owning organization or leased to another such nonprofit corporation or charitable organization, and

b.   Appropriated exclusively for public parks and drives.

(7a) (Effective for taxes imposed for taxable years beginning on or after July 1, 2011, and expiring for taxes imposed for taxable years beginning on or after July 1, 2016) Real and personal property that meets each of the following requirements:

a. It is a contiguous tract of land previously (i) used primarily for commercial or industrial purposes and (ii) damaged significantly as a result of a fire or explosion.

b. It was donated to a nonprofit corporation formed under the provisions of Chapter 55A of the General Statutes by an entity other than an affiliate, as defined in G.S. 105-163.010.

c. No portion is or has been leased or sold by the nonprofit corporation.

(8) a. Real and personal property that is used or, if under construction, is to be used exclusively for air cleaning or waste disposal or to abate, reduce, or prevent the pollution of air or water (including, but not limited to, waste lagoons and facilities owned by public or private utilities built and installed primarily for the purpose of providing sewer service to areas that are predominantly residential in character or areas that lie outside territory already having sewer service), if the Department of Environment and Natural Resources or a local air pollution control program for air-cleaning devices located in an area where the Environmental Management Commission has certified a local air pollution control program pursuant to G.S. 143-215.112 furnishes a certificate to the tax supervisor of the county in which the property is situated or to be situated stating that the Environmental Management Commission or local air pollution control program has found that the described property:

1. Has been or will be constructed or installed;

2. Complies with or that plans therefor which have been submitted to the Environmental Management Commission or local air pollution control program indicate that it will comply with the requirements of the Environmental Management Commission or local air pollution control program;

3. Is being effectively operated or will, when completed, be required to operate in accordance with the terms and conditions of the permit, certificate of approval, or other document of approval issued by the Environmental Management Commission or local air pollution control program; and

4. Has or, when completed, will have as its primary rather than incidental purpose the reduction of water pollution resulting from the discharge of sewage and waste or the reduction of air pollution resulting from the emission of air contaminants.

a1. Sub-subdivision a. of this subdivision shall not apply to an animal waste management system, as defined in G.S. 143-215.10B, unless the Environmental Management Commission determines that the animal waste management system will accomplish all of the following:

1. Eliminate the discharge of animal waste to surface waters and groundwater through direct discharge, seepage, or runoff.

2. Substantially eliminate atmospheric emissions of ammonia.

3. Substantially eliminate the emission of odor that is detectable beyond the boundaries of the parcel or tract of land on which the farm is located.

4. Substantially eliminate the release of disease-transmitting vectors and airborne pathogens.

5. Substantially eliminate nutrient and heavy metal contamination of soil and groundwater.

b. Real or personal property that is used or, if under construction, is to be used exclusively for recycling or resource recovering of or from solid waste, if the Department of Environment and Natural Resources furnishes a certificate to the tax supervisor of the county in which the property is situated stating the Department of Environment and Natural Resources has found that the described property has been or will be constructed or installed, complies or will comply with the rules of the Department of Environment and Natural Resources, and has, or will have as its primary purpose recycling or resource recovering of or from solid waste.

c. Tangible personal property that is used exclusively, or if being installed, is to be used exclusively, for the prevention or reduction of cotton dust inside a textile plant for the protection of the health of the employees of the plant, in accordance with occupational safety and health standards adopted by the State of North Carolina pursuant to Article 16 of G.S. Chapter 95. Notwithstanding the exclusive use requirement of this sub-subdivision, all parts of a ventilation or air conditioning system that are integrated into a system used for the prevention or reduction of cotton dust, except for chillers and cooling towers, are excluded from taxation under this sub-subdivision. The Department of Revenue shall adopt guidelines to assist the tax supervisors in administering this exclusion.

    d.   Real or personal property that is used or, if under construction, is to be used by a major recycling facility as defined in G.S. 105-129.25 predominantly for recycling or resource recovering of or from solid waste, if the Department of Environment and Natural Resources furnishes a certificate to the tax supervisor of the county in which the property is situated stating the Department of Environment and Natural Resources has found that the described property has been or will be constructed or installed for use by a major recycling facility, complies or will comply with the rules of the Department of Environment and Natural Resources, and has, or will have as a purpose recycling or resource recovering of or from solid waste.

(9)   through (11) Repealed by Session Laws 1987, c. 813, s. 5.

(12)   Real property that (i) is owned by a nonprofit corporation or association organized to receive and administer lands for conservation purposes, (ii) is exclusively held and used for one or more of the purposes listed in this subdivision, and (iii) produces no income or produces income that is incidental to and not inconsistent with the purpose or purposes for which the land is held and used. The taxes that would otherwise be due on land classified under this subdivision shall be a lien on the real property of the taxpayer as provided in G.S. 105-355(a). The taxes shall be carried forward in the records of the taxing unit or units as deferred taxes. The deferred taxes for the preceding five fiscal years are due and payable in accordance with G.S. 105-277.1F when the property loses its eligibility for deferral as a result of a disqualifying event. A disqualifying event occurs when the property (i) is no longer exclusively held and used for one or more of the purposes listed in this subdivision, (ii) produces income that is not incidental to and consistent with the purpose or purposes for which the land is held and used, or (iii) is sold or transferred without an easement recorded at the time of sale that requires perpetual use of the land for one or more of the purposes listed in this subdivision and that prohibits any use of the land that would generate income that is not incidental to and consistent with the purpose or purposes for which the land is held and used. In addition to the provisions in G.S. 105-277.1F, all liens arising under this subdivision are extinguished upon the real property being sold or transferred to a local, state, or federal government unit for conservation purposes or subject to an easement recorded at the time of sale that requires perpetual use of the land for one or

more of the purposes listed in this subdivision. The purposes allowed under this subdivision are any of the following:

a.   Used for an educational or scientific purpose as a nature reserve or park in which wild nature, flora and fauna, and biotic communities are preserved for observation and study. For purposes of this sub-subdivision, the terms "educational purpose" and "scientific purpose" are defined in G.S. 105-278.7(f).

b.   Managed under a written wildlife habitat conservation agreement with the North Carolina Wildlife Resources Commission.

c.   Managed under a forest stewardship plan developed by the Forest Stewardship Program.

d.   Used for public access to public waters or trails.

e.   Used for protection of water quality and subject to a conservation agreement under the provision of the Conservation and Historic Preservation Agreements Act, Article 4, Chapter 121 of the General Statutes.

f.   Held by a nonprofit land conservation organization for sale or transfer to a local, state, or federal government unit for conservation purposes.

(13)   Repealed by Session Laws 1973, c. 904.

(14)   Motor vehicles chassis belonging to nonresidents, which chassis temporarily enters the State for the purpose of having a body mounted thereon.

(15)   Upon the date on which each county's next general reappraisal of real property under the provisions of G.S. 105-286(a) becomes effective, standing timber, pulpwood, seedlings, saplings, and other forest growth. (The purpose of this classification is to encourage proper forest management practices and to develop and maintain the forest resources of the State.)

(16)   Non-business Property. - As used in this subdivision, the term "non-business property" means personal property that is used by the owner of the property for a purpose other than the production of income and is not used in connection with a business. The term includes household furnishings, clothing, pets, lawn tools, and lawn equipment. The term does not include motor vehicles, mobile homes, aircraft, watercraft, or engines for watercraft.

(17) Real and personal property belonging to the American Legion, Veterans of Foreign Wars, Disabled American Veterans, or to any similar veterans organizations chartered by the Congress of the United States or organized and operated on a statewide or nationwide basis, and any post or local organization thereof, when used exclusively for meeting or lodge purposes by said organization, together with such additional adjacent real property as may be necessary for the convenient and normal use of the buildings thereon. Notwithstanding the exclusive-use requirement hereinabove established, if a part of a property that otherwise meets this subdivision's requirements is used for a purpose that would require that it not be listed, appraised, assessed or taxed if the entire property were so used, that part, according to its value, shall not be listed, appraised, assessed or taxed. The fact that a building or facility is incidentally available to and patronized by the general public, so far as there is no material amount of business or patronage with the general public, shall not defeat the classification granted by this section.

(18) Real and personal property belonging to the Grand Lodge of Ancient, Free and Accepted Masons of North Carolina, the Prince Hall Masonic Grand Lodge of North Carolina, their subordinate lodges and appendant bodies including the Ancient and Arabic Order Nobles of the Mystic Shrine, and the Ancient Egyptian Order Nobles of the Mystic Shrine, when used exclusively for meeting or lodge purposes by said organization, together with such additional adjacent real property as may be necessary for the convenient normal use of the buildings thereon. Notwithstanding the exclusive-use requirement hereinabove established, if a part of a property that otherwise meets this subdivision's requirements is used for a purpose that would require that it not be listed, appraised, assessed or taxed if the entire property were so used, that part, according to its value, shall not be listed, appraised, assessed or taxed. The fact that a building or facility is incidentally available to and patronized by the general public, so far as there is no material amount of business or patronage with the general public, shall not defeat the classification granted by this section.

(19) Real and personal property belonging to the Loyal Order of Moose, the Benevolent and Protective Order of Elks, the Knights of Pythias, the Odd Fellows, the Woodmen of the World, and similar fraternal or civic orders and organizations operated for nonprofit benevolent, patriotic, historical, charitable, or civic purposes, when used exclusively for meeting or lodge purposes by the organization, together with as much additional adjacent real property as may be necessary for the convenient normal use of the buildings. Notwithstanding the exclusive-use requirement of this subdivision, if a part of a property that

otherwise meets this subdivision's requirements is used for a purpose that would require that it not be listed, appraised, assessed, or taxed if the entire property were so used, that part, according to its value, shall not be listed, appraised, assessed, or taxed. The fact that a building or facility is incidentally available to and patronized by the general public, so far as there is no material amount of business or patronage with the general public, shall not defeat the classification granted by this section. Nothing in this subdivision shall be construed so as to include social fraternities, sororities, and similar college, university, or high school organizations in the classification for exclusion from ad valorem taxes.

(19a) (Effective for taxes imposed for taxable years beginning on or after July 1, 2013) Improvements to real property that are (i) owned by social fraternities, sororities, and similar college, university, or high school organizations and (ii) located on land owned by or allocated to The University of North Carolina or one if its constituent institutions.

(20) Real and personal property belonging to Goodwill Industries and other charitable organizations organized for the training and rehabilitation of disabled persons when used exclusively for training and rehabilitation, including commercial activities directly related to such training and rehabilitation.

(21) Repealed by Session Laws 2008-107, s. 28.11(a), effective for taxes imposed for taxable years beginning on or after July 1, 2009.

(22) Repealed by Session Laws 1987, c. 813, s. 5.

(23) Tangible personal property imported from outside the United States and held in a Foreign Trade Zone for the purpose of sale, manufacture, processing, assembly, grading, cleaning, mixing or display and tangible personal property produced in the United States and held in a Foreign Trade Zone for exportation, either in its original form or as altered by any of the above processes.

(24) Cargo containers and container chassis used for the transportation of cargo by vessels in ocean commerce.

The term "container" applies to those nondisposable receptacles of a permanent character and strong enough for repeated use and specially designed to facilitate the carriage of goods, by one or more modes of transport, one of which shall be by ocean vessels, without intermediate reloadings and fitted with devices permitting its ready handling particularly in the transfer from one transport mode to another.

(24a) Aircraft that is owned or leased by an interstate air courier, is apportioned under G.S. 105-337 to the air courier's hub in this State, and is used in the air courier's operations in this State. For the purpose of this subdivision, the terms "interstate air courier" and "hub" have the meanings provided in G.S. 105-164.3.

(25) Tangible personal property shipped into this State for the purpose of repair, alteration, maintenance or servicing and reshipment to the owner outside this State.

(26) For the tax year immediately following transfer of title, tangible personal property manufactured in this State for the account of a nonresident customer and held by the manufacturer for shipment. For the purpose of this subdivision, the term "nonresident" means a taxpayer having no place of business in North Carolina.

(27), (28) Repealed by Session Laws 1983, c. 643, s. 1.

(29) Real property and easements wholly and exclusively held and used for nonprofit historic preservation purposes by a nonprofit historical association or institution, including real property owned by a nonprofit corporation organized for historic preservation purposes and held by its owner exclusively for sale under an historic preservation agreement to be prepared and recorded, at the time of sale, under the provisions of the Conservation and Historic Preservation Agreements Act, Article 4, Chapter 121 of the General Statutes of North Carolina.

(29a) Land that is within an historic district and is held by a nonprofit corporation organized for historic preservation purposes for use as a future site for an historic structure that is to be moved to the site from another location. Property may be classified under this subdivision for no more than five years. The taxes that would otherwise be due on land classified under this subdivision shall be a lien on the real property of the taxpayer as provided in G.S. 105-355(a). The taxes shall be carried forward in the records of the taxing unit or units as deferred taxes. The deferred taxes are due and payable in accordance with G.S. 105-277.1F when the property loses its eligibility for deferral as a result of a disqualifying event. A disqualifying event occurs when an historic structure is not moved to the property within five years from the first day of the fiscal year the property was classified under this subdivision. In addition to the provisions in G.S. 105-277.1F, all liens arising under this subdivision are extinguished upon the location of an historic structure on the site within the time period allowed under this subdivision.

(30)   Repealed by Session Laws 1987, c. 813, s. 5.

(31)   Intangible personal property other than a leasehold interest that is in exempted real property and is not excluded under subdivision (31e) of this section. This subdivision does not affect the taxation of software not otherwise excluded by subdivision (40) of this section.

(31a)   through (31d) Repealed by Session Laws 1997-23, s. 3.

(31e)   A leasehold interest in real property that is exempt under G.S. 105-278.1 and is used to provide affordable housing for employees of the unit of government that owns the property.

(32)   Recodified as G.S. 105-278.6A by Session Laws 1998-212, s. 29A.18(a), effective for taxes imposed for taxable years beginning on or after July 1, 1998.

(32a)   Inventories owned by contractors.

(33)   Inventories owned by manufacturers.

(34)   Inventories owned by retail and wholesale merchants.

(35)   Severable development rights, as defined in G.S. 136-66.11(a), when severed and evidenced by a deed recorded in the office of the register of deeds pursuant to G.S. 136-66.11(c).

(36)   Repealed by Session Laws 2001-474, s. 8, effective November 29, 2001.

(37)   Poultry and livestock and feed used in the production of poultry and livestock.

(38)   Repealed by Session Laws 2001-474, s. 8, effective November 29, 2001.

(39) Real and personal property that is: (i) owned by a nonprofit corporation organized upon the request of a State or local government unit for the sole purpose of financing projects for public use, (ii) leased to a unit of State or local government whose property is exempt from taxation under G.S. 105-278.1, and (iii) used in whole or in part for a public purpose by the unit of State or local government. If only part of the property is used for a public purpose, only that part is excluded from the tax. This subdivision does not apply if any distributions are made to members, officers, or directors of the nonprofit corporation.

(39a) A correctional facility, including construction in progress, that is located on land owned by the State and is constructed pursuant to a contract with the State, and any leasehold interest in the land owned by the State upon which the correctional facility is located.

(40) (Effective for taxes imposed for taxable years beginning before July 1, 2014) Computer software and any documentation related to the computer software. As used in this subdivision, the term "computer software" means any program or routine used to cause a computer to perform a specific task or set of tasks. The term includes system and application programs and database storage and management programs.

The exclusion established by this subdivision does not apply to computer software and its related documentation if the computer software meets one or more of the following descriptions:

a. It is embedded software. "Embedded software" means computer instructions, known as microcode, that reside permanently in the internal memory of a computer system or other equipment and are not intended to be removed without terminating the operation of the computer system or equipment and removing a computer chip, a circuit, or another mechanical device.

b. It is purchased or licensed from a person who is unrelated to the taxpayer and it is capitalized on the books of the taxpayer in accordance with generally accepted accounting principles, including financial accounting standards issued by the Financial Accounting Standards Board. A person is unrelated to a taxpayer if (i) the taxpayer and the person are not subject to any common ownership, either directly or indirectly, and (ii) neither the taxpayer nor the person has any ownership interest, either directly or indirectly, in the other.

This subdivision does not affect the value or taxable status of any property that is otherwise subject to taxation under this Subchapter.

The provisions of the exclusion established by this subdivision are not severable. If any provision of this subdivision or its application is held invalid, the entire subdivision is repealed.

(40) (Effective for taxes imposed for taxable years beginning on or after July 1, 2014) Computer software and any documentation related to the computer software. As used in this subdivision, the term "computer software" means any program or routine used to cause a computer to perform a specific task or set of tasks. The term includes system and application programs and database storage and management programs.

The exclusion established by this subdivision does not apply to computer software and its related documentation if the computer software meets one or more of the following descriptions:

a. It is embedded software. "Embedded software" means computer instructions, known as microcode, that reside permanently in the internal memory of a computer system or other equipment and are not intended to be removed without terminating the operation of the computer system or equipment and removing a computer chip, a circuit, or another mechanical device.

b. It is purchased or licensed from a person who is unrelated to the taxpayer and it is capitalized on the books of the taxpayer in accordance with generally accepted accounting principles, including financial accounting standards issued by the Financial Accounting Standards Board. A person is unrelated to a taxpayer if (i) the taxpayer and the person are not subject to any common ownership, either directly or indirectly, and (ii) neither the taxpayer nor the person has any ownership interest, either directly or indirectly, in the other. The foregoing does not include development of software or any modifications to software, whether done internally by the taxpayer or externally by a third party, to meet the customer's specified needs.

This subdivision does not affect the value or taxable status of any property that is otherwise subject to taxation under this Subchapter.

The provisions of the exclusion established by this subdivision are not severable. If any provision of this subdivision or its application is held invalid, the entire subdivision is repealed.

(41) Repealed by Session Laws 2012-120, s. 1(a), effective October 1, 2012.

(42) A vehicle that is offered at retail for short-term lease or rental and is owned or leased by an entity engaged in the business of leasing or renting vehicles to the general public for short-term lease or rental. For the purposes of this subdivision, the term "short-term lease or rental" shall have the same meaning as in G.S. 105-187.1, and the term "vehicle" shall have the same meaning as in G.S. 153A-156(e) and G.S. 160A-215.1(e). A gross receipts tax as set forth by G.S. 153A-156 and G.S. 160A-215.1 is substituted for and replaces the ad valorem tax previously levied on these vehicles.

(42a) Heavy equipment on which a gross receipts tax may be imposed under G.S. 153A-156.1 and G.S. 160A-215.2.

(43) Real or tangible personal property that is subject to a capital lease pursuant to G.S. 115C-531.

(44) Free samples of drugs that are required by federal law to be dispensed only on prescription and are given to physicians and other medical practitioners to dispense free of charge in the course of their practice.

(45) Eighty percent (80%) of the appraised value of a solar energy electric system. For purposes of this subdivision, the term "solar energy electric system" means all equipment used directly and exclusively for the conversion of solar energy to electricity.

(46) (Effective for taxes imposed for taxable years beginning on or after July 1, 2013) Real property that is occupied by a charter school and is wholly and exclusively used for educational purposes as defined in G.S. 105-278.4(f) regardless of the ownership of the property. (1939, c. 310, s. 303; 1961, c. 1169, s. 8; 1967, c. 1185; 1971, c. 806, s. 1; c. 1121, s. 3; 1973, cc. 290, 451; c. 476, s. 128; c. 484; c. 695, s. 1; c. 790, s. 1; cc. 904, 962, 1028, 1034, 1077; c. 1262, s. 23; c. 1264, s. 1; 1975, cc. 566, 755; c. 764, s. 6; 1977, c. 771, s. 4; c. 782, s. 2; c. 1001, ss. 1, 2; 1977, 2nd Sess., c. 1200, s. 4; 1979, c. 200, s. 1; 1979, 2nd Sess., c. 1092; 1981, c. 86, s. 1; 1981 (Reg. Sess., 1982), c. 1244, ss. 1, 2; 1983, c. 643, ss. 1, 2; c. 693; 1983 (Reg. Sess., 1984), c. 1060; 1985, c. 510, s. 1; c. 656, s. 37; 1985 (Reg. Sess., 1986), c. 982, s. 18; 1987, c. 356; c. 622, s. 2; c. 747, s. 8; c. 777, s. 6; c. 813, ss. 5, 6, 22; c. 850, s. 17; 1987 (Reg. Sess., 1988), c. 1041, s. 1.1; 1989, c. 148, s. 4; c. 168, s. 6; c. 705; c. 723, s. 1; c. 727, ss. 28, 29; 1991, c. 717, s. 1; 1991 (Reg. Sess., 1992), c. 975, s. 2; 1993, c. 459, s. 2; 1993 (Reg. Sess., 1994), c. 745, s. 39; 1995, c. 41, s. 2; c. 509, s. 51; 1995 (Reg. Sess., 1996), c. 646, s. 12; 1997-23, ss. 1, 3, 9; 1997-443, s. 11A.119(a); 1997-456, s. 27; 1998-55, ss. 10, 18; 1998-212, s.

29A.18(a); 1999-337, s. 35(a); 2000-2, s. 1; 2000-18, s. 1, 2000-140, ss. 71, 72(a); 2001-84, s. 3; 2001-427, s. 15(a); 2001-474, s. 8; 2002-104, s. 1; 2003-284, s. 43A.1; 2007-477, s. 1; 2007-527, s. 37; 2008-35, s. 2.1; 2008-107, s. 28.11(a); 2008-134, s. 72; 2008-144, s. 1; 2008-146, ss. 4.1, 5.1; 2008-171, ss. 7(a), (b); 2009-445, s. 21; 2010-95, s. 15; 2011-123, s. 1; 2011-274, s. 1; 2012-120, s. 1(a); 2013-259, s. 1; 2013-355, s. 3; 2013-375, s. 3(a).)

§ 105-275.1: Repealed by Session Laws 2001-424, s. 34.15, as amended by Session Laws 2002-126, 30A.1, effective July 1, 2002.

§ 105-275.2: Repealed by Session Laws 2001-424, s. 34.15, as amended by Session Laws 2002-126, 30A.1, effective July 1, 2002.

§ 105-276. Taxation of intangible personal property.

Intangible personal property that is not excluded from taxation under G.S. 105-275 is subject to this Subchapter. The exclusion of a class of intangible personal property from taxation under G.S. 105-275 does not affect the appraisal or assessment of real property and tangible personal property. (1939, c. 310, s. 601; 1971, c. 806, s. 1; 1973, c. 1180; 1985, c. 656, s. 38; 1987, c. 813, s. 8; 1995, c. 41, s. 6; 1997-23, s. 2.)

§ 105-277. Property classified for taxation at reduced rates; certain deductions.

(a) through (c) Repealed by Session Laws 1987, c. 813, s. 9, effective for taxable years beginning on or after January 1, 1988.

(d) All bona fide indebtedness incurred in the purchase of fertilizer and fertilizer materials owing by a taxpayer as principal debtor may be deducted from the total value of all fertilizer and fertilizer materials as are held by such taxpayer for his own use in agriculture during the current year.

(e) Repealed by Session Laws 1987, c. 813, s. 9, effective for taxable years beginning on or after January 1, 1988.

(f) Repealed by Session Laws 1977, c. 869, s. 1.

(g) Buildings equipped with a solar energy heating or cooling system, or both, are hereby designated a special class of property under authority of Article V, Sec. 2(2) of the North Carolina Constitution. Such buildings shall be assessed for taxation in accordance with each county's schedules of value for buildings equipped with conventional heating or cooling systems and no additional value shall be assigned for the difference in cost between a solar energy heating or cooling system and a conventional system typically found in the county. As used in this classification, the term "system" includes all controls, tanks, pumps, heat exchangers and other equipment used directly and exclusively for the conversion of solar energy for heating or cooling. The term "system" does not include any land or structural elements of the building such as walls and roofs nor other equipment ordinarily contained in the structure.

(h) Private Water Companies. - Contributions in aid of construction and acquisition adjustments. In assessing the property of any private water company, there shall be excluded that portion of the investment of the company represented by contributions in aid of construction and by acquisition adjustments which is designated a special class of property under Article V, Sec. 2(2) of the Constitution. "Investment," "contributions in aid of construction" and "acquisition adjustment" shall have the meanings as those terms are defined in the Uniform System of Accounts specified by the North Carolina Utilities Commission for use by such private water company.

(i) Repealed by Session Laws 1987, c. 622, s. 5. (1947, c. 1026; 1955, c. 697, s. 1; 1961, c. 1169, ss. 6, 7, 71/2; 1963, c. 940; 1971, c. 806, s. 1; 1973, c. 511, s. 4; c. 695, s. 2; 1975, c. 578; 1977, c. 869, s. 1; c. 965; 1979, c. 605, s. 1; 1985, c. 440; c. 656, ss. 52, 52.1; 1985 (Reg. Sess., 1986), c. 947, s. 5; 1987, c. 622, s. 5; c. 813, s. 9; 2003-416, s. 20.)

§ 105-277.001: Repealed by Session Laws 2001-424, s. 34.15, as amended by Session Laws 2002-126, 30A.1, effective July 1, 2002.

§ 105-277.01. Certain farm products classified for taxation at reduced valuation.

Farm products (including crops but excluding poultry and other livestock) held by or for a cooperative stabilization or marketing association or corporation to which they have been delivered, conveyed, or assigned by the original producer for the purpose of sale are hereby designated a special class of property under authority of Article V, Sec. 2(2), of the North Carolina Constitution. Before being assessed for taxation the appraised valuation of farm products so classified shall be reduced by the amount of any unpaid loan or advance made or granted thereon by the United States government, an agency of the United States government, or a cooperative stabilization or marketing association or corporation. (1973, c. 695, s. 3.)

§ 105-277.1. Elderly or disabled property tax homestead exclusion.

(a) Exclusion. - A permanent residence owned and occupied by a qualifying owner is designated a special class of property under Article V, Sec. 2(2) of the North Carolina Constitution and is taxable in accordance with this section. The amount of the appraised value of the residence equal to the exclusion amount is excluded from taxation. The exclusion amount is the greater of twenty five thousand dollars ($25,000) or fifty percent (50%) of the appraised value of the residence. An owner who receives an exclusion under this section may not receive other property tax relief.

A qualifying owner is an owner who meets all of the following requirements as of January 1 preceding the taxable year for which the benefit is claimed:

(1) Is at least 65 years of age or totally and permanently disabled.

(2) Has an income for the preceding calendar year of not more than the income eligibility limit.

(3) Is a North Carolina resident.

(a1) Temporary Absence. - An otherwise qualifying owner does not lose the benefit of this exclusion because of a temporary absence from his or her permanent residence for reasons of health, or because of an extended absence while confined to a rest home or nursing home, so long as the residence is unoccupied or occupied by the owner's spouse or other dependent.

(a2) Income Eligibility Limit. - For the taxable year beginning on July 1, 2008, the income eligibility limit is twenty-five thousand dollars ($25,000). For taxable years beginning on or after July 1, 2009, the income eligibility limit is the amount for the preceding year, adjusted by the same percentage of this amount as the percentage of any cost-of-living adjustment made to the benefits under Titles II and XVI of the Social Security Act for the preceding calendar year, rounded to the nearest one hundred dollars ($100.00). On or before July 1 of each year, the Department of Revenue must determine the income eligibility amount to be in effect for the taxable year beginning the following July 1 and must notify the assessor of each county of the amount to be in effect for that taxable year.

(b)	Definitions. - The following definitions apply in this section:

(1)	Code. - The Internal Revenue Code, as defined in G.S. 105-228.90.

(1a)	Income. - All moneys received from every source other than gifts or inheritances received from a spouse, lineal ancestor, or lineal descendant. For married applicants residing with their spouses, the income of both spouses must be included, whether or not the property is in both names.

(1b)	Owner. - A person who holds legal or equitable title, whether individually, as a tenant by the entirety, a joint tenant, or a tenant in common, or as the holder of a life estate or an estate for the life of another. A manufactured home jointly owned by husband and wife is considered property held by the entirety.

(2)	Repealed by Session Laws 1993, c. 360, s. 1.

(2a)	Repealed by Session Laws 1985 (Reg. Sess., 1986), c. 982, s. 20.

(3)	Permanent residence. - A person's legal residence. It includes the dwelling, the dwelling site, not to exceed one acre, and related improvements. The dwelling may be a single family residence, a unit in a multi-family residential complex, or a manufactured home.

(3a)	Property tax relief. - The property tax homestead exclusion provided in this section, the property tax homestead circuit breaker provided in G.S. 105-277.1B, or the disabled veteran property tax homestead exclusion provided in G.S. 105-277.1C.

(4)	Totally and permanently disabled. - A person is totally and permanently disabled if the person has a physical or mental impairment that substantially precludes him or her from obtaining gainful employment and appears reasonably certain to continue without substantial improvement throughout his or her life.

(c) Application. - An application for the exclusion provided by this section should be filed during the regular listing period, but may be filed and must be accepted at any time up to and through June 1 preceding the tax year for which the exclusion is claimed. When property is owned by two or more persons other than husband and wife and one or more of them qualifies for this exclusion, each owner must apply separately for his or her proportionate share of the exclusion.

(1) Elderly Applicants. - Persons 65 years of age or older may apply for this exclusion by entering the appropriate information on a form made available by the assessor under G.S. 105-282.1.

(2) Disabled Applicants. - Persons who are totally and permanently disabled may apply for this exclusion by (i) entering the appropriate information on a form made available by the assessor under G.S. 105-282.1 and (ii) furnishing acceptable proof of their disability. The proof must be in the form of a certificate from a physician licensed to practice medicine in North Carolina or from a governmental agency authorized to determine qualification for disability benefits. After a disabled applicant has qualified for this classification, the applicant is not required to furnish an additional certificate unless the applicant's disability is reduced to the extent that the applicant could no longer be certified for the taxation at reduced valuation.

(d) Ownership by Spouses. - A permanent residence owned and occupied by husband and wife is entitled to the full benefit of this exclusion notwithstanding that only one of them meets the age or disability requirements of this section.

(e) Other Multiple Owners. - This subsection applies to co-owners who are not husband and wife. Each co-owner of a permanent residence must apply separately for the exclusion allowed under this section.

When one or more co-owners of a permanent residence qualify for the exclusion allowed under this section and none of the co-owners qualifies for the exclusion allowed under G.S. 105-277.1C, each co-owner is entitled to the full amount of the exclusion allowed under this section. The exclusion allowed to one co-owner may not exceed the co-owner's proportionate share of the valuation of the property, and the amount of the exclusion allowed to all the co-owners may not exceed the exclusion allowed under this section.

When one or more co-owners of a permanent residence qualify for the exclusion allowed under this section and one or more of the co-owners qualify for the exclusion allowed under G.S. 105-277.1C, each co-owner who qualifies for the exclusion under this section is entitled to the full amount of the exclusion. The exclusion allowed to one co-owner may not exceed the co-owner's proportionate share of the valuation of the property, and the amount of the exclusion allowed to all the co-owners may not exceed the greater of the exclusion allowed under this section and the exclusion allowed under G.S. 105-277.1C. (1971, c. 932, s. 1; 1973, c. 448, s. 1; 1975, c. 881, s. 2; 1977, c. 666, s. 1; 1979, c. 356, s. 1; c. 846, s. 1; 1981, c. 54, s. 1; c. 1052, s. 1; 1985, c. 656, ss. 44, 45; 1985 (Reg. Sess., 1986), c. 982, ss. 19, 20; 1987, c. 45, s. 1; 1993, c. 360, s. 1; 1996, 2nd Ex. Sess., c. 18, s. 15.1(a); 2001-308, s. 1; 2007-484, s. 43.7T(a), (b); 2007-497, ss. 1.1, 2.1, 2.2; 2008-35, s. 3; 2008-107, s. 28.11(c)-(f), (i); 2009-445, s. 22(a).)

§ 105-277.1A: Repealed by Session Laws 2001-424, s. 34.15, as amended by Session Laws 2002-126, 30A.1, effective July 1, 2002.

§ 105-277.1B. Property tax homestead circuit breaker.

(a) Classification. - A permanent residence owned and occupied by a qualifying owner is designated a special class of property under Article V, Section 2(2) of the North Carolina Constitution and is taxable in accordance with this section.

(b) Definitions. - The definitions provided in G.S. 105-277.1 apply to this section.

(c) Income Eligibility Limit. - The income eligibility limit provided in G.S. 105-277.1(a2) applies to this section.

(d) Qualifying Owner. - For the purpose of qualifying for the property tax homestead circuit breaker under this section, a qualifying owner is an owner who meets all of the following requirements as of January 1 preceding the taxable year for which the benefit is claimed:

(1) The owner has an income for the preceding calendar year of not more than one hundred fifty percent (150%) of the income eligibility limit specified in subsection (c) of this section.

(2) The owner has owned the property as a permanent residence for at least five consecutive years and has occupied the property as a permanent residence for at least five years.

(3) The owner is at least 65 years of age or totally and permanently disabled.

(4) The owner is a North Carolina resident.

(e) Multiple Owners. - A permanent residence owned and occupied by husband and wife is entitled to the full benefit of the property tax homestead circuit breaker notwithstanding that only one of them meets the length of occupancy and ownership requirements and the age or disability requirement of this section. When a permanent residence is owned and occupied by two or more persons other than husband and wife, no property tax homestead circuit breaker is allowed unless all of the owners qualify and elect to defer taxes under this section.

(f) Tax Limitation. - A qualifying owner may defer the portion of the principal amount of tax that is imposed for the current tax year on his or her permanent residence and exceeds the percentage of the qualifying owner's income set out in the table in this subsection. If a permanent residence is subject to tax by more than one taxing unit and the total tax liability exceeds the tax limit imposed by this section, then both the taxes due under this section and the taxes deferred under this section must be apportioned among the taxing units based upon the ratio each taxing unit's tax rate bears to the total tax rate of all units.

Income Over	Income Up To	Percentage
-0-	Income Eligibility Limit	4.0%
Income Eligibility Limit	150% of Income Eligibility Limit	5.0%

(g) Temporary Absence. - An otherwise qualifying owner does not lose the benefit of this circuit breaker because of a temporary absence from his or her permanent residence for reasons of health, or because of an extended absence while confined to a rest home or nursing home, so long as the residence is unoccupied or occupied by the owner's spouse or other dependent.

(h) Deferred Taxes. - The difference between the taxes due under this section and the taxes that would have been payable in the absence of this section are a lien on the real property of the taxpayer as provided in G.S. 105-355(a). The difference in taxes must be carried forward in the records of each taxing unit as deferred taxes. The deferred taxes for the preceding three fiscal years are due and payable in accordance with G.S. 105-277.1F when the property loses its eligibility for deferral as a result of a disqualifying event described in subsection (i) of this section. On or before September 1 of each year, the collector must send to the mailing address of a residence on which taxes have been deferred a notice stating the amount of deferred taxes and interest that would be due and payable upon the occurrence of a disqualifying event.

(i) Disqualifying Events. - Each of the following constitutes a disqualifying event:

(1) The owner transfers the residence. Transfer of the residence is not a disqualifying event if (i) the owner transfers the residence to a co-owner of the residence or, as part of a divorce proceeding, to his or her spouse and (ii) that individual occupies or continues to occupy the property as his or her permanent residence.

(2) The owner dies. Death of the owner is not a disqualifying event if (i) the owner's share passes to a co-owner of the residence or to his or her spouse and (ii) that individual occupies or continues to occupy the property as his or her permanent residence.

(3) The owner ceases to use the property as a permanent residence.

(j) Gap in Deferral. - If an owner of a residence on which taxes have been deferred under this section is not eligible for continued deferral for a tax year, the deferred taxes are carried forward and are not due and payable until a disqualifying event occurs. If the owner of the residence qualifies for deferral after one or more years in which he or she did not qualify for deferral and a disqualifying event occurs, the years in which the owner did not qualify are disregarded in determining the preceding three years for which the deferred taxes are due and payable.

(k) Repealed by Session Laws 2008-35, s. 1.2, effective July 1, 2008.

(I) Creditor Limitations. - A mortgagee or trustee that elects to pay any tax deferred by the owner of a residence subject to a mortgage or deed of trust does not acquire a right to foreclose as a result of the election. Except for requirements dictated by federal law or regulation, any provision in a mortgage, deed of trust, or other agreement that prohibits the owner from deferring taxes on property under this section is void.

(m) Construction. - This section does not affect the attachment of a lien for personal property taxes against a tax-deferred residence.

(n) Application. - An application for property tax relief provided by this section should be filed during the regular listing period, but may be filed and must be accepted at any time up to and through June 1 preceding the tax year for which the relief is claimed. Persons may apply for this property tax relief by entering the appropriate information on a form made available by the assessor under G.S. 105-282.1. (2007-484, s. 43.7T(b); 2007-497, s. 2.3; 2008-35, s. 1.2; 2009-445, s. 22(b).)

§ 105-277.1C. Disabled veteran property tax homestead exclusion.

(a) Classification. - A permanent residence owned and occupied by a qualifying owner is designated a special class of property under Article V, Section 2(2) of the North Carolina Constitution and is taxable in accordance with this section. The first forty-five thousand dollars ($45,000) of appraised value of the residence is excluded from taxation. A qualifying owner who receives an exclusion under this section may not receive other property tax relief.

(b) Definitions. - The following definitions apply in this section:

(1) Disabled veteran. - A veteran of any branch of the Armed Forces of the United States whose character of service at separation was honorable or under honorable conditions and who satisfies one of the following requirements:

a. As of January 1 preceding the taxable year for which the exclusion allowed by this section is claimed, the veteran had received benefits under 38 U.S.C. § 2101.

b. The veteran has received a certification by the United States Department of Veterans Affairs or another federal agency indicating that, as of

January 1 preceding the taxable year for which the exclusion allowed by this section is claimed, he or she has a service-connected, permanent, and total disability.

    c.   The veteran is deceased and the United States Department of Veterans Affairs or another federal agency has certified that, as of January 1 preceding the taxable year for which the exclusion allowed by this section is claimed, the veteran's death was the result of a service-connected condition.

(2)   Repealed by Session Laws 2009-445, s. 22(c), effective for taxes imposed for taxable years beginning on or after July 1, 2009.

(3)   Permanent residence. - Defined in G.S. 105-277.1.

(4)   Property tax relief. - Defined in G.S. 105-277.1.

(4a)   Qualifying owner. - An owner, as defined in G.S. 105-277.1, who is a North Carolina resident and one of the following:

    a.   A disabled veteran.

    b.   The surviving spouse of a disabled veteran who has not remarried.

(5), (6) Repealed by Session Laws 2009-445, s. 22(c), effective for taxes imposed for taxable years beginning on or after July 1, 2009.

(7)   Service-connected. - Defined in 38 U.S.C. § 101.

(c)   Temporary Absence. - An owner does not lose the benefit of this exclusion because of a temporary absence from his or her permanent residence for reasons of health or because of an extended absence while confined to a rest home or nursing home, so long as the residence is unoccupied or occupied by the owner's spouse or other dependent.

(d)   Ownership by Spouses - A permanent residence owned and occupied by husband and wife is entitled to the full benefit of this exclusion notwithstanding that only one of them meets the requirements of this section.

(e)   Other Multiple Owners. - This subsection applies to co-owners who are not husband and wife. Each co-owner of a permanent residence must apply separately for the exclusion allowed under this section.

When one or more co-owners of a permanent residence qualify for the exclusion allowed under this section and none of the co-owners qualifies for the exclusion allowed under G.S. 105-277.1, each co-owner is entitled to the full amount of the exclusion allowed under this section. The exclusion allowed to one co-owner may not exceed the co-owner's proportionate share of the valuation of the property, and the amount of the exclusion allowed to all the co-owners may not exceed the exclusion allowed under this section.

When one or more co-owners of a permanent residence qualify for the exclusion allowed under this section and one or more of the co-owners qualify for the exclusion allowed under G.S. 105-277.1, each co-owner who qualifies for the exclusion allowed under this section is entitled to the full amount of the exclusion. The exclusion allowed to one co-owner may not exceed the co-owner's proportionate share of the valuation of the property, and the amount of the exclusion allowed to all the co-owners may not exceed the greater of the exclusion allowed under this section and the exclusion allowed under G.S. 105-277.1.

(f) Application. - An application for the exclusion allowed under this section should be filed during the regular listing period, but may be filed and must be accepted at any time up to and through June 1 preceding the tax year for which the exclusion is claimed. An applicant for an exclusion under this section must establish eligibility for the exclusion by providing a copy of the veteran's disability certification or evidence of benefits received under 38 U.S.C. § 2101. (2008-107, s. 28.11(b); 2009-445, s. 22(c); 2010-95, s. 16; 2010-96, s. 41.)

§ 105-277.1D. (Effective for taxes imposed for taxable years beginning on or after July 1, 2010. See note for repeal.) Inventory property tax deferral.

(a) Classification. - A residence constructed by a builder and owned by the builder or a business entity of which the builder is a member, as defined in G.S. 105-277.2, is designated a special class of property under Section 2(2) of Article V of the North Carolina Constitution and is taxable in accordance with this section. For purposes of this section, a "residence" is an improvement, other than remodeling, renovating, rehabilitating, or refinishing, by a builder to real property that is intended to be sold and used as an individual's residence, that is unoccupied, and for which a certificate of occupancy authorized by law has been issued.

(b) Deferred Taxes. - An owner may defer the portion of tax imposed on real property that represents the increase in value of the property attributable solely to improvements resulting from the construction by the builder of a residence on the property. The difference between the taxes due under this section and the taxes that would have been payable in the absence of this section are a lien on the real property of the taxpayer as provided in G.S. 105-355(a). The difference in taxes for the fiscal years preceding the current tax year shall be carried forward in the records of the taxing unit or units as deferred taxes. The deferred taxes are due and payable in accordance with G.S. 105-277.1F when the property loses its eligibility for deferral because of the occurrence of a disqualifying event. A disqualifying event occurs at the earliest of (i) when the owner transfers the residence, (ii) when the residence is occupied by the owner or by someone other than the owner with the owner's consent, (iii) five years from the time the improved property was first subject to being listed for taxation by the owner, or (iv) three years from the time the improved property first received the property tax benefit provided by this section. On or before September 1 of each year, the collector shall notify each owner to whom a tax deferral has previously been granted of the accumulated sum of deferred taxes and interest.

(c) Creditor Limitations. - A mortgagee or trustee that elects to pay any tax deferred by the owner subject to a mortgage or deed of trust does not acquire a right to foreclose as a result of the election. Except for requirements dictated by federal law or regulation, any provision in a mortgage, deed of trust, or other agreement that prohibits the owner from deferring taxes on property under this section is void.

(d) Construction. - This section does not affect the attachment of a lien for personal property taxes against a tax-deferred residence.

(e) Application. - An application for property tax relief provided by this section should be filed during the regular listing period but may be filed after the regular listing period upon a showing of good cause by the applicant for failure to make a timely application, as determined and approved by the board of equalization and review or, if that board is not in session, by the board of county commissioners. An untimely application approved under this subsection applies only to property taxes levied by the county or municipality in the calendar year in which the untimely application is filed. Decisions of the county board may be appealed to the Property Tax Commission. Persons may apply for this property tax relief by entering the appropriate information on a form made available by the assessor under G.S. 105-282.1. (2009-308, s. 2; 2010-140, s. 1.)

§ 105-277.1E. Reserved for future codification purposes.

§ 105-277.1F. Uniform provisions for payment of deferred taxes.

(a) Scope. - This section applies to the following deferred tax programs:

(1) G.S. 105-275(12), real property owned by a nonprofit corporation held as a protected natural area.

(1a) G.S. 105-275(29a), historic district property held as future site of historic structure.

(2) G.S. 105-277.1B, the property tax homestead circuit breaker.

(2a) (See note for repeal) G.S. 105-277.1D, the inventory property tax deferral.

(3) G.S. 105-277.4(c), present-use value property.

(4) G.S. 105-277.14, working waterfront property.

(4a) G.S. 105-277.15, wildlife conservation land.

(4b) (Effective for taxes imposed for taxable years beginning on or after July 1, 2013) G.S. 105-277.15A, site infrastructure land.

(5) G.S. 105-278(b), historic property.

(6) G.S. 105-278.6(e), nonprofit property held as future site of low- or moderate-income housing.

(b) Payment. - Taxes deferred on property under a deferral program listed in subsection (a) of this section are due and payable on the day the property loses its eligibility for the deferral program as a result of a disqualifying event. If only a part of property for which taxes are deferred loses its eligibility for deferral, the assessor must determine the amount of deferred taxes that apply to that part and that amount is due and payable. Interest accrues on deferred taxes as if they had been payable on the dates on which they would have originally become due.

The tax for the fiscal year that begins in the calendar year in which the deferred taxes are due and payable is computed as if the property had not been classified for that year. A lien for deferred taxes is extinguished when the taxes are paid.

All or part of the deferred taxes that are not due and payable may be paid to the tax collector at any time without affecting the property's eligibility for deferral. A partial payment is applied first to accrued interest. (2008-35, s. 2.2; 2008-107, s. 28.11(h); 2008-171, s. 2; 2009-308, s. 3; 2011-274, s. 2; 2012-79, s. 1.9; 2013-130, s. 3.)

§ 105-277.2. Agricultural, horticultural, and forestland - Definitions.

The following definitions apply in G.S. 105-277.3 through G.S. 105-277.7:

(1) Agricultural land. - Land that is a part of a farm unit that is actively engaged in the commercial production or growing of crops, plants, or animals under a sound management program. Agricultural land includes woodland and wasteland that is a part of the farm unit, but the woodland and wasteland included in the unit must be appraised under the use-value schedules as woodland or wasteland. A farm unit may consist of more than one tract of agricultural land, but at least one of the tracts must meet the requirements in G.S. 105-277.3(a)(1), and each tract must be under a sound management program. If the agricultural land includes less than 20 acres of woodland, then the woodland portion is not required to be under a sound management program. Also, woodland is not required to be under a sound management program if it is determined that the highest and best use of the woodland is to diminish wind erosion of adjacent agricultural land, protect water quality of adjacent agricultural land, or serve as buffers for adjacent livestock or poultry operations.

(1a) Business entity. - A corporation, a general partnership, a limited partnership, or a limited liability company.

(2) Forestland. - Land that is a part of a forest unit that is actively engaged in the commercial growing of trees under a sound management program. Forestland includes wasteland that is a part of the forest unit, but the wasteland included in the unit must be appraised under the use-value schedules as wasteland. A forest unit may consist of more than one tract of forestland, but at least one of the tracts must meet the requirements in G.S. 105-277.3(a)(3), and each tract must be under a sound management program.

(3) Horticultural land. - Land that is a part of a horticultural unit that is actively engaged in the commercial production or growing of fruits or vegetables or nursery or floral products under a sound management program. Horticultural land includes woodland and wasteland that is a part of the horticultural unit, but the woodland and wasteland included in the unit must be appraised under the use-value schedules as woodland or wasteland. A horticultural unit may consist of more than one tract of horticultural land, but at least one of the tracts must meet the requirements in G.S. 105-277.3(a)(2), and each tract must be under a sound management program. If the horticultural land includes less than 20 acres of woodland, then the woodland portion is not required to be under a sound management program. Also, woodland is not required to be under a sound management program if it is determined that the highest and best use of the woodland is to diminish wind erosion of adjacent horticultural land or protect water quality of adjacent horticultural land. Land used to grow horticultural and agricultural crops on a rotating basis or where the horticultural crop is set out or planted and harvested within one growing season, may be treated as agricultural land as described in subdivision (1) of this section when there is determined to be no significant difference in the cash rental rates for the land.

(4) Individually owned. - Owned by one of the following:

a. An individual.

b. A business entity that meets all of the following conditions:

1. Its principal business is farming agricultural land, horticultural land, or forestland.

2. All of its members are, directly or indirectly, individuals who are actively engaged in farming agricultural land, horticultural land, or forestland or a relative of one of the individuals who is actively engaged. An individual is indirectly a member of a business entity that owns the land if the individual is a member of a business entity or a beneficiary of a trust that is part of the ownership structure of the business entity that owns the land.

3. It is not a corporation whose shares are publicly traded, and none of its members are corporations whose shares are publicly traded.

4. If it leases the land, all of its members are individuals and are relatives. Under this condition, "principal business" and "actively engaged" include leasing.

c. A trust that meets all of the following conditions:

1. It was created by an individual who owned the land and transferred the land to the trust.

2. All of its beneficiaries are, directly or indirectly, individuals who are the creator of the trust or a relative of the creator. An individual is indirectly a beneficiary of a trust that owns the land if the individual is a beneficiary of another trust or a member of a business entity that has a beneficial interest in the trust that owns the land.

d. A testamentary trust that meets all of the following conditions:

1. It was created by an individual who transferred to the trust land that qualified in that individual's hands for classification under G.S. 105-277.3.

2. At the date of the creator's death, the creator had no relatives.

3. The trust income, less reasonable administrative expenses, is used exclusively for educational, scientific, literary, cultural, charitable, or religious purposes as defined in G.S. 105-278.3(d).

e. Tenants in common, if each tenant would qualify as an owner if the tenant were the sole owner. Tenants in common may elect to treat their individual shares as owned by them individually in accordance with G.S. 105-302(c)(9). The ownership requirements of G.S. 105-277.3(b) apply to each tenant in common who is an individual, and the ownership requirements of G.S. 105-277.3(b1) apply to each tenant in common who is a business entity or a trust.

(4a) Member. - A shareholder of a corporation, a partner of a general or limited partnership, or a member of a limited liability company.

(5) Present-use value. - The value of land in its current use as agricultural land, horticultural land, or forestland, based solely on its ability to produce income and assuming an average level of management. A rate of nine percent (9%) shall be used to capitalize the expected net income of forestland. The capitalization rate for agricultural land and horticultural land is to be determined by the Use-Value Advisory Board as provided in G.S. 105-277.7.

(5a) Relative. - Any of the following:

a. A spouse or the spouse's lineal ancestor or descendant.

b. A lineal ancestor or a lineal descendant.

c. A brother or sister, or the lineal descendant of a brother or sister. For the purposes of this sub-subdivision, the term brother or sister includes stepbrother or stepsister.

d. An aunt or an uncle.

e. A spouse of an individual listed in paragraphs a. through d. For the purpose of this subdivision, an adoptive or adopted relative is a relative and the term "spouse" includes a surviving spouse.

(6) Sound management program. - A program of production designed to obtain the greatest net return from the land consistent with its conservation and long-term improvement.

(7) Unit. - One or more tracts of agricultural land, horticultural land, or forestland. Multiple tracts must be under the same ownership and be of the same type of classification. If the multiple tracts are located within different counties, they must be within 50 miles of a tract qualifying under G.S. 105-277.3(a). (1973, c. 709, s. 1; 1975, c. 746, s. 1; 1985, c. 628, s. 1; c. 667, ss. 1, 4; 1987, c. 698, s. 1; 1995, c. 454, s. 1; 1995 (Reg. Sess., 1996), c. 646, s. 17; 1998-98, s. 24; 2002-184, s. 1; 2004-8, s. 1; 2005-313, ss. 1, 2; 2008-146, s. 2.1.)

§ 105-277.3. Agricultural, horticultural, and forestland - Classifications.

(a) Classes Defined. - The following classes of property are designated special classes of property under authority of Section 2(2) of Article V of the North Carolina Constitution and must be appraised, assessed, and taxed as provided in G.S. 105-277.2 through G.S. 105-277.7.

(1) Agricultural land. - Individually owned agricultural land consisting of one or more tracts, one of which satisfies the requirements of this subdivision. For agricultural land used as a farm for aquatic species, as defined in G.S. 106-758, the tract must meet the income requirement for agricultural land and must consist of at least five acres in actual production or produce at least 20,000 pounds of aquatic species for commercial sale annually, regardless of acreage.

For all other agricultural land, the tract must meet the income requirement for agricultural land and must consist of at least 10 acres that are in actual production. Land in actual production includes land under improvements used in the commercial production or growing of crops, plants, or animals.

To meet the income requirement, agricultural land must, for the three years preceding January 1 of the year for which the benefit of this section is claimed, have produced an average gross income of at least one thousand dollars ($1,000). Gross income includes income from the sale of the agricultural products produced from the land, any payments received under a governmental soil conservation or land retirement program, and the amount paid to the taxpayer during the taxable year pursuant to P.L. 108-357, Title VI, Fair and Equitable Tobacco Reform Act of 2004.

(2)   Horticultural land. - Individually owned horticultural land consisting of one or more tracts, one of which consists of at least five acres that are in actual production and that, for the three years preceding January 1 of the year for which the benefit of this section is claimed, have met the applicable minimum gross income requirement. Land in actual production includes land under improvements used in the commercial production or growing of fruits or vegetables or nursery or floral products. Land that has been used to produce evergreens intended for use as Christmas trees must have met the minimum gross income requirements established by the Department of Revenue for the land. All other horticultural land must have produced an average gross income of at least one thousand dollars ($1,000). Gross income includes income from the sale of the horticultural products produced from the land and any payments received under a governmental soil conservation or land retirement program.

(3)   Forestland. - Individually owned forestland consisting of one or more tracts, one of which consists of at least 20 acres that are in actual production and are not included in a farm unit.

(b)   Individual Ownership Requirements. - In order to come within a classification described in subsection (a) of this section, land owned by an individual must also satisfy one of the following conditions:

(1)   It is the owner's place of residence.

(2)   It has been owned by the current owner or a relative of the current owner for the four years preceding January 1 of the year for which the benefit of this section is claimed.

(3) At the time of transfer to the current owner, it qualified for classification in the hands of a business entity or trust that transferred the land to the current owner who was a member of the business entity or a beneficiary of the trust, as appropriate.

(b1) Entity Ownership Requirements. - In order to come within a classification described in subsection (a) of this section, land owned by a business entity must meet the requirements of subdivision (1) of this subsection and land owned by a trust must meet the requirements of subdivision (2) of this subsection.

(1) Land owned by a business entity must have been owned by one or more of the following for the four years immediately preceding January 1 of the year for which the benefit of this section is claimed:

a. The business entity.

b. A member of the business entity.

c. Another business entity whose members include a member of the business entity that currently owns the land.

(2) Land owned by a trust must have been owned by the trust or by one or more of its creators for the four years immediately preceding January 1 of the year for which the benefit of this section is claimed.

(b2) Exceptions to Ownership Requirements. - Notwithstanding the provisions of subsections (b) and (b1) of this section, land may qualify for classification in the hands of the new owner if all of the conditions listed in either subdivision of this subsection are met, even if the new owner does not meet all of the ownership requirements of subsections (b) and (b1) of this section with respect to the land.

(1) Continued use. - If the land qualifies for classification in the hands of the new owner under the provisions of this subdivision, then any deferred taxes remain a lien on the land under G.S. 105-277.4(c), the new owner becomes liable for the deferred taxes, and the deferred taxes become payable if the land fails to meet any other condition or requirement for classification. Land qualifies for classification in the hands of the new owner if all of the following conditions are met:

a. The land was appraised at its present use value at the time title to the land passed to the new owner.

b. The new owner acquires the land and continues to use the land for the purpose for which it was classified under subsection (a) of this section while under previous ownership.

c. The new owner has timely filed an application as required by G.S. 105-277.4(a) and has certified that the new owner accepts liability for any deferred taxes and intends to continue the present use of the land.

(2) Expansion of existing unit. - Land qualifies for classification in the hands of the new owner if, at the time title passed to the new owner, the land was not appraised at its present-use value but was being used for the same purpose and was eligible for appraisal at its present-use value as other land already owned by the new owner and classified under subsection (a) of this section. The new owner must timely file an application as required by G.S. 105-277.4(a).

(c) Repealed by Session Laws 1995, c. 454, s. 2.

(d) Exception for Conservation Reserve Program. - Land enrolled in the federal Conservation Reserve Program authorized by 16 U.S.C. Chapter 58 is considered to be in actual production, and income derived from participation in the federal Conservation Reserve Program may be used in meeting the minimum gross income requirements of this section either separately or in combination with income from actual production. Land enrolled in the federal Conservation Reserve Program must be assessed as agricultural land if it is planted in vegetation other than trees, or as forestland if it is planted in trees.

(d1) Exception for Easements on Qualified Conservation Lands Previously Appraised at Use Value. - Property that is appraised at its present-use value under G.S. 105-277.4(b) shall continue to qualify for appraisal, assessment, and taxation as provided in G.S. 105-277.2 through G.S. 105-277.7 as long as (i) the property is subject to an enforceable conservation easement that would qualify for the conservation tax credit provided in G.S. 105-130.34 and G.S. 105-151.12, without regard to actual production or income requirements of this section; and (ii) the taxpayer received no more than seventy-five percent (75%) of the fair market value of the donated property interest in compensation. Notwithstanding G.S. 105-277.3(b) and (b1), subsequent transfer of the property does not extinguish its present-use value eligibility as long as the property remains subject to an enforceable conservation easement that qualifies for the conservation tax credit provided in G.S. 105-130.34 and G.S. 105-151.12. The exception provided in this subsection applies only to that part of the property that is subject to the easement.

(d2)   Wildlife Exception. - When an owner of land classified under this section does not transfer the land and the land becomes eligible for classification under G.S. 105-277.15, no deferred taxes are due. The deferred taxes remain a lien on the land and are payable in accordance with G.S. 105-277.15.

(d3)   (Effective for taxes imposed for taxable years beginning on or after July 1, 2013) Site Infrastructure Exception. - When an owner of land classified under this section (i) does not transfer the land and the land becomes eligible for classification under G.S. 105-277.15A or (ii) does transfer the land but the land becomes eligible for classification under G.S. 105-277.15A within six months of the transfer, no deferred taxes are due. The deferred taxes remain a lien on the land and are payable in accordance with G.S. 105-277.15A.

(e)   Exception for Turkey Disease. - Agricultural land that meets all of the following conditions is considered to be in actual production and to meet the minimum gross income requirements:

(1)   The land was in actual production in turkey growing within the preceding two years and qualified for present use value treatment while it was in actual production.

(2)   The land was taken out of actual production in turkey growing solely for health and safety considerations due to the presence of Poult Enteritis Mortality Syndrome among turkeys in the same county or a neighboring county.

(3)   The land is otherwise eligible for present use value treatment.

(f)   Sound Management Program for Agricultural Land and Horticultural Land. - If the property owner demonstrates any one of the following factors with respect to agricultural land or horticultural land, then the land is operated under a sound management program:

(1)   Enrollment in and compliance with an agency-administered and approved farm management plan.

(2)   Compliance with a set of best management practices.

(3) Compliance with a minimum gross income per acre test.

(4) Evidence of net income from the farm operation.

(5) Evidence that farming is the farm operator's principal source of income.

(6) Certification by a recognized agricultural or horticultural agency within the county that the land is operated under a sound management program.

Operation under a sound management program may also be demonstrated by evidence of other similar factors. As long as a farm operator meets the sound management requirements, it is irrelevant whether the property owner received income or rent from the farm operator.

(g) Sound Management Program for Forestland. - If the owner of forestland demonstrates that the forestland complies with a written sound forest management plan for the production and sale of forest products, then the forestland is operated under a sound management program. (1973, c. 709, s. 1; 1975, c. 746, s. 2; 1983, c. 821; c. 826; 1985, c. 667, ss. 2, 3, 6.1; 1987, c. 698, ss. 2-5; 1987 (Reg. Sess., 1988), c. 1044, s. 13.1; 1989, cc. 99, 736, s. 1; 1989 (Reg. Sess., 1990), c. 814, s. 29; 1995, c. 454, s. 2; 1997-272, s. 1; 1998-98, s. 22; 2001-499, s. 1; 2002-184, s. 2; 2005-293, s. 1; 2005-313, s. 3; 2007-484, s. 43.7T(c); 2007-497, s. 3.1; 2008-146, s. 2.2; 2008-171, ss. 4, 5; 2011-9, s. 1; 2013-130, s. 2.)

§ 105-277.4. Agricultural, horticultural and forestland - Application; appraisal at use value; appeal; deferred taxes.

(a) Application. - Property coming within one of the classes defined in G.S. 105-277.3 is eligible for taxation on the basis of the value of the property in its present use if a timely and proper application is filed with the assessor of the county in which the property is located. The application must clearly show that the property comes within one of the classes and must also contain any other relevant information required by the assessor to properly appraise the property at its present-use value. An initial application must be filed during the regular listing period of the year for which the benefit of this classification is first claimed, or within 30 days of the date shown on a notice of a change in valuation made pursuant to G.S. 105-286 or G.S. 105-287. A new application is not required to be submitted unless the property is transferred or becomes ineligible for use-value appraisal because of a change in use or acreage. An application required due to transfer of the land may be submitted at any time during the calendar year but must be submitted within 60 days of the date of the property's transfer.

(a1) Late Application. - Upon a showing of good cause by the applicant for failure to make a timely application as required by subsection (a) of this section, an application may be approved by the board of equalization and review or, if that board is not in session, by the board of county commissioners. An untimely application approved under this subsection applies only to property taxes levied by the county or municipality in the calendar year in which the untimely application is filed. Decisions of the county board may be appealed to the Property Tax Commission.

(b) Appraisal at Present-use Value. - Upon receipt of a properly executed application, the assessor must appraise the property at its present-use value as established in the schedule prepared pursuant to G.S. 105-317. In appraising the property at its present-use value, the assessor must appraise the improvements located on qualifying land according to the schedules and standards used in appraising other similar improvements in the county. If all or any part of a qualifying tract of land is located within the limits of an incorporated city or town, or is property annexed subject to G.S. 160A-37(f1) or G.S. 160A-49(f1), the assessor must furnish a copy of the property record showing both the present-use appraisal and the valuation upon which the property would have been taxed in the absence of this classification to the collector of the city or town. The assessor must also notify the tax collector of any changes in the appraisals or in the eligibility of the property for the benefit of this classification. Upon a request for a certification pursuant to G.S. 160A-37(f1) or G.S.160A-49(f1), or any change in the certification, the assessor for the county where the land subject to the annexation is located must, within 30 days, determine if the land meets the requirements of G.S. 160A-37(f1)(2) or G.S. 160A-49(f1)(2) and report the results of its findings to the city.

(b1) Appeal. - Decisions of the assessor regarding the qualification or appraisal of property under this section may be appealed to the county board of equalization and review or, if that board is not in session, to the board of county commissioners. An appeal must be made within 60 days after the decision of the assessor. If an owner submits additional information to the assessor pursuant to G.S. 105-296(j), the appeal must be made within 60 days after the assessor's decision based on the additional information. Decisions of the county board may be appealed to the Property Tax Commission.

(c) Deferred Taxes. - Land meeting the conditions for classification under G.S. 105-277.3 must be taxed on the basis of the value of the land for its present use. The difference between the taxes due on the present-use basis and the taxes that would have been payable in the absence of this classification, together with any interest, penalties, or costs that may accrue thereon, are a lien on the real property of the taxpayer as provided in G.S. 105-355(a). The difference in taxes must be carried forward in the records of the taxing unit or units as deferred taxes. The deferred taxes for the preceding three fiscal years are due and payable in accordance with G.S. 105-277.1F when the property loses its eligibility for deferral as a result of a disqualifying event. A disqualifying event occurs when the land fails to meet any condition or requirement for classification or when an application is not approved.

(d) Exceptions. - Notwithstanding the provisions of subsection (c) of this section, if property loses its eligibility for present use value classification solely due to one of the following reasons, no deferred taxes are due and the lien for the deferred taxes is extinguished:

(1) There is a change in income caused by enrollment of the property in the federal conservation reserve program established under 16 U.S.C. Chapter 58.

(2) The property is conveyed by gift to a nonprofit organization and qualifies for exclusion from the tax base pursuant to G.S. 105-275(12) or G.S. 105-275(29).

(3) The property is conveyed by gift to the State, a political subdivision of the State, or the United States.

(e) Repealed by Session Laws 1997-270, s. 3, effective July 3, 1997. (1973, c. 709, s. 1; c. 905; c. 906, ss. 1, 2; 1975, c. 62; c. 746, ss. 3-7; 1981, c. 835; 1985, c. 518, s. 1; c. 667, ss. 5, 6; 1987, c. 45, s. 1; c. 295, s. 5; c. 698, s. 6; 1987 (Reg. Sess., 1988), c. 1044, s. 13.2; 1995, c. 443, s. 4; c. 454, s. 3; 1997-270, s. 3; 1998-98, s. 23; 1998-150, s. 1; 2001-499, s. 2; 2002-184, s. 3; 2005-313, s. 4; 2006-30, s. 4; 2008-35, s. 2.3.)

§ 105-277.5. Agricultural, horticultural and forestland - Notice of change in use.

Not later than the close of the listing period following a change which would disqualify all or a part of a tract of land receiving the benefit of this classification, the property owner shall furnish the assessor with complete information regarding such change. Any property owner who fails to notify the assessor of changes as aforesaid regarding land receiving the benefit of this classification shall be subject to a penalty of ten percent (10%) of the total amount of the deferred taxes and interest thereon for each listing period for which the failure to report continues. (1973, c. 709, s. 1; 1975, c. 746, s. 8; 1987, c. 45, s. 1.)

§ 105-277.6. Agricultural, horticultural and forestland - Appraisal; computation of deferred tax.

(a) In determining the amount of the deferred taxes herein provided, the assessor shall use the appraised valuation established in the county's last general revaluation except for any changes made under the provisions of G.S. 105-287.

(b) In revaluation years, as provided in G.S. 105-286, all property entitled to classification under G.S. 105-277.3 shall be reappraised at its true value in money and at its present use value as of the effective date of the revaluation. The two valuations shall continue in effect and shall provide the basis for deferred taxes until a change in one or both of the appraisals is required by law. The present use-value schedule, standards, and rules shall be used by the tax assessor to appraise property receiving the benefit of this classification until the next general revaluation of real property in the county as required by G.S. 105-286.

(c) Repealed by Session Laws 1987, c. 295, s. 2. (1973, c. 709, s. 1; 1975, c. 746, ss. 9, 10; 1987, c. 45, s. 1, c. 295, s. 2.)

§ 105-277.7. Use-Value Advisory Board.

(a) Creation and Membership. - The Use-Value Advisory Board is established under the supervision of the Agricultural Extension Service of North Carolina State University. The Director of the Agricultural Extension Service of North Carolina State University shall serve as the chair of the Board. The Board shall consist of the following additional members, to serve ex officio:

(1) A representative of the Department of Agriculture and Consumer Services, designated by the Commissioner of Agriculture.

(2) A representative of the North Carolina Forest Service of the Department of Agriculture and Consumer Services, designated by the Director of that Division.

(3) A representative of the Agricultural Extension Service at North Carolina Agricultural and Technical State University, designated by the Director of the Extension Service.

(4) A representative of the North Carolina Farm Bureau Federation, Inc., designated by the President of the Bureau.

(5) A representative of the North Carolina Association of Assessing Officers, designated by the President of the Association.

(6) The Director of the Property Tax Division of the North Carolina Department of Revenue or the Director's designee.

(7) A representative of the North Carolina Association of County Commissioners, designated by the President of the Association.

(8) A representative of the North Carolina Forestry Association, designated by the President of the Association.

(b) Staff. - The Agricultural Extension Service at North Carolina State University must provide clerical assistance to the Board.

(c) Duties. - The Board must annually submit to the Department of Revenue a recommended use-value manual. In developing the manual, the Board may consult with federal and State agencies as needed. The manual must contain all of the following:

(1) The estimated cash rental rates for agricultural lands and horticultural lands for the various classes of soils found in the State. The rental rates must recognize the productivity levels by class of soil or geographic area, and the crop as either agricultural or horticultural. The rental rates must be based on the rental value of the land to be used for agricultural or horticultural purposes when those uses are presumed to be the highest and best use of the land. The recommended rental rates may be established from individual county studies or from contracts with federal or State agencies as needed.

(2) The recommended net income ranges for forestland furnished to the Board by the Forestry Section of the North Carolina Cooperative Extension Service. These net income ranges may be based on up to six classes of land within each Major Land Resource Area designated by the United States Soil Conservation Service. In developing these ranges, the Forestry Section must consider the soil productivity and indicator tree species or stand type, the average stand establishment and annual management costs, the average rotation length and timber yield, and the average timber stumpage prices.

(3) The capitalization rates adopted by the Board prior to February 1 for use in capitalizing incomes into values. The capitalization rate for forestland shall be nine percent (9%). The capitalization rate for agricultural land and horticultural land must be no less than six percent (6%) and no more than seven percent (7%). The incomes must be in the form of cash rents for agricultural lands and horticultural lands and net incomes for forestlands.

(4) The value per acre adopted by the Board for the best agricultural land. The value may not exceed one thousand two hundred dollars ($1,200).

(5) Recommendations concerning any changes to the capitalization rate for agricultural land and horticultural land and to the maximum value per acre for the best agricultural land and horticultural land based on a calculation to be determined by the Board. The Board shall annually report these recommendations to the Revenue Laws Study Committee and to the President Pro Tempore of the Senate and the Speaker of the House of Representatives.

(6) Recommendations concerning requirements for horticultural land used to produce evergreens intended for use as Christmas trees when requested to do so by the Department. (1973, c. 709, s. 1; 1975, c. 746, s. 11; 1985, c. 628, s. 2; 1989, c. 727, s. 218(44); c. 736, s. 2; 1997-261, s. 109; 1997-443, s. 11A.119(a); 2002-184, s. 4; 2005-313, s. 5; 2005-386, s. 1.3; 2011-145, s. 13.25(oo); 2013-155, s. 7.)

§ 105-277.8. (Effective for taxes imposed for taxable years beginning before July 1, 2012) Taxation of property of nonprofit homeowners' association.

(a) The value of real and personal property owned by a nonprofit homeowners' association shall be included in the appraisals of property owned by members of the association and shall not be assessed against the association if:

(1)   All property owned by the association is held for the use, benefit, and enjoyment of all members of the association equally;

(2)   Each member of the association has an irrevocable right to use and enjoy, on an equal basis, all property owned by the association, subject to any restrictions imposed by the instruments conveying the right or the rules, regulations, or bylaws of the association; and

(3)   Each irrevocable right to use and enjoy all property owned by the association is appurtenant to taxable real property owned by a member of the association.

The assessor may allocate the value of the association's property among the property of the association's members on any fair and reasonable basis.

(b)   As used in this section, "nonprofit homeowners' association" means a homeowners' association as defined in § 528(c) of the Internal Revenue Code. (1979, c. 686, s. 1; 1987, c. 130.)

§ 105-277.8. (Effective for taxes imposed for taxable years beginning on or after July 1, 2012) Taxation of property of nonprofit homeowners' association.

(a)   Except as provided in subsection (a1) of this section, the value of real and personal property owned by a nonprofit homeowners' association shall be included in the appraisals of property owned by members of the association and shall not be assessed against the association if each of the following requirements is met:

(1)   All property owned by the association is held for the use, benefit, and enjoyment of all members of the association equally.

(2)   Each member of the association has an irrevocable right to use and enjoy, on an equal basis, all property owned by the association, subject to any restrictions imposed by the instruments conveying the right or the rules, regulations, or bylaws of the association.

(3) Each irrevocable right to use and enjoy all property owned by the association is appurtenant to taxable real property owned by a member of the association.

The assessor may allocate the value of the association's property among the property of the association's members on any fair and reasonable basis.

(a1) The value of extraterritorial common property shall be subject to taxation only in the jurisdiction in which it is entirely contained and only in the amount of the local tax of the jurisdiction in which it is entirely contained. The value of any property taxed pursuant to this subsection, as determined by the latest schedule of values, shall not be included in the appraisals of property owned by members of the association that are referenced in subsection (a) of this section or otherwise subject to taxation. The assessor for the jurisdiction that imposes a tax pursuant to this subsection shall provide notice of the property, the value, and any other information to the assessor of any other jurisdiction so that the real properties owned by the members of the association are not subject to taxation for that value. The governing board of a nonprofit homeowners' association with property subject to taxation under this subsection shall provide annually to each member of the association the amount of tax due on the property, the value of the property, and, if applicable, the means by which the association will recover the tax due on the property from the members.

(b) As used in this section, "nonprofit homeowners' association" means a homeowners' association as defined in § 528(c) of the Internal Revenue Code, and "extraterritorial common property" means real property that is (i) owned by a nonprofit homeowners association that meets the requirements of subdivisions (1) through (3) of subsection (a) of this section and (ii) entirely contained within a taxing jurisdiction that is different from that of the taxable real property owned by members of the association and providing the appurtenant rights to use and enjoy the association property. (1979, c. 686, s. 1; 1987, c. 130; 2012-157, s. 1.)

§ 105-277.9. (Effective for taxes imposed for taxable years beginning before July 1, 2011) Taxation of property inside certain roadway corridors.

Real property that lies within a transportation corridor marked on an official map filed under Article 2E of Chapter 136 of the General Statutes is designated a special class of property under Article V, Sec. 2(2) of the North Carolina

Constitution and is taxable at twenty percent (20%) of the general tax rate levied on real property by the taxing unit in which the property is situated if:

(1)   As of January 1, no building or other structure is located on the property; and

(2)   The property has not been subdivided, as defined in G.S. 153A-335 or G.S. 160A-376, since it was included in the corridor. (1987, c. 747, s. 22; 1998-184, s. 2.)

§ 105-277.9. (Effective for taxes imposed for taxable years beginning on or after July 1, 2011) Taxation of property inside certain roadway corridors.

Real property that lies within a transportation corridor marked on an official map filed under Article 2E of Chapter 136 of the General Statutes is designated a special class of property under Article V, Sec. 2(2) of the North Carolina Constitution and is taxable at twenty percent (20%) of the appraised value of the property if each of the following requirements is met:

(1)   As of January 1, no building or other structure is located on the property.

(2)   The property has not been subdivided, as defined in G.S. 153A-335 or G.S. 160A-376, since it was included in the corridor. (1987, c. 747, s. 22; 1998-184, s. 2; 2011-30, s. 1.)

§ 105-277.9A. (Effective for taxes imposed for taxable years beginning on or after July 1, 2011. See note for delayed repeal.) Taxation of improved property inside certain roadway corridors.

(a)   Reduced Assessment. - Real property on which a building or other structure is located and that lies within a transportation corridor marked on an official map filed under Article 2E of Chapter 136 of the General Statutes is designated a special class of property under Section 2(2) of Article V of the North Carolina Constitution and is taxable at fifty percent (50%) of the appraised value of the property if the property has not been subdivided, as defined in G.S. 153A-335 or G.S. 160A-376, since it was included in the corridor.

(b)   Sunset. - This section is repealed effective for taxes imposed for taxable years beginning on or after July 1, 2021. (2011-30, s. 2.)

§ 105-277.10. Taxation of precious metals used or held for use directly in manufacturing or processing by a manufacturer.

Precious metals, including rhodium and platinum, used or held for use directly in manufacturing or processing by a manufacturer as part of industrial machinery is designated a special class of property under Article V, Sec. 2(2) of the North Carolina Constitution and shall be assessed for taxation in accordance with this section. The classified property shall be assessed at the lower of its true value or the manufacturer's original cost less depreciation. The original cost of the classified property shall be adjusted by the index factor, if any, that applies in assessing the industrial machinery with which the property is used, and the depreciable life of the classified property shall be the life assigned to the industrial machinery with which the property is used. The residual value of the classified property may not exceed twenty-five percent (25%) of the manufacturer's original cost. (1989, c. 674, s. 1.)

§ 105-277.11. Taxation of property subject to a development financing district agreement.

Property that is in a development financing district established pursuant to G.S. 160A-515.1 or G.S. 158-7.3 and that is subject to an agreement entered into pursuant to G.S. 159-108, shall, pursuant to Article V, Section 14 of the North Carolina Constitution, be assessed for taxation at the greater of its true value or the minimum value established in the agreement.(2003-403, s. 21.)

§ 105-277.12. Antique airplanes.

(a)   For the purpose of this section, the term "antique airplane" means an airplane that meets all of the following conditions:

(1)   It is registered with the Federal Aviation Administration and is a model year 1954 or older.

(2)   It is maintained primarily for use in exhibitions, club activities, air shows, and other public interest functions.

(3)   It is used only occasionally for other purposes.

(4)   It is used by the owner for a purpose other than the production of income.

(b)   Antique airplanes are designated a special class of property under Article V, Sec. 2(2) of the North Carolina Constitution and shall be assessed for taxation in accordance with this section. An antique airplane shall be assessed at the lower of its true value or five thousand dollars ($5,000). (1997-355, s. 1.)

§ 105-277.13. Taxation of improvements on brownfields.

(a)   Qualifying improvements on brownfields properties are designated a special class of property under Article V, Sec. 2(2) of the North Carolina Constitution and shall be appraised, assessed, and taxed in accordance with this section. An owner of land is entitled to the partial exclusion provided by this section for the first five taxable years beginning after completion of qualifying improvements made after the later of July 1, 2000, or the date of the brownfields agreement. After property has qualified for the exclusion provided by this section, the assessor for the county in which the property is located shall annually appraise the improvements made to the property during the period of time that the owner is entitled to the exclusion.

(b)   For the purposes of this section, the terms "qualifying improvements on brownfields properties" and "qualifying improvements" mean improvements made to real property that is subject to a brownfields agreement entered into by the Department of Environment and Natural Resources and the owner pursuant to G.S. 130A-310.32.

(c)   The following table establishes the percentage of the appraised value of the qualified improvements that is excluded based on the taxable year:

Year	Percent of Appraised Value Excluded
Year 1	90%
Year 2	75%
Year 3	50%
Year 4	30%

Year 5   10%.

(2000-158, s. 1.)

§ 105-277.14. Taxation of working waterfront property.

(a)   Definitions. - The following definitions apply in this section:

(1)   Coastal fishing waters. - Defined in G.S. 113-129.

(2)   Commercial fishing operation. - Defined in G.S. 113-168.

(3)   Fish processing. - Processing fish, as defined in G.S. 113-129, for sale.

(4)   Working waterfront property. - Any of the following property that has, for the most recent three-year period, produced an average gross income of at least one thousand dollars ($1,000):

a.   A pier that extends into coastal fishing waters and limits access to those who pay a fee.

b.   Real property that is adjacent to coastal fishing waters and is primarily used for a commercial fishing operation or fish processing, including adjacent land that is under improvements used for one of these purposes.

(b)   Classification. - Working waterfront property is designated a special class of property under Section 2(2) of Article V of the North Carolina Constitution and must be appraised, assessed, and taxed on the basis of the value of the property in its present use rather than on its true value. Working waterfront property includes land reasonably necessary for the convenient use of the property.

(c)   Deferred Taxes. - The difference between the taxes that are due on working waterfront property taxed on the basis of its present use and that would be due if the property were taxed on the basis of its true value is a lien on the property. The difference in taxes must be carried forward in the records of each taxing unit as deferred taxes. The deferred taxes for the preceding three fiscal years are due and payable in accordance with G.S. 105-277.1F when the property loses its eligibility for deferral as a result of a disqualifying event. A disqualifying event occurs when the property no longer qualifies as working waterfront property.

(d) Repealed by Session Laws 2009-445, s. 23(b), effective August 7, 2009. (2007-485, s. 1; 2008-35, s. 2.4; 2009-445, s. 23(b).)

§ 105-277.15. Taxation of wildlife conservation land.

(a) Definitions. - The following definitions apply in this section:

(1) Business entity. - Defined in G.S. 105-277.2.

(2) Family business entity. - A business entity whose members are, directly or indirectly, individuals and are relatives. An individual is indirectly a member of a business entity if the individual is a member of a business entity or a beneficiary of a trust that is part of the ownership structure of the business entity.

(3) Family trust. - A trust that was created by an individual and whose beneficiaries are, directly or indirectly, individuals who are the creator of the trust or a relative of the creator. An individual is indirectly a beneficiary of a trust if the individual is a beneficiary of another trust or a member of a business entity that has a beneficial interest in the trust.

(4) Member. - Defined in G.S. 105-277.2.

(5) Relative. - Defined in G.S. 105-277.2.

(b) Classification. - Wildlife conservation land is designated a special class of property under Article V, Section 2(2) of the North Carolina Constitution and must be appraised, assessed, and taxed in accordance with this section. Wildlife conservation land classified under this section must be appraised and assessed as if it were classified under G.S. 105-277.3 as agricultural land.

(c) Requirements. - Land qualifies as wildlife conservation land if it meets the following size, ownership, and use requirements:

(1) Size. - The land must consist of at least 20 contiguous acres.

(2) Ownership. - The land must be owned by an individual, a family business entity, or a family trust and must have been owned by the same owner for the previous five years, except as follows:

a. If the land is owned by a family business entity, the land meets the ownership requirement if the land was owned by one or more members of the family business entity for the required time.

b. If the land is owned by a family trust, the land meets the ownership requirement if the land was owned by one or more beneficiaries of the family trust for the required time.

c. If an owner acquires land that was classified as wildlife conservation land under this section when it was acquired and the owner continues to use the land as wildlife conservation land, then the land meets the ownership requirement if the new owner files an application and signs the wildlife habitat conservation agreement in effect for the property within 60 days after acquiring the property.

(3) Use. - The land must meet all of the following requirements:

a. The land must be managed under a written wildlife habitat conservation agreement with the North Carolina Wildlife Resources Commission that is in effect as of January 1 of the year for which the benefit of this section is claimed and that requires the owner to do one or more of the following:

1. Protect an animal species that lives on the land and, as of January 1 of the year for which the benefit of this section is claimed, is on a North Carolina protected animal list published by the Commission under G.S. 113-333.

2. Conserve any of the following priority animal wildlife habitats: longleaf pine forest, early successional habitat, small wetland community, stream and riparian zone, rock outcrop, or bat cave.

b. It must have been classified under G.S. 105-277.3 when the wildlife habitat conservation agreement was signed or the owner must demonstrate to both the Wildlife Resources Commission and the assessor that the owner used the land for a purpose specified in the signed wildlife habitat conservation agreement for three years preceding the January 1 of the year for which the benefit of this section is claimed.

(d) Restrictions. - The following restrictions apply to the classification allowed under this section:

(1) No more than 100 acres of an owner's land in a county may be classified under this section.

(2) Land owned by a business entity is not eligible for classification under this section if the business entity is a corporation whose shares are publicly traded or one of its members is a corporation whose shares are publicly traded.

(e) Deferred Taxes. - The difference between the taxes that are due on wildlife conservation land classified under this section and that would be due if the land were taxed on the basis of its true value is a lien on the property. The difference in taxes must be carried forward in the records of each taxing unit as deferred taxes. The deferred taxes for the preceding three fiscal years are due and payable in accordance with G.S. 105-277.1F when the land loses its eligibility for deferral as a result of a disqualifying event. A disqualifying event occurs when the property no longer qualifies as wildlife conservation land.

(f) Exceptions to Payment. - No deferred taxes are due in the following circumstances and the deferred taxes remain a lien on the land:

(1) When the owner of wildlife conservation land that was previously classified under G.S. 105-277.3 before the wildlife habitat conservation agreement was signed does not transfer the land and the land again becomes eligible for classification under G.S. 105-277.3. In this circumstance, the deferred taxes are payable in accordance with G.S. 105-277.3.

(2) When land that is classified under this section is transferred to an owner who signed the wildlife habitat conservation agreement in effect for the land at the time of the transfer and the land remains classified under this section. In this circumstance, the deferred taxes are payable in accordance with this section.

(g) Exceptions to Payment and Lien. - Notwithstanding subsection (e) of this section, if land loses its eligibility for deferral solely due to one of the following reasons, no deferred taxes are due and the lien for the deferred taxes is extinguished:

(1) The property is conveyed by gift to a nonprofit organization and qualifies for exclusion from the tax base under G.S. 105-275(12) or G.S. 105-275(29).

(2) The property is conveyed by gift to the State, a political subdivision of the State, or the United States.

(h) Administration. - An owner who applies for the classification allowed under this section must attach a copy of the owner's written wildlife habitat agreement required under subsection (c) of this section. An owner who fails to notify the county assessor when land classified under this section loses its eligibility for classification is subject to a penalty in the amount set in G.S. 105-277.5. (2008-171, s. 1.)

§ 105-277.15A. (Effective for taxes imposed for taxable years beginning on or after July 1, 2013) Taxation of site infrastructure land.

(a) Classification. - Site infrastructure land is designated a special class of property under Section 2(2) of Article V of the North Carolina Constitution and must be appraised, assessed, and taxed in accordance with this section.

(b) Requirements. - Land qualifies as site infrastructure land if it meets the following size and use requirements:

(1) Size. - The land must consist of at least 100 contiguous acres.

(2) Use. - The land must meet all of the following requirements:

a. It must be zoned for industrial use, office use, or both.

b. A building permit for a primary building or structure must not have been issued for the land, and there is no primary building or structure on the land.

c. It must be classified under G.S. 105-277.3 or have been classified under G.S. 105-277.3 within the previous six months.

(c) Deferred Taxes. - An owner may defer a portion of tax imposed on site infrastructure land that represents the sum of the increase in value of the property attributable solely to improvements made to the site infrastructure land, if any, and the difference between the true value of the site infrastructure land and the value of the site infrastructure land as if it were classified under G.S. 105-277.3 as agricultural land. The difference between the taxes due under this section and the taxes that would have been payable in the absence of this section is a lien on the site infrastructure land as provided in G.S. 105-355(a).

The difference in taxes must be carried forward in the records of each taxing unit as deferred taxes. The deferred taxes are due and payable in accordance with G.S. 105-277.1F when the site infrastructure land loses its eligibility for deferral because of the occurrence of a disqualifying event as follows:

(1) The deferred taxes for the preceding five fiscal years are due and payable when an amount equal to the deferred taxes is not invested in improvements to make the land suitable for industrial use, office use, or both within five years from the first day of the fiscal year the property was classified under this section.

(2) The deferred taxes for the preceding five fiscal years are due and payable when the minimum investment required by subdivision (1) of this subsection is timely made, but the land has been classified under this section for 10 years.

(3) All deferred taxes are due and payable when some or all of the site infrastructure land is rezoned for a use other than for industrial use, office use, or both.

(4) The deferred taxes for the preceding year are due and payable when the land is transferred or when a building permit for a primary building or structure for the land is issued.

(d) Notice. - On or before September 1 of each year, the collector shall notify each owner to whom a tax deferral has previously been granted of the accumulated sum of deferred taxes and interest. An owner who fails to notify the county assessor when land classified under this section loses its eligibility for classification is subject to a penalty in the amount set in G.S. 105-277.5.

(e) Exception to Payment. - No deferred taxes are due in the following circumstances, and the deferred taxes remain a lien on the land:

(1) When the owner of site infrastructure land that was previously classified under G.S. 105-277.3 does not transfer the land, and the land again becomes eligible for classification under G.S. 105-277.3. In this circumstance, the deferred taxes are payable in accordance with G.S. 105-277.3.

(2) When a portion of the site infrastructure land is transferred for industrial use, office use, or both or has issued for the land a building permit for a primary building or structure for industrial use, office use, or both, and the remainder of

the site infrastructure land no longer meets the size requirement of this section. In this circumstance, the deferred taxes for the remainder are payable in accordance with this section without application of the size requirement of subdivision (b)(1) of this section.

(f) Application. - An application for property tax relief provided by this section should be filed during the regular listing period but may be filed after the regular listing period upon a showing of good cause by the applicant for failure to make a timely application, as determined and approved by the board of equalization and review or, if that board is not in session, by the board of county commissioners. An untimely application approved under this subsection applies only to property taxes levied by the county or municipality in the calendar year in which the untimely application is filed. Decisions of the county board may be appealed to the Property Tax Commission. Persons may apply for this property tax relief by entering the appropriate information on a form made available by the assessor under G.S. 105-282.1. An application for property tax relief provided by this section may not be approved for any portion of site infrastructure land which has previously lost eligibility for the program.

(g) Report. - On August 1 of each year, the Secretary shall report to the Department of Commerce the number and location of site infrastructure lands qualified under this section. (2013-130, s. 1.)

§ 105-277.16. Taxation of low-income housing property.

A North Carolina low-income housing development to which the North Carolina Housing Finance Agency allocated a federal tax credit under section 42 of the Code is designated a special class of property under Article V, Section 2(2) of the North Carolina Constitution and must be appraised, assessed, and taxed in accordance with this section. The assessor must use the income approach as the method of valuation for property classified under this section and must take rent restrictions that apply to the property into consideration in determining the income attributable to the property. The assessor may not consider income tax credits received under section 42 of the Code or under G.S. 105-129.42 in determining the income attributable to the property. (2008-146, s. 3.1; 2008-187, s. 47.6.)

§ 105-277.17. Taxation of community land trust property.

(a) Classification. - Community land trust property is designated a special class of property under Section 2(2) of Article V of the North Carolina Constitution and must be appraised, assessed, and taxed in accordance with this section.

(b) Definitions. - The following definitions apply in this section:

(1) Community land trust developer. - A nonprofit housing development entity that is an exempt organization under section 501(c)(3) of the Code and that transfers community land trust property to a qualifying owner.

(2) Community land trust property. - Improvements to real property that meet all of the following conditions:

a. A fee or leasehold interest in the improvements is transferred subject to resale restrictions contained in a long-term ground lease of not less than 99 years.

b. The community land trust developer retains an interest in the property pursuant to the deed of conveyance or the long-term ground lease.

(3) Ground lease. - A lease between the community land trust developer of a dwelling site, as landlord, and the owner or lessee of a permanent residence constructed on the dwelling site, as tenant. The leasehold interest of the tenant in the dwelling site includes an undivided interest and nonexclusive easement for ingress and egress to the dwelling site and for the use and enjoyment of the common areas and community facilities, if any.

(4) Income. - Defined in G.S. 105-277.1(b).

(5) Initial investment basis. - The most recent sales price, excluding any silent mortgage amount, of community land trust property.

(6) Qualifying owner. - A North Carolina resident who (i) occupies, as owner or lessee, community land trust property as a permanent residence and (ii) is part of a household, the annual income of which at the time of transfer and adjusted for family size is not more than one hundred percent (100%) of the local area median family income as defined by the most recent figures published by the U.S. Department of Housing and Urban Development.

(7) Resale restrictions. - Binding restrictions that affect the price at which a qualifying owner's interest in community land trust property can be transferred for value to a subsequent qualifying owner or the community land trust developer.

(8) Silent mortgage amount. - The amount of debt incurred by a qualifying owner that is represented by a deed of trust or leasehold deed of trust on community land trust property and that earns no interest and requires no repayment prior to satisfaction of any interest-earning mortgage or a subsequent transfer of the property, whichever occurs first.

(9) Transfer. - Any method of disposing of an interest in real property.

(c) Valuation. - The initial appraised value of community land trust property in the year the property first qualifies for classification under this section is the initial investment basis. In subsequent general reappraisals, the value of the community land trust property shall not exceed the sum of the restricted capital gain amount and the initial investment basis. The restricted capital gain amount is the market value of the community land trust property that would be established for the current general reappraisal if not for this classification (i) adjusted to the maximum sales price permitted pursuant to the resale restrictions effective for a hypothetical sale occurring on the date of reappraisal, if less, and (ii) subtracting the initial investment basis and any silent mortgage amount. (2009-481, s. 1.)

§ 105-278. Historic properties.

(a) Real property designated as a historic property by a local ordinance adopted pursuant to former G.S. 160A-399.4 or designated as a historic landmark by a local ordinance adopted pursuant to G.S. 160A-400.5 is designated a special class of property under authority of Article V, Sec. 2(2) of the North Carolina Constitution. Property so classified shall be taxed uniformly as a class in each local taxing unit on the basis of fifty percent (50%) of the true value of the property as determined pursuant to G.S. 105-285 and 105-286, or 105-287.

(b) The difference between the taxes due on the basis of fifty percent (50%) of the true value of the property and the taxes that would have been payable in the absence of the classification provided for in subsection (a) shall be a lien on the property of the taxpayer as provided in G.S. 105-355(a). The taxes shall be carried forward in the records of the taxing unit or units as deferred taxes. The deferred taxes for the preceding three fiscal years are due and payable in accordance with G.S. 105-277.1F when the property loses the benefit of this classification as a result of a disqualifying event. A disqualifying event occurs when there is a change in an ordinance designating a historic property or a change in the property, other than by fire or other natural disaster, that causes the property's historical significance to be lost or substantially impaired. In addition to the provisions in G.S. 105-277.1F, no deferred taxes are due and all liens arising under this subsection are extinguished when the property's historical significance is lost or substantially impaired due to fire or other natural disaster. (1977, c. 869, s. 2; 1981, c. 501; 1989, c. 706, s. 3.1; 2005-435, s. 38; 2006-162, s. 28; 2008-35, s. 2.5; 2010-95, s. 17.)

§ 105-278.1. Exemption of real and personal property owned by units of government.

(a)   Real and personal property owned by the United States and, by virtue of federal law, not subject to State and local taxes shall be exempted from taxation.

(b)   Real and personal property belonging to the State, counties, and municipalities is exempt from taxation.

(c)   For purposes of this section:

(1)   A specified unit of government (federal, State, or local) includes its departments, institutions, and agencies.

(2)   By way of illustration but not by way of limitation, the following boards, commissions, authorities, and institutions are units of State government:

a.   The State Marketing Authority established by G.S. 106-529.

b.   The Board of Governors of the University of North Carolina incorporated under the provisions of G.S. 116-3 and known as "The University of North Carolina."

c.   The North Carolina Museum of Art made an agency of the State under G.S. 140-5.12.

(3) By way of illustration but not by way of limitation, the following boards, commissions, authorities, and institutions are units of local government of this State:

a. An airport authority, board, or commission created as a separate and independent body corporate and politic by an act of the General Assembly.

b. An airport authority, board, or commission created as a separate and independent body corporate and politic by one or more counties or municipalities or combinations thereof under the authority of an act of the General Assembly.

c. A hospital authority created under G.S. 131E-17.

d. A housing authority created under G.S. 157-4 or G.S. 157- 4.1.

e. A municipal parking authority created under G.S. 160-477.

f. A veterans' recreation authority created under G.S. 165-26. (1973, c. 695, s. 4; 1987, c. 777, s. 1; 2005-435, s. 39.)

§ 105-278.2. Burial property.

(a) Real property set apart for burial purposes shall be exempted from taxation unless it is owned and held for purposes of (i) sale or rental or (ii) sale of burial rights therein.

(b) Taxable real property set apart for human burial purposes is hereby designated a special class of property under authority of Article V, Section 2(2) of the North Carolina Constitution, and it shall be assessed for taxation taking into consideration the following:

(1) The effect on its value by division and development into burial plots;

(2) Whether it is irrevocably dedicated for human burial purposes by plat recorded with the Register of Deeds in the county in which the land is located; and

(3) Whether the owner is prohibited or restricted by law or otherwise from selling, mortgaging, leasing or encumbering the same.

(c) For purposes of this section, the term "real property" includes land, tombs, vaults, monuments, and mausoleums, and the term "burial" includes entombment. (1973, c. 695, s. 4; 1987, c. 724.)

§ 105-278.3. Real and personal property used for religious purposes.

(a) Buildings, the land they actually occupy, and additional adjacent land reasonably necessary for the convenient use of any such building shall be exempted from taxation if wholly owned by an agency listed in subsection (c), below, and if:

(1) Wholly and exclusively used by its owner for religious purposes as defined in subsection (d)(1), below; or

(2) Occupied gratuitously by one other than the owner and wholly and exclusively used by the occupant for religious, charitable, or nonprofit educational, literary, scientific, or cultural purposes.

(b) Personal property shall be exempted from taxation if wholly owned by an agency listed in subsection (c), below, and if:

(1) Wholly and exclusively used by its owner for religious purposes; or

(2) Gratuitously made available to one other than the owner and wholly and exclusively used by the possessor for religious, charitable, or nonprofit educational, literary, scientific, or cultural purposes.

(c) The following agencies, when the other requirements of this section are met, may obtain exemption for their properties:

(1) A congregation, parish, mission, or similar local unit of a church or religious body; or

(2) A conference, association, presbytery, diocese, district, synod, or similar unit comprising local units of a church or religious body.

(d) Within the meaning of this section:

(1)   A religious purpose is one that pertains to practicing, teaching, and setting forth a religion. Although worship is the most common religious purpose, the term encompasses other activities that demonstrate and further the beliefs and objectives of a given church or religious body. Within the meaning of this section, the ownership and maintenance of a general or promotional office or headquarters by an owner listed in subdivision (2) of subsection (c), above, is a religious purpose and the ownership and maintenance of residences for clergy, rabbis, priests or nuns assigned to or serving a congregation, parish, mission or similar local unit, or a conference, association, presbytery, diocese, district, synod, province or similar unit of a church or religious body or residences for clergy on furlough or unassigned, is also a religious purpose. However, the ownership and maintenance of residences for other employees is not a religious purpose for either a local unit of a church or a religious body or a conference, association, presbytery, diocese, district, synod, or similar unit of a church or religious body. Provided, however, that where part of property which otherwise qualifies for the exemption provided herein is made available as a residence for an individual who provides guardian, janitorial and custodial services for such property, or who oversees and supervises qualifying activities upon and in connection with said property, the entire property shall be considered as wholly and exclusively used for a religious purpose.

(2)   A charitable purpose is one that has humane and philanthropic objectives; it is an activity that benefits humanity or a significant rather than limited segment of the community without expectation of pecuniary profit or reward. The humane treatment of animals is also a charitable purpose.

(3)   An educational purpose is one that has as its objective the education or instruction of human beings; it comprehends the transmission of information and the training or development of the knowledge or skills of individual persons.

(4)   A literary purpose is one that pertains to letters or literature, especially writing, publishing, and the study of literature. It includes the literature of the stage and screen as well as the performance or exhibition of works based on literature.

(5)   A cultural purpose is one that is conducive to the enlightenment and refinement of taste acquired through intellectual and aesthetic training, education, and discipline.

(6) A scientific purpose is one that yields knowledge systematically through research, experimentation or other work done in one or more of the natural sciences.

(e) Notwithstanding the exclusive-use requirement of subsection (a), above, if part of a property that otherwise meets that subsection's requirements is used for a purpose that would require exemption if the entire property were so used, the valuation of the part so used shall be exempted from taxation.

(f) The fact that a building or facility is incidentally available to and patronized by the general public, so long as there is no material amount of business or patronage with the general public, shall not defeat the exemption granted by this section.

(g) Notwithstanding the exclusive-use requirement of subsection (a), above, any parking lot wholly owned by an agency listed in subsection (c), above, may be used for parking without removing the tax exemption granted in this section; provided, the total charge for said uses shall not exceed that portion of the actual maintenance expenditures for the parking lot reasonably estimated to have been made on account of said uses. This subsection shall apply beginning with the taxable year that commences on January 1, 1978. (1973, c. 695, s. 4; c. 1421; 1975, c. 848; 1977, c. 867; 2005-435, s. 59(a).)

Vision Books Order Form

Fax Orders:	1-704-299-5965
Phone Orders:	1-704-898-0770
E-mail Orders:	www.visionbooks.org
Mail Orders:	Vision Books, LLC P.O. Box 42406 Charlotte, NC 28215

Shipp To:
Name_____
Address_____
City_____State_____Zip_____
Phone_____Fax_____
Email_____@_____

Bill To: We can bill a third party on your behalf.
Name_____
Address_____
City_____State_____Zip_____
Phone___(_____)_____Fax_____
Email_____@_____

Pamphlet Number ($15.00 Each)	Qty	Total Cost
_____	_____	_____
_____	_____	_____
_____	_____	_____
_____	_____	_____
_____	_____	_____
_____	_____	_____
_____	_____	_____
_____		
<u>Full Volume Set 1-92</u>	<u>92 Pamphlets</u>	<u>1,380.00</u>

Free Shipping Shipping & Handling on Full Volume Orders
Add $1.00 Shipping & Handling per pamphlet $_____

Total Cost $_____

Thank you for your support. Management!

DID YOU ENJOY THIS BOOK?

Vision Books, LLC would like to hear from you! If you or someone you know has been fasely imprisoned, we would like to hear your story. If the 'North Carolina Criminal Law and Procedure' has had an effect in your life or if you have suggestions, we would like to hear from you. Send your letters to:

Vision Books, LLC
Attn: Staff Writers
P.O. Box 42406
Charlotte, NC 28215
Email: staff@visionbooks.org

Order Additional Copies:

Fax Orders: 1-980-299-5965

Phone Orders: 1-704-898-0770

E-mail Orders: www.visionbooks.org

Mail Orders: Vision Books, LLC
                    P.O. Box 42406
                    Charlotte, NC 28215

www.ingramcontent.com/pod-product-compliance
Lightning Source LLC
Chambersburg PA
CBHW051630170526
45167CB00001B/135